More praise for *In the Arena*

"With America's free society being strangled by progressives and bureaucrats at home and America's leadership assaulted by Islamists and globalists abroad, Pete Hegseth lays out a citizen-led road map for rejecting decline and forging another American century."

—Mark Levin, nationally syndicated radio host and
#1 *New York Times* bestselling author of *Plunder and Deceit*

"Pete Hegseth has written an impassioned, wide-ranging book that is a rallying cry for engaged patriots to get in the arena, where we belong."

—Rich Lowry, editor of *National Review*

"Pete Hegseth just can't seem to stop serving his country. He has defended America and then served its defenders. And now, in this extraordinary book, he shows how civic rhetoric, properly understood, can help recover civic spirit. This intellectual case for active patriotism could hardly be more timely."

—Yuval Levin, editor of *National Affairs*

"Pete Hegseth has written a contemporary update to Theodore Roosevelt's iconic 'man in the arena' speech, one that makes for insightful and important reading."

—Ambassador John Bolton, former U.S. Ambassador to the UN

"*In the Arena* is a timely reminder of citizenship's call to defend the American experiment. Pete Hegseth reminds us we're each capable of the enduring commitment to advance freedom, whether through military service or by pursuing the American dream here at home."

—Senator Tom Cotton (R-AK), Iraq and Afghanistan veteran

"Pete Hegseth tells the hard truths about what America needs, at home and overseas, to make the 21st century an American century. A must-read for patriots who want to fight for a free and strong America."

—Kimberly Guilfoyle, FOX News co-host of
The Five and author of *Making the Case*

"Be careful picking up this book, because it will motivate you to take action. This book grabs you by the shirt collar. Pete Hegseth makes an impassioned and informed case for a tough-minded foreign policy as only he can. Pete already went to war for us—read *In the Arena* and find out why."

—S. E. Cupp, CNN commentator and author of
Losing Our Religion: The Liberal Media's Attack on Christianity

"In this engaging, well-written book, drawing on the courageous virtues Teddy Roosevelt championed a century ago, Hegseth exhorts America to renew herself. It is a challenge . . . and an inspiration."

—Andrew C. McCarthy, *National Review* contributing editor and
New York Times bestselling author of *The Grand Jihad*

"Every page, clear and concise, forces the reader to pause and to think: What sort of America do we want, and how do we get there? A smart, combat-proven soldier with a resounding message, Pete Hegseth is a modern-day Teddy Roosevelt. He writes with verve."

—Bing West, bestselling author of
One Million Steps: A Marine Platoon at War

"America needs this book now more than ever. Pete Hegseth brilliantly resurrects one of the finest speeches in history and illustrates how a great republic is maintained through citizenry, family, honesty, and patriotism."

—Robert J. O'Neill, SEAL Team Six

"Pete Hegseth has written a book that's at once informative and inspiring, educational and captivating. His hero Teddy Roosevelt would have enjoyed it. So will you."

—William Kristol, editor of *The Weekly Standard*

"This book gives voice to our generation's fight and makes a convincing case for applying the lessons we learned—strength, resolve, and leadership, among the many—to a continued world of dangerous threats. If you love America, and are concerned about our future, you should read this book."

—Congressman Adam Kinzinger (R-IL),
Iraq and Afghanistan veteran

"Pete Hegseth, who was among those who bravely risked their lives for our beloved nation in Iraq and Afghanistan, has given us a fine book explaining what it means to be "in the arena" and why it is critical for all of us to stand up and speak out for limited government and fidelity to the Constitution and the fundamental freedoms it protects."

—Robert P. George, author of *Conscience and Its Enemies*

"A wake-up call from an American patriot, soldier, and father that our nation's greatness depends on each one of us getting into the fight."

—Buck Sexton, TheBlaze radio and television host
and former CIA officer

"Hegseth breaks down the poignant truths of an iconic American hero. This is a must-read for anybody who desires to know what America really stands for and the underlying principles that make our country great."

—Congressman Duncan Hunter (R-CA),
Iraq and Afghanistan veteran

In the
ARENA

Good Citizens, a Great Republic,
and How One Speech
Can Reinvigorate America

★ ★ ★

PETE HEGSETH

THRESHOLD EDITIONS

New York   London   Toronto   Sydney   New Delhi

Threshold Editions
An Imprint of Simon & Schuster, Inc.
1230 Avenue of the Americas
New York, NY 10020

Copyright © 2016 by Pete Hegseth

First Threshold Editions hardcover edition May 2016

THRESHOLD EDITIONS and colophon are
trademarks of Simon & Schuster, Inc.

For information about special discounts for bulk purchases,
please contact Simon & Schuster Special Sales at
1-866-506-1949 or business@simonandschuster.com.

The Simon & Schuster Speakers Bureau can bring authors to your live event. For more information or to book an event, contact the Simon & Schuster Speakers Bureau at 1-866-248-3049 or visit our website at www.simonspeakers.com.

Interior design by Akasha Archer

Manufactured in the United States of America

1 3 5 7 9 10 8 6 4 2

Library of Congress Cataloging-in-Publication Data

ISBN 978-1-4767-4934-1
ISBN 978-1-4767-4937-2 (ebook)

For my three sons, Gunner, Boone, & Rex:
May you fear God, love America,
and serve both unapologetically.

CONTENTS

★ ★ ★

PART III
THE POWER OF LOOKING AHEAD | THE FUTURE
OF OUR REPUBLIC

AN INVITATION

★ ★ ★

The Man in the Arena

Like every soldier of every generation, I have a few Army-issue
green duffle bags that travel with me everywhere—from my home
state of Minnesota to Guantanamo Bay, from the sands of Iraq and
Afghanistan to the sinkhole of American politics, Washington, D.C.
Always stuffed inside one of those duffle bags is a piece of plain white
copy paper encased in a durable black plastic frame. Inside is a quote,
printed in plain font. The words, known by many, come from a speech
delivered in 1910 by former president Teddy Roosevelt at a famous
university in Paris, France. Following a yearlong African safari—an intentional hiatus from American politics—Roosevelt was at the height
of his postpresidential popularity when he gave the speech. He titled
it "Citizenship in a Republic," and it contained the quote in my plastic
frame:

> It is not the critic who counts; not the man who points out how the
> strong man stumbles, or where the doer of deeds could have done them bet-
> ter. The credit belongs to the man who is actually in the arena, whose face
> is marred by dust and sweat and blood; who strives valiantly; who errs,

who comes short again and again, because there is no effort without error and shortcoming; but who does actually strive to do the deeds; who knows great enthusiasms, the great devotions; who spends himself in a worthy cause; who at the best knows in the end the triumph of high achievement, and who at the worst, if he fails, at least fails while daring greatly, so that his place shall never be with those cold and timid souls who neither know victory nor defeat.

Teddy Roosevelt's words—commonly known as "The Man in the Arena"—challenge me every day when I wake up and every night when I lay my head down, every time I succeed and every time I fail.

Am I striving valiantly?
Is my face marred by dust and sweat and blood?
Am I spending myself in a worthy cause?
Am I daring greatly?
Am I in the arena?

In June 2004, with America at war, I found myself stepping off a plane in Guantanamo Bay, Cuba. The first thing that struck me about "Gitmo" was the signature dry heat of the Cuban coast—followed by an authentic sense of purpose. Guarding detainees at Guantanamo Bay, while not combat in Iraq or Afghanistan, was a controversial and highly scrutinized mission, a legal-limbo-land that housed some of the world's most dangerous Islamic militants. I was proud to be there. We'd be there for eleven months, a *long* eleven months, mostly confronting early mornings, late nights, monotony, menial tasks—and banana rats, the freakishly large rodents that roam Gitmo. The arena is a dirty place, always is.

Squinting in the midday sun, my infantry platoon—hailing from the New Jersey Army National Guard—descended the long stairway from the plane, saluted a general at the bottom, and shuffled into an Air Force hangar. After falling into quick formation, we dropped our duffle bags with a simultaneous thud. For at least a minute, it was silent, and I stood behind my thirty-four men, absorbing the new surroundings. I had no idea what to expect—and did my best to hide a nervous energy. During that silence I remember looking down at my two extremely full green duffle bags and noticing the corner of that black frame sticking out from one of them. I took a deep breath.

What I didn't realize at the time was the direct connection Teddy Roosevelt's words inside that black frame had to the reason I was standing on *American* soil on the island of Cuba. I knew that Guantanamo Bay was leased from the Cuban government for two thousand dollars a year, and that the communist government under Fidel Castro had refused to cash the checks since the Cuban Revolution ended in 1959. But my knowledge stopped there, as revealed by the first line of my journal entry from that day—"nothing but a desert by the sea"; the observation of an infantryman more consumed with finding the new chow hall than mulling the significance of an international flash point.

Following victory in the Spanish-American War, Guantanamo Bay became sovereign United States soil when President Teddy Roosevelt signed the Cuban-American Treaty of Relations in 1903. The treaty outlined seven U.S.-dictated terms for the withdrawal of U.S. troops from Cuba—the seventh of which allowed for the lease of Cuban land to the United States for "naval stations." Soon thereafter, Naval Station Guantanamo Bay was born—seventy-one square miles of American soil and sea on the island of Cuba.

Those who deem the post-9/11 detention facility at Guantanamo Bay controversial would view the 1898 war that gave birth to its existence as equally controversial. The Spanish-American War was brief, but consequential. Following the mystifying sinking of the U.S. battleship *Maine* off the coast of Havana, calls from hawkish Democrats and anti-Spanish journalists—*"Remember the Maine!"*—led America to war. Isolationists (dubbed "anti-imperialists" then) decried the war, and the U.S. military was ill-prepared for tough combat in the hot climate (sound familiar?).

But thanks to the ineptitude of the Spaniards, and some good fortune for the Americans, Cuban independence was quickly secured—and along with it, American regional dominance. Lasting less than four months and costing three thousand American lives (2,500 from disease), the "splendid little war" reshuffled the global chessboard. A younger, confident, and increasingly powerful America asserted itself against an experienced Spanish foe—effectively ending the Spanish Empire in the Caribbean.

On one of Cuba's rolling hills—located just forty miles from where my green duffle bag landed in Guantanamo Bay—the trajectory of the free world was changed forever. On San Juan Hill, a decisive battle was won and a future president forged. Charging up a gradual hillside in the sweltering July heat of 1898, Colonel Teddy Roosevelt and his volunteer "Rough Riders" were met with withering Spanish gunfire. While unheralded Buffalo Soldiers bore the brunt of the fight and a new technology—the Gatling machine gun—substantially aided the Americans, all accounts of the battle place Colonel Roosevelt at the front of the charge up San Juan Hill. It was a daring maneuver that earned Teddy Roosevelt the Medal of Honor and catapulted him into the American consciousness.

Standing atop San Juan Hill with his Rough Riders—an iconic photo in American history—Teddy Roosevelt became a national figure. He returned home a war hero, an emblem of American guts, swagger, and strength. He was elected governor of New York as a Republican the following year, elected vice president in 1900 (coining the phrase "speak softly and carry a big stick"), and, following the assassination of recently reelected William McKinley, he assumed the presidency on September 14, 1901. Three years later he would earn the presidency in his own right, winning the popular vote decisively. Upon leaving the presidency and choosing his presidential successor, Teddy embarked on a yearlong African safari—physically distancing himself from domestic politics. He was America's international celebrity, her rugged exemplar.

On his way home from Africa in 1910, Teddy Roosevelt toured

Europe, greeting adoring crowds from city to city. In many ways the myth was as large as the man. Everyone wanted to meet the American cowboy, the Rough Rider. *Does he really carry a big stick?* they wondered. He personified the confidence of the young American nation as it entered the twentieth century, and Europe took notice. One of his final stops before heading home to record-breaking crowds in New York City was at the leading university in Paris. It was there, at the Grand Amphitheatre at the Sorbonne, that he delivered "Citizenship in a Republic."

Which brings me back me to the words inside that black frame in my green duffle bag. Words that have forged my life's path, and words that chart the course for America's reinvigoration. Words that invited me to enter *the* arena, and words that still challenge:

> *Am I striving valiantly?*
> *Is my face marred by dust and sweat and blood?*
> *Am I spending myself in a worthy cause?*
> *Am I daring greatly?*
> *Am I in the arena?*

Are *you*? Our fragile and imperiled American experiment asks.

INTRODUCTION

★ ★ ★

The Strong Man Stumbles

It's important to note that Roosevelt gave his "Citizenship in a Republic" speech in France not as president of the United States, not as an elected official, not as a candidate, and not as a soldier. Roosevelt instead spoke as a citizen who had seen the greatest heights of his republic. Through the crucible of war, and after a meteoric political career, 1910 was an "in-between time" for Teddy Roosevelt. He was two years removed from the end of his two Republican terms in the Oval Office and his failed effort to return to the White House under the banner of the Progressive (or "Bull Moose") Party in 1912 still lay two years ahead. Positioned between his Republican presidency and Progressive candidacy, and following a year on African safari disconnected from civilization, the speech was mostly free of partisan patronage. Roosevelt spoke with a clear and detached mind, doing his rhetorical best to both confront the worst manifestations of developed societies while elevating the timeless, if inconvenient, principles needed to cultivate the "good citizens" and "good patriots" of Great Republics.

In his opening words, Roosevelt presented himself to the audience as a humble representative from a rugged "new world," while also paying homage to the ancient academic institution he was addressing. "This [Sorbonne] was the most famous university of medieval Europe at a time when no one dreamed that there was a New World to discover," said Roosevelt. Yet it is clear Roosevelt was eager to use his pulpit at the Sorbonne—also known as the University of Paris—to suggest that Americans might have something to teach the French about republics and citizenship. When Roosevelt took the stage to speak, the American republic was 134 years old, while France's "Third Republic" was just 40 years young.

As Americans, we often take for granted the stability of our republic, but the famous Frenchman Alexis de Tocqueville originally called us a "great experiment." In our minds, we rarely contemplate the alternatives; *of course* the American republic has lasted since 1776. *Of course* we won a revolutionary war against the world's preeminent empire. *Of course* we have always survived challenges—divisions over self-rule, slavery, the brutal Civil War, the surprise attack on Pearl Harbor, the civil rights era, Vietnam, and terror on 9/11. We tell this to ourselves even as so many other democratic "experiments"—even "great republics" like France—have slowly crumbled under the weight of human nature, hubris, and history.

At the time Roosevelt spoke, France's efforts at republican government had twice before fallen into chaos—replaced for long periods by the return of absolute rule by monarchs and emperors. The Third French Republic to which Roosevelt spoke would also eventually come to an end—under the jackboot of Hitler's Nazi invasion in 1940. As Roosevelt reminded his audience, republican governance has never been inevitable, and what makes freedom—and America—truly exceptional is the willingness of each generation to actively perpetuate it.

Most Americans remember only the famous "man in the arena" quote from the speech—a quote worth knowing, memorizing, and jamming into your duffle bag of life. But the entire speech has prophetic resonance that should serve as a wake-up call—and blueprint for action—for America today. Roosevelt's 1910 speech serves as the frame for this book.

But this book is not about Teddy Roosevelt. These pages do not seek to defend or litigate Roosevelt's life, policies, political philosophy, or historical significance. Dozens of historians have done that work before me. I also have no illusions regarding Roosevelt's reputation among my fellow conservatives. Glenn Beck summarized their sentiment a few years ago, saying, "Are you a Theodore Roosevelt Republican? Because if you are, may history forget that you were my countryman." Others say worse. While I proudly count Roosevelt as my fellow countryman, I recognize his unfortunate political metamorphosis. I entered this project, and submit it to you now, with eyes wide open about Teddy Roosevelt the man, the leader, and the president—especially regarding the negative manifestations of his legacy. These include his leftward lurch from Republican reformer to founder of the Progressive Party, laying the groundwork for the modern administrative and regulatory state, an extraconstitutional view of executive power, and the active re-distribution of wealth by the state. Roosevelt's 1912 third-party can-didacy also gave the world the misfortune of Woodrow Wilson's two terms as president. To say that Roosevelt failed "while daring greatly," on many occasions and in many ways, is an understatement.

That said, this book is not about the life, times, and policies of Teddy Roosevelt. Instead, the namesake of this book—*In the Arena*—centers on a 140-word quote that personally propels my life, and ulti-mately an 8,750-word speech that, if heeded, could powerfully propel America into a new century. I don't agree with every word or assertion of the speech—and neither will you—but America desperately needs to hear the exhortation it contains.

America at the dawn of the twentieth century was a nation just start-ing to feel its oats. Nobody embodied that spirit more than Theodore Roosevelt. If getting off to a good start is important, then Roosevelt was responsible—more than any other man—for making his century an "American Century." Nestled between a decade of mass immigra-tion and economic depression in the 1890s and a world war that would reshape the globe in 1914, the first decade of the twentieth century and, more important, the man who led it shot America into the pole position.

Roosevelt's political ideology and governing philosophy are both pragmatic and principled, utterly defying neat categorization. Those who look for the historical Teddy will find many shades: Roosevelt the "law-and-order" New York Police Commissioner. Roosevelt the Cowboy. Roosevelt the Big-Government Progressive. Roosevelt the Conservative. Roosevelt the Imperialist. Roosevelt the Compromiser. Roosevelt the Agitator. Roosevelt the Republican Reformer. Colonel Roosevelt the Warrior. Roosevelt the Peacemaker. A man who seemed to welcome the prospect of armed conflict and sought the crucible of the battlefield himself, he was also awarded a Nobel Prize—for peace. On the domestic front, Roosevelt—a New York silver spoon aristocrat—pushed a "Square Deal" that took aim at cronyism and entrenched interests in an effort to make sure the little guy got a fair shake. He was an American, many shades over.

Despite the apparent contradictions, however, three attributes best define Teddy Roosevelt the man, the leader, and the politician—and those same three elements dominate his speech at the Sorbonne. These three elements brought him from a sickly and frail childhood in upper-crust Manhattan to the heat of battle on San Juan Hill, and from the devastation of losing his wife and child on the very same day in 1884 to the halls of the White House seventeen years later. Three core characteristics and beliefs—American *citizenship, strength,* and *action*—put Teddy Roosevelt on Mount Rushmore next to Washington, Lincoln, and Jefferson.

History is deceptive in the certainty it delivers, but the twentieth century was never destined to be an American century—it could have been, just as likely, another British century or a new French, Russian, or German century. Instead, largely on the back of the American ethos Roosevelt established, America dominated the twentieth century. His words from that moment in time—1910, at the grandest of academic stages in France—serve as a historical compass for how America today can continue to follow his lead and make the twenty-first century another American century. Across the mighty Atlantic Ocean and overlooking a brave new century, Roosevelt's guiding principles— citizenship, strength, and action—echo through every word of his speech: *Be good. Be strong. Get in the Arena.* His words, and those principles, are needed in America today more than ever.

The question is, will we heed his words? Will we elevate duties over rights? Will we perpetuate good citizenship? Will we recapture the rugged and virile spirit that built America? Will we raise our children plentifully and unapologetically? Will we perpetuate real "equality of opportunity"? Will we overcome the cynics and critics? Will America commit to winning the wars we must fight? Will we produce "good patriots" or rudderless citizens of the world? The fate of America—and the free world—ultimately hangs on those questions, and this one: will our citizens, whose shoulders upon which great republics rise and fall, get back in the arena?

As Teddy says in the speech,

> *A democratic republic such as ours—an effort to realize [in] its full sense government by, of, and for the people—represents the most gigantic of all possible social experiments, the one fraught with great responsibilities alike for good and evil. The success of republics like yours and like ours means the glory, and our failure the despair, of mankind; and for you and for us the question of the quality of the individual citizen is supreme.*

This republic is ours—yours and mine—if we can keep it.

Through this speech, it is as if citizen Teddy Roosevelt— achievements, warts, and all—is reaching through the annals of history, grabbing each American citizen by the shirt collar, and growling: *Wake up! Remember! Don't apologize! Have courage! Work hard! Rub some dirt on it! Be patriotic! Be industrious! Be . . . American!*

His call to action is the call of this book. My own humble journey—

which in no way compares to Roosevelt's—thus far validates his recipe for the revitalization of our nation's greatness. Our task now is to convince all Americans to get out of a defensive crouch and into the arena.

But what is the arena? While we each make unique contributions—driven by talents, passions, and circumstances—there is no *my* arena, *his* arena, *her* arena, or *your* arena. There is only *the* arena. This book, as with Teddy's speech, is not a "you do you!" argument; it is the exact opposite. The arena is not a grab bag of personal priorities; nor is it a physical location, or specific vocation. Instead, the arena—locally or globally, large or small—represents the principled and selfless pursuit, advancement, and defense of the American experiment; a cause larger than any of us, gifted to all of us at America's founding, and enshrined in the Declaration of Independence and Constitution. The principles and perpetuation of human freedom, limited self-government, rule of law, God-given rights, equal opportunity, and free enterprise were entrusted to us by average citizens of their day, and how we fight in the arena—and how many of us fight—matters as much today as it did in 1776 and 1910.

For me, the arena has included tours in Afghanistan, Iraq, and Guantanamo Bay. It has included cultural clashes on Ivy League campuses, firefights in Iraq, political confrontations on Capitol Hill, and media battles on FOX News and MSNBC. It has also included plenty of failures, through every twist and turn of life. For you, the arena could look much different—but no less important. The arena for you could be starting or running a small (or large!) business, local civic action, perpetuating patriotic observances, supporting a principled candidate, leading a Boy Scout troop, coaching youth football, or volunteering at your church. Your contribution to the arena could be your day job, or it could be the cause, business, civic organization, or campaign you incubate in your free time. In an American civil society built by rugged individuals with shared values, we will all have different talents, interests, and passions—all of which lead us down different paths, toward different pursuits, and to different levels of involvement. But all of those paths lead to only *one* American arena. You are either in it, or you are watching others shape it.

Of course, entering and affecting the arena is easier said than done. It was not easy in 1910 and is not easy today. Modern America and her citizens face a mountain of obstacles to our collective experiment in individual human freedom and flourishing: a massive, sprawling, and impenetrable federal bureaucracy; broken public institutions and status quo politics; declining American virtues and fractured families; the conflation of amoral and uncontroversial causes with existential civic action; a corrupt, crony, and arrogant so-called elite political and business class; smaller paychecks, huge debts, and higher costs; opportunity inequality and social immobility; demographic challenges and diminished national identity; sprawling international institutions and shrinking American sovereignty; weakened military readiness and new, dangerous, and asymmetric Islamist threats. America's educational, government, and civic institutions have been manipulated—in nearly every way—by a postmodern cultural seduction that has made our government exponentially larger and our citizens emasculatingly smaller.

It's enough to make you want to throw up your hands, pull all our troops home, declare a thirty-hour workweek, and just become an inconsequential European welfare state already!

That is, like clockwork, the way great civilizations and republics have trended throughout human history; they go through seasons—from infancy to growth to peak and eventually to decline, slowly or quickly. Many speculate that America, as well as the Western civilization we lead, has reached its peak and is on the slow decline. In fact, when surveyed, an overwhelming number of Americans today believe America is in decline. Unarguably, America is certainly older, more entrenched, and more institutionalized than the younger version Teddy Roosevelt inhabited. In 1910, Secretary of the Navy Roosevelt could resign, recruit a band of cowboys and college students (the "Rough Riders"), train them for a few weeks in Texas, and deploy to fight America's enemies. He could even receive official decorations for it. More rules, more regulations, and more scrutiny make something like that nearly impossible today, not just in the Defense Department, but across America's governmental and economic landscape. Red tape, regulations, and risk aversion have a tendency to add up. What is young always ages; it's a fact of life and history.

In this case, the weight of history is both the largest impediment to the twenty-first century being an American century *and* the reason we must make it one. The most likely scenario for our country is the inevitable decline that has met every great power in human history, including the French Republic Teddy Roosevelt addressed. Many great powers have risen, but all have fallen—followed by their influence and ideas. Even the most robust and principled actions may not be enough to prevent an unfortunate decline of America. But, here again, history comes knocking—because those who live in the real world (not the world we wish we had) and recognize human nature (not modern "social constructs") understand a simple truth:

History is not over. It is never over.

History is also not inevitable. With all of its cruel twists and tragedies, villains and violence, human history and the imperfect humans who make it barrel forward without a predetermined moral compass. While political freedom and free markets seem like the norm to us today, less than 1 percent of human beings who have ever walked planet earth have ever lived free. Most have been subjects or slaves or subordinate to their family, clan, religion, or economic station in life. Most never conceived of voting for their leader, let alone voting fairly. And while freedom has increased in the West since our founders threw off the chains of tyranny from Great Britain, it has increased precisely because America was strong, principled, and increasingly assertive. With America on the scene, as imperfect as we may be, freedom has a champion.

But what if America weren't the strongest? What if we could not lead—morally, economically, politically, or militarily? If not America, who would it be? At the time of Teddy Roosevelt's speech, the United Kingdom was still the West's dominant power. Then, exhausted after two world wars, our British friends took a knee and handed us the keys to the free world, a leadership role that we embraced. But what if America, intentionally or unintentionally, took a knee today? What if we didn't lead? What if—saddled by mountains of debt, sprawling bureaucracies, and entitled citizens—we were not capable of leading? The free world doesn't have a deep bench; in fact, we have *no* bench. As we are witnessing right now, a world without America in the lead is a world fundamentally adrift, thrust back into the uncertain high seas of history. As we are witnessing today, the real world is unforgiving—and history is unfinished.

In order for the twenty-first century to be an American century, our citizens, institutions, and leaders must find ways to overcome the challenges of our time. We can neither shrink from addressing the democratic, demographic, and deadly serious problems of our time nor find ourselves locked into never-ending political knife fights. If the twenty-first century is not unambiguously an American century, then it will not be a free century. Political freedom can be marginalized, free markets gamed, and free speech snuffed out. Whether it's morally vacuous globalists, the ascendant, ambitious, and aggressive Chinese civilization, or an unholy mix of Islamists—the enemies of real human freedom are powerful, and they are swarming. America is the last best hope for the free world; and if we don't prevent her decline now, then we are failing to prevent the decline of the entire free world—at least what's left of it.

Is Teddy Roosevelt grabbing your shirt collar yet?

At home, we need Roosevelt's "good citizens." The virtues that make America the free world's guarantor, and the military might that underwrites that guarantee, are right, good, and true—and worth fighting for. Those virtues start at home, and are in short supply in today's America. Familiar refrains—from the ideological Left, the fractured Right, and a "war weary" nation—do not sufficiently answer the challenges of the twenty-first century. A renewed and informed formulation of what makes America special, and therefore exceptional, is needed to fortify the defense of our fragile freedoms and reawaken the spirit of American citizenship and leadership.

In order to advocate for both our highest virtues at home and for-tify a skeptical public toward an assertive posture in the world, we need to get out from underneath well-worn cultural wars and address a deeper and more insidious civic shortfall: an American public, as Teddy put it, that is "far more conscious of its rights rather than of its duties and blind to its own shortcomings." Ultimately, great republics rise—and fall—on the backs of ordinary citizens; it's an empowering, yet harrowing, truth. Moreover, the tireless pursuit of equal opportu-nity, economic freedom, and civic-mindedness ought be the passion of those seeking to empower all Americans, defending and perpetuating a tiny American Dream that drives the massive engine of prosperity and power.

Being a great nation first requires forging "good citizens"—a re-education America must undertake. The word *reeducation* is used in-tentionally, to denote both the bottom-up swell *and* the top-down intentionality with which such a task must be undertaken. Too many Americans, young and old, don't understand what makes America spe-cial and, as such, are easily swayed by cheap, seductive, and failed for-mulations of governance, economics, and human nature.

Abroad, we desperately need Roosevelt's "good patriots." Following fifteen years of difficult combat operations since 9/11, the advance-ment of American values and interests abroad faces a multitude of internal obstacles that Teddy knew well. First is the "foolish cosmopol-itan" who sees nothing exceptional about America, and instead believes international institutions and "mutual understanding" will unleash perpetual peace. This is the modern Left's "Coexist" crowd, personi-fied by Barack Obama's "blame America first" foreign policy approach.

Second, on the other end of the ideological spectrum, are isolationists (dubbed "anti-imperialists" by Roosevelt and rebranded as "restraint" advocates today) who seek to neuter America's "will and the power," believing that American intervention is unnecessary and unhelpful—espousing the belief that restraining American action minimizes overseas threats. The third obstacle is outright "citizens of the world" whose "international feeling swamps . . . national feeling." Our campuses and media are filled with such sentiment, undercutting commitment to American values. Instead, as Roosevelt noted forcefully in the speech, our citizenry must be "good patriots" before we hope to constructively engage the world.

My experience in Iraq and Afghanistan, like that of millions more Americans on other battlefields, supports Roosevelt's assertions. Conventional wisdom holds that the wars in Iraq and Afghanistan were a fiasco; no doubt mistakes were made and outcomes murky. However, especially in Iraq, great triumphs were also achieved and hard-won lessons learned—if not in the White House or on Capitol Hill. I will argue, forcefully, that in light of the world we live in today, the Iraq War teaches us more about what *to do* than what *not to do*. My take on the wars in Afghanistan and Libya, by contrast, are different. The 9/11 generation looks at the world with eyes wide open, knowing, in Roosevelt's words, "there is no effort without error and shortcoming." And like Colonel Roosevelt standing atop San Juan Hill, we have learned that only American resolve—not unilateral retreat or shortsighted restraint—can ensure the twenty-first century is free and prosperous.

I was a college student when the attacks of 9/11 occurred, an event that will forever shape the trajectory of my life. I was a soldier in Samarra, Iraq, the day a different type of 9/11-scale attack occurred: the bombing of the Samarra Golden Mosque, which sent Iraq spiraling downward in a cycle of bloody sectarian violence. I remember hearing the explosion in Samarra that morning and quickly realizing that the war—and the world—would soon change. The Golden Mosque attack, like 9/11, was perpetrated by elements of Al Qaeda.

As I experienced on the ground, the 2007 troop surge and change of U.S. strategy in Iraq was the effective application of American power needed to forge a good outcome for Americans and Iraqis, whereas the precipitous withdrawal of U.S. troops, and abandonment of strategic gains, was not. The lessons of that effort—as well as the benefit of hindsight—demonstrate that an engaged, aggressive, and strong America is more effective than a timid and apologetic America that "leads from behind." Both the nexus of the Islamic State, and our ongoing fight against them, tragically tell the same story.

Reviving American exceptionalism—which includes understanding *why America is exceptional*—will require building a principled but pragmatic movement focused on the restoration of American citizenship and opportunity at home and leadership in a dangerous, disorderly, and ideologically volatile world abroad. For some of us, this is not an entirely new challenge. Since 9/11, a small few—so many of whom did so much more than me—have resolutely fought vicious enemies in distant lands, dutifully fighting controversial wars while America grew "weary," self-interested politicians phoned in solutions to mounting problems, and critics sniped from the sidelines. In doing so—with the support of Americans in the arena at home—warriors of our generation dared greatly and found solutions that, as Teddy Roosevelt said, "can in practice be realized." Like Teddy in 1910—a man who earned both a Medal of Honor and a Nobel Peace Prize—we meet the world as it is (not as we wish it was) and fight to make it better.

But we look out at America today and realize that, tragically, the spirit of Teddy Roosevelt's speech has been snuffed out. At home we teach our kids to be environmental evangelists but not economically self-sufficient. We give our kids a fifth-place trophy but not the tough love of failure that breeds development, improvement, and ultimately earned success. We put our kids in bike helmets and pink ribbons but we don't gird them for the hellish threats of systemic Islamic intolerance and female subjugation. We teach them to be unbendingly tolerant, without teaching them that America is the world's ultimate melting pot—where race, class, and gender ought have no bearing on your ability to succeed as a "citizen of the republic." We teach them that war is hell but not that injustice and subjugation are far worse. We are a "coexist culture," taught to tolerate the militant dogma of blind multiculturalism while marginalizing the timeless, unique, and color-blind values America was built on. A popular postmodern bumper sticker reads, *Think globally, act locally*. Reviving Teddy Roosevelt will require an American citizenry that not only rips off that sticker, but replaces it with one Teddy would proudly approve of: *Think locally, act globally*.

The ethos of Teddy Roosevelt in 1910 provides a blueprint for fortifying the spirit of 1776 in 2016—thinking locally, but acting globally in the twenty-first century. The thrust of this book is unabashedly conservative, but only in the sense that it reinforces the principles of America's founding and the citizenship espoused by Roosevelt. Otherwise, my argument intentionally attempts to avoid modern litmus tests because America needs a clear lens through which to view entrenched and stale political characterizations, lest we doom ourselves to status quo gridlock and inevitable decline. We need to transcend the old formulations of political allegiance—and special interests on both the left and right—in order to save our great republic. With America and the Constitution as our lodestar, we need a restorative revolt against a stale political class in Washington, D.C., that has empowered itself while simultaneously running modern America into the ground.

The arena is not about Republicans and Democrats. And it's not about Teddy Roosevelt. It's about America.

This book calls every generation to be Teddy Roosevelt's modern "men in the arena"—tireless and unafraid to meet the challenges of a new century at home and abroad. We are called to know the "great enthusiasms, the great devotions" that come with "daring greatly" for a "worthy cause," and for America to be restored we must all—some of us *again*—lace up our boots and fight. Ask yourself this question: *If not me, then who?* If not freedom-loving and engaged citizens, then who will fight for the America our founders entrusted to us? It's not going to be your neighbor, who watches Netflix reruns every night and spends the weekend "slaying" dragons on World of Warcraft. If we wait for others to enter the arena for us, then America's fate is sealed. The fate of great republics is directly tied to the goodness of their citizens, and together we must be the "good citizens" and "good patriots" that Roosevelt describes. And when we fight, we need to fight to win—no matter what. We could ultimately fail in the protection and preservation of our American experiment, but at least it would be for the same worthy cause Teddy Roosevelt articulated a century ago.

I used to say, frequently, that *I fought so that my kids won't have to.* It was an honest statement, a hopeful one. We all want to slay the real dragons of our time so our kids can live freely, prosperously, and peacefully. But I no longer say that, and neither should you. It is a comfy platitude with no grounding in reality. Not because the soil my generation spilled blood on in Iraq was eventually lost to an even more vicious Islamic State enemy, but because, on a much larger scale, if we believe it, we deceive ourselves—and the next generation. We must confront the big challenges and threats of our time, for the sake of our kids and the world they will inherit.

I didn't fight so my kids won't have to. I fought knowing that my three sons, and your sons, daughters, grandsons, and granddaughters, will have to fight for freedom as well. Teddy Roosevelt fought on San Juan Hill and his three sons served in World War I—with his youngest, Quentin, killed in combat over German skies. I can't imagine what it would be like for any of my three sons—Gunner, Boone, or Rex—to give their life for this country. I hope they never have to, but I also hope—if it ever came to that—they would be willing to serve, fight, and die for something greater than themselves. Our republic requires such men (and women).

As we fight for the American way of life, we don't do so angrily, blindly, or arrogantly. As we fight, we learn—and we adapt. We learn with clear eyes about the world we live in, not the world we wished we lived in; at the same time, to borrow a sentiment popularized by Robert F. Kennedy, we don't merely see things as they are and ask, "Why?" We dream things that never were and ask, "Why not?" We are not unconstrained utopians, but we must be aspirational and hopeful. We view America—her promise and her role—through an intellectually honest lens, but also refuse to cede to mindless, moral equivalency. We see her flaws, but we choose to dwell on her virtues and the limitless potential of her citizens. We are grateful to live in the greatest country in the world. We learn the hard lessons of our battlefields, but choose to resolutely overcome them—militarily and politically—in pursuit of outcomes that advance our security and American interests. We are not cogs in an American empire, but instead engaged citizens in the ongoing American experiment. And we do it all with a grateful spirit and humble hearts, reminded of our fallen nature and utter humanity.

This invitation to enter the arena comes from someone with failures and flaws galore. I have failed—professionally and personally— at every turn of my life; saved only by the redemptive grace of Jesus Christ. I have failed my God, my family, and my organizations in private, in public, and in trying ways. If you're looking for the perfect person to carry the day, or the perfect moment to get off the couch neither is coming. Our founding fathers understood this. Men are not angels; we are all fallen, and our system of government must reflect this reality. Every human being is capable of wonderful goodness, but also utter wickedness; and if we were each judged by our lowest moments in life, we'd all be destined for the gates of hell. These flaws, and the other complications and excuses of life, will always give us a reason not to act, not to fight, and not to enter the arena. They represent our inner resistance—they make cowards of even the strongest among us. Overcoming our own failures, temptations, weaknesses, and excuses requires both being humble about them, and owning them (*it's my fault, not yours!*).

Otherwise, the excuses—personal, professional, or circumstantial—never end and we never act. And, with our country in peril and the world in chaos, our inaction is action. One of those moments for me was July 13, 2005. I had just returned from my deployment to Guantanamo Bay, Cuba, and was back to my day job in New York City. I was seated at my crammed desk space on the thirty-eighth floor of the investment firm Bear Stearns in midtown Manhattan, drinking my morning coffee and reading the *Wall Street Journal*. My three computer screens were on, but my head was scanning the newspaper headlines instead. It was just like any other morning, until my eyes froze on a blurb in the "What's News" section. The passage read: *"A suicide bomber attacked a crowd of children gathered near U.S. troops passing out candy in a Shiite area of Baghdad, killing 27 people, including 18 children and a soldier."* I read the sentence over and over. And then read further. Twelve of the dead were kids younger than thirteen years old, and the soldier was a twenty-four-year-old American from rural Georgia. As the day progressed, images of escalating violence in Iraq dominated the news coverage on the television above my desk. As a low-level equity capital markets analyst, I was paid good money to be analyzing initial public offerings—but I could not get my mind out of Iraq.

That was the day I decided to try to volunteer to deploy to Iraq. I immediately jumped on my email, contacting anyone I knew on active duty who was headed there. I had very few connections but used the few that I had. As fortune would have it, one of the men I emailed was my former platoon trainer from the Infantry Officer Basic Course at Fort Benning; he was now a company commander in the storied Rakkasans brigade of the 101st Airborne Division and needed a new Second Platoon leader. He told me, in a near-immediate email response, that if I could navigate the Army bureaucracy and get there within eight weeks, he would like to have me. We both knew it was a long shot, but he got approval through his chain of command, and I through mine. After much paperwork and with only a few days to spare, my packet was stalled somewhere in the Pentagon labyrinth. Against the advice of many, I refused to wait—and called in a favor from the only general I knew, a man I had met only once. He unclogged the approval process, and the transfer was done. The day my deployment orders were cut, I received a phone call on my Bear Stearns landline from a blocked number; it was a full-bird colonel in the personnel department of the Pentagon. He said, "Your orders to join the 101st for their tour in Iraq have been cut. I don't know who you think you are, or how you made this happen—but don't fuck this up, Lieutenant." I apologized and thanked him, both of which are better than asking for permission. Less than two months later—having joined the unit at Fort Campbell and conducted final training in Kuwait—I was leading an infantry platoon in Baghdad, Iraq.

That day at Bear Stearns, I cut out that paragraph from the *Wall Street Journal*, laminated it, and have carried it ever since. I carried it with me every day in Iraq, next to Teddy Roosevelt's quote. And I still carry it with me today in my wallet. It reminds me of the stakes of our fight against Islamism, but it also reminds me that—no matter the obstacles—there is always a way into the arena. Don't make excuses. Don't allow people to tell you that it can't happen. There is always an exception, always a path, always a way to navigate the labyrinth of life.

Barriers to entering the arena not only lie within but also come from others. Entering the arena also means being maliciously attacked, professionally and personally. In Iraq, we knew every patrol, convoy, or mission could quickly turn violent or bloody. Our enemy attacked from the shadows, usually melting away into the civilian population and rarely fighting us toe-to-toe. Islamic insurgents hoped their attacks would deter us from continuing the fight, mentally testing us day after day. The calculation, if not the medium, is much the same at home. Personal attacks come in an entirely different form than combat, but the perpetrators seek the same insidious mental impact. They want you to quit, and whether online or in person, critics snipe from the sidelines—flagrantly and falsely impugning your motives, character, and family. Most hide behind their computers, bravely taking to their Twitter and Facebook accounts to take below-the-belt shots from the cheap seats. But others will confront you—either by shouting or whispering—in intensely personal ways.

I first experienced baseless personal attacks when, just months after returning from a combat tour in Iraq and mere weeks after starting to advocate for the Iraq surge, the left-wing website Daily Kos published a highly publicized article about me titled "Phonied-Up Republican Soldier." The article attacked my military service, the personal appearance of my (ex-) wife, and even accused me of breaking the law. I had not attacked them and I certainly wasn't well-known. The article was unprovoked, completely uninformed, and devoid of any factual substance—a complete smear and hit job. Others like it would follow. The organized and ideological Left saw me as a threat and tried to hit me early and often. They attacked then, and still attack today. I know they, and others, will never stop. But when attacked in the media or in person, I always remember two things: First, nobody is physically shooting at me—so it can always be worse (until the new domestic threat of the Islamic State, of course). And, second, they are attacking because they perceive a threat—which means we're on the right track. Being attacked isn't fun, nor is it easy—especially the first few times; but pushing through the resistance is critical to being in the arena.

The critics will be ferocious, shameless, and many, but, as Teddy Roosevelt so powerfully articulated in his speech, "it is not the critic who counts," it is those actually *still* in the arena—spending their lives, their fortunes, and their sacred honors for a worthy cause. Every American citizen must find his or her hill—literal or metaphorical—inside the arena. They must hold it, defend it, fight for it, and then seek to take other hills. With each passing day and generation, it becomes even more important that, as free people, we win—lest we doom ourselves, as Ronald Reagan famously said, to "spend[ing] our sunset years telling our children and our children's children what it was once like in the United States where men were free."

My kids will be taught to be freedom fighters, in one capacity or another. Maybe they'll carry a rifle, and I hope they do. But they may also carry the balance sheet of a capitalist, the notepad of a patriotic journalist, or the clipboard of a freedom activist. No matter what they carry, they will carry with them the weight of history—the weight of American responsibility. They will be taught to seek *the* arena.

If you believe America's best days are behind us, this book is not for you. But if you believe in the America our founders bequeathed to us, and are looking for inspiration to fight for it, then I hope you'll turn the page. This book is for American citizens and freedom lovers— right or left, white or black, male or female, rich or poor, straight or gay, old or young—who believe the next century can be, and ought be, an American century. Teddy Roosevelt stood at the beginning of a new century and boldly charged ahead. His unique speech—which I physically carried into battle and back home again—provided America's guiding star then, as it does today. The principles, warnings, and exhortations from his speech provide modern-day Americans with a timeless lens through which to examine the current state of affairs in America, the perils of our current course, and hope for the future of our country and the free world.

History is not over.

Pick up your green duffle bag, with that black frame inside, and get in the arena.

PART I

★ ★ ★

The Good Citizen | Roosevelt's Speech and Our Republic

ONE

★ ★ ★

Hold Your Own: The Virtues and Duties of Citizenship

With you here, and with us in my own home, in the long run, success or failure will be conditioned upon the way in which the average man, the average woman, does his or her duty, first in the ordinary, every-day affairs of life, and next in those great occasional crises which call for heroic virtues. The average citizen must be a good citizen if our republics are to succeed. The stream will not permanently rise higher than the main source; and the main source of national power and national greatness is found in the average citizenship of the nation.

Self-restraint, self-mastery, common sense, the power of accepting individual responsibility and yet of acting in conjunction with others, courage and resolution—these are the qualities which mark a masterful people. Without them no people can control itself, or save itself from being controlled from the outside.

—TEDDY ROOSEVELT, 1910

Confidence in the face of risk.

—DEFINITION OF *MANLINESS*, HARVEY MANSFIELD, PROFESSOR OF GOVERNMENT, HARVARD UNIVERSITY

The photograph online struck me. The Islamic State fighter—with a long beard, military camouflage, and Rambo-style ammunition belts across his chest—stands atop an American-made Humvee, clutching a Quran in one hand and an AK-47 rifle in the other. It's high noon and the vehicle is parked in the middle of a busy street. Throngs of civilians surround him. He is gesturing forcefully, his eyes determined, and the crowd is hanging on his every word. Hours earlier, he and fellow fighters had captured the small Syrian city from regime forces. It was a fierce fight, but another victory for the Islamic State. With God on his side and the wind at his back, he is a conquering warrior. He is a soldier of Allah. He does not want a job, or a city council seat; he wants an Islamic caliphate. He is fighting for something greater than himself. He is fighting for his god. He is alive, but willing to die. He is a man, and he is in an arena. The wrong arena, but an arena nonetheless.

The photograph struck me because I recognize that fighter, even though I've never met him. I am drawn to him, because I relate to him. I deplore what he stands for, what he does, and how he does it. He is a soldier of hate, subjugation, and sheer evil. But I understand his passions. Like many other veterans and freedom advocates—who also despise every other aspect of Islamists—I relate more with the passions of that fighter than I do selfish, lazy, and disengaged so-called United States citizens. Apathetic, self-indulgent, and coddled Americans often feel to me like aliens from another planet who lucked out and landed in America. Many Americans know nothing of where freedom comes from, don't appreciate how special it is, and refuse to do their part to advance it. They are not men or women in an arena; they are masters of their parents' basement, heroes of an alternate video game universe, or perpetual victims of a cruel world. They fight for nothing. They are not alive, and see nothing worth dying for. They are not men, and while they may occupy space in America, they are not in *any* arena—even though they live in the greatest country in human history.

I was first drawn to Teddy Roosevelt and his historic speech exclusively by the "man in the arena" quote. Especially following the September 11, 2001, attacks, the quote—in that black frame and eventually in my green duffle bag—spoke to my deepest desires and instincts for action. Hearing the story of San Juan Hill and Teddy Roosevelt's Rough Riders drew me even closer to the quote. More than anything else, whether on the battlefield or in the public square, I wanted to be the man in the quote. I wanted a "face marred by dust and sweat and blood." I wanted to be one who "strives valiantly" and "knows great enthusiasms, the great devotions." I believed in America and stood for broad conservative principles, but was—initially—drawn to the sheer action, the sheer relevance, of the arena. Young men and women are drawn to action and causes. Causes are intoxicating; they give your life purpose and meaning. It's why young people around the world are usually the ones protesting, chanting, "raising awareness," or waving signs; it's why some join violent street gangs, and others join the Islamic State. Had I been born elsewhere, either of those could have been me.

The action—and honor—of an arena is also why I joined the military. Each summer, I watched the veterans of Wanamingo, a small farming town in southern Minnesota where my parents grew up, walk down the wide main street during the Memorial Day parade (which ended, fittingly, at Memorial Park to remember the fallen). The veterans, some in old and ill-fitting uniforms and others fresh out of the service, walked proudly while the citizens of Wanamingo stood, clapped, and honored them. My grandfather Alton, an Army corporal who served in postwar Germany, was among the men marching. As he passed he would always smile humbly. The ritual left an imprint on my brain, but more so my heart. My other grandfather, Milton, a Navy ensign who died before I was born, also wore the nation's uniform, serving in Guam during World War II. His memories, and old uniform, were often revived on those holidays as well. Otherwise, with no veterans on either my father's or mother's side (most were too young to be drafted in Vietnam), I did not come from a military family. That parade, and the patriotism and pride it exuded, led me to want to do something honorable and worthy of admiration. I wanted to be in the fight. I didn't *really* understand the price of freedom, but I understood that those who fought for it were held in high esteem and that those who lost their lives for it were remembered. It drew me to military service—and because I was fortunate enough to live in the United States, eventually into the most important of arenas.

Roosevelt would certainly recognize my impulse for action, as it was his story, and the story of tens of millions of other Americans. But Roosevelt would also recognize—in form if not in kind—the Islamic State fighter perched atop his Humvee, clutching a rifle, and exhorting the crowd. Alone, action is a value-neutral construct, and Roosevelt understood that. Action can be good, but it can also be very bad. This simple fact is why his famous speech was not titled "Man in the Arena," as is popularly thought. Roosevelt understood that being a man of action and in *an* arena is not enough. Fighting for something has some measure of inherent dignity, but what you fight for is exponentially more important. The Islamic State fighter certainly does not have a "timid soul," but *his* arena is a cesspool of death, destruction, and slavery. *His* arena belongs only in Dante's ninth circle of treacherous Hell. This example—like Nazism or communism before it—is where Roosevelt would passionately assert the converse of his famous quote: the critic *does* count, the *cause* must also be worthy, and having a *cold soul* validates neither victory nor defeat. Being "manly" (for men or women) has always mattered—but only if the fight is just, right, and true.

This is the point at which Roosevelt's lens widens considerably. His speech was not titled "Man in the Arena" but instead "Citizenship in a Republic." Citizenship is the indispensable ingredient to successful republics. The principle also works in reverse. Nonrepublics don't have, or need, citizens. Roosevelt writes,

> *Under other forms of government, under the rule of one man or very few men, the quality of the leaders is all-important. If, under such gov-*

ernments, the quality of the rulers is high enough, then the nations for generations lead a brilliant career, and add substantially to the sum of world achievement, no matter how low the quality of average citizen; because the average citizen is an almost negligible quantity in working out the final results of that type of national greatness.

Great leaders are central to advancing a republic, but not sufficient, a fact that has allowed our experiment in self-governance to survive so many mediocre leaders. Being in the arena requires active *citizenship* in pursuit of individual freedom, impartial justice, and equal opportunity; the pursuit of a *republic*. Only advancing, in some form, the fragile American experiment places someone in the arena Roosevelt spoke about. That is citizenship, and only that preserves our republic. America's citizenry must unapologetically understand and embody what makes America exceptional. Roosevelt homed in on that central characteristic and we should, too: "The average citizen must be a good citizen if our republics are to succeed." A great America requires *good citizens*, who know her, believe in her, and will fight for her; good citizens who, when necessary, can muster the fortitude to drive a stake through the heart of that fanatical Islamic State fighter. As my good friend and Gold Star mother Karen Vaughn says often, "Our enemies fight because they hate what is in front of them, but Americans fight because we love what is behind us."

Today, 147 of the world's 206 countries use the word *republic* as part of their official name—an impressive number, until you see some of the names on the roster: People's *Republic* of China, *Republic* of Cuba, Islamic *Republic* of Iran, Democratic People's *Republic* of Korea (otherwise known as North Korea), and *Republic* of the Sudan; a list of RINOs—Republics In Name Only—if I've ever seen one. Use of the word may be widespread, but true implementation of the principles is rare. Merriam-Webster defines *republic* as "a government in which supreme power resides in a body of citizens entitled to vote and is exercised by elected officers and representatives responsible to them and governing according to the law." There is that word again—*citizens*—front and center. The textbook definition includes bedrock republican principles of voting, elected representatives, and the rule of law—but before all of that is the "supreme power" of the "body of citizens."

But what does the word *citizen* really mean? The definition of *citizen*—someone who legally belongs to a country and has the rights and protections of that country—tells us very little. As do the modern criteria for citizenship in the United States, either through birth or through allegiance. Those physically born in the United States (with some important dispute) or born to United States citizens abroad (with some caveats and exceptions) are considered American citizens at the time of birth. Likewise, individuals who seek United States citizenship—through a process of application, residence, time, status, and declared allegiance—can become naturalized citizens of the United States. Properly understood, citizens of either process inherit a basic set of rights—"life, liberty, and the pursuit of happiness"—enshrined in the Declaration of Independence, the Constitution, and the Bill of Rights. American citizens have the right to reside and work in the United States, a right to equal justice, the right to vote for their representatives, and the right to run for that same office—along with scores of other liberties. They also incur basic obligations like jury duty, paying taxes, and potential conscription into military service. Finally, American citizens are afforded the protection of the U.S. government from foreign and domestic threats.

These rights, duties, and benefits of American citizenship are, in and of themselves, impressive. Political, economic, and religious freedom, elected and accessible representatives, juries of peers, public education, and the world's most powerful military are things very few people on earth have ever experienced. These things are part of what makes America, by definition, exceptional. However, American citizenship can easily devolve—and has—into a transactional relationship where expansive rights and generous benefits are afforded to citizens in exchange for superficial and easily avoidable duties to the American experiment in self-government. Paying your taxes, voting in a presidential election every four years, and doing jury duty twice in one's life may meet the technical definition of citizenship, but certainly not the spirit. It is also not sufficient for a republic to succeed in the long term. As Teddy Roosevelt pointed out, the perpetuation of America's exceptional experiment in citizen empowerment is not possible merely through disinterested participation. Great republics, like America, require not just citizens, but "good citizens."

According to polling conducted by the American Enterprise Institute in 2010, roughly two-thirds of Americans said loving one's country was enough to be a good citizen. Certainly loving your country—being a "good patriot," as Roosevelt called it at the Sorbonne—is a necessary precondition for good citizenship. Love of country is a beautiful thing and might compel someone to hang a flag in their yard, cheer for our athletes in the Olympics, or maybe even buy an American-made car—all of which are welcome sentiments. But the *feeling* of patriotism is little comfort, and utterly insufficient, if it is not conjoined with the attributes of "good citizens." Many of those who hang flags, chant "U-S-A" every four years, and buy American cars have already been seduced into the kind of counterproductive cultural complacency described later in this section. Loving America does not necessarily equate to fighting for her. This is especially true in light of the cultural decline that has occurred in America, and good citizens will be needed to reverse this trend, not government. By its very nature, government and its bureaucracy grow, justifying and expanding its existence by purporting to solve every conceivable crisis, ill, or "social injustice." Only good citizens can reverse this growth. Good citizenship is patriotism in action, and it is good citizenship—not government—that is, as Roosevelt called it, "the main source of national power and national greatness."

This point cannot be overstated. Quite simply, good citizens are the only antidote to bad and big government. The smaller, more selfish, and more slavish the citizen, the larger, more paternalistic, and more dictatorial the government. Small citizens—either those not engaged at all, or those who only chant "U-S-A" and check the box every four years—are the enablers of nefarious, insatiable, and unchecked centralized power. Eventually, if power is left unchecked, small citizens eventually turn into mere subjects, exchanging their minimal civic duties for the small securities of government-granted, and therefore government-limited, freedom. The old adage still holds true—he who takes the king's money eventually does the king's bidding. On the flip side, however, the more engaged, more selfless, and more informed the citizen becomes, the smaller, less intrusive, and more restrained government becomes. Good citizens—informed about America's founding ideals and willing to act accordingly—are the thin line between freedom and tyranny. In a republic, the good citizen is the only guarantor of good governance.

So who is this "good citizen"? And are *you* willing to be one?

After a brief introduction to his French audience, Roosevelt begins: "Today I shall speak to you on the subject of individual citizenship." He starts by talking about "average citizens" before quickly transitioning to the phrase "good citizen," stating his simple—but powerful—thesis: *"The average citizen must be a good citizen if our republics are to succeed."* Average is not good enough for republics and therefore not good enough for Roosevelt. He also lays out an important bifurcation, saying the success of a republic depends on citizens doing their duty, "first in the ordinary, every-day affairs of life, and next in those great occasional crises which call for heroic virtues." Good citizenship is a daily and ordinary exercise, not merely a response to extraordinary crises. This is an important point that permeates the entire speech. Heroic virtues are vitally important but are secondary compared to the "homely virtues" that "stand at the bottom of character" for a good citizen. Moreover, the ability to muster—and *sustain*—heroic virtues in times of crisis is dependent upon the ability to undergird them through good citizenship in everyday life. It is the ordinary—the vast majority of men, women, and days—that Roosevelt addresses first.

"In short, the good citizen in a republic must realize that they ought to possess two sets of qualities, and that neither avails without the other. He must have those qualities which make for *efficiency*; and that he also must have those qualities which direct the efficiency into channels for the *public good*," says Roosevelt. *Efficiency* and the *public good*—probably not the words you expected. *Public good* maybe, but *efficiency* is a word most often associated with lightbulbs and starting pitchers—not citizenship. For Roosevelt, efficiency means intentional action without wasting substantial time or energy; it means an active life full of meaning and purpose. In great republics, there is little place for "inefficient" average citizens who are simply "harmless," "sluggish," or "timid." Every society contains a range of physical and mental abilities, with some citizens naturally more capable than others. Roosevelt is specifically calling out those average citizens—with the physical and mental ability to contribute at their level and station in life—to maximize their personal contributions. He sums it up by saying the "good citizen" must "be able to hold his own." Holding your own is a relative measure, not an absolute one, but it is nonetheless a powerful measure. It is a measure we can *all* live up to. Efficient citizens productively contribute in the manner, and to the degree, that they are capable of—they maximize themselves, their family, and their country.

Roosevelt further clarifies what "holding your own" means for the good citizen, saying the "ordinary, every-day qualities include the will and the power to work, to fight at need, and to have plenty of healthy children." Even before these, "above mind and above body . . . stands character," the bedrock of any good citizen. Good, efficient citizens work hard, fight when necessary, have large and strong families, and possess strong character. *Work, Fight, Children,* and *Character*—the four ingredients for free, efficient, and good citizens. While character is the baseline for all of them, no ingredient is less important than another, and each places an obligation on the individual, not government. The government plays a role in enabling each ingredient, but only the citizen makes them possible and keeps them healthy. Citizenship is *first* about what men, women, and their families achieve; it is not about what those men, women, and children provide for the government. Those other obligations—to community and country—are important, but come during the "public good" portion of the civic equation. Before we point to the government or others, we must first hold our own. This understanding of good citizenship is the key to fixing our upside-down civic culture.

WORK

Roosevelt starts by addressing work, saying, "The need that the average man [or woman, of course] shall work is so obvious as hardly to warrant insistence." But then, speaking to elite men of leisure in Paris, France, he insists:

> *The man's foremost duty is owed to himself and his family; and he can do this duty only by earning money, by providing what is essential to material well-being; it is only after this has been done that he can hope to build a higher superstructure on the solid material foundation; it is only after this has been done that he can help in his movements for the general well-being. He must pull his own weight first, and only after this can his surplus strength be of use to the general public.*

Notice how Roosevelt frames work—not as a right, but as a duty. It's a duty not only to one's self, but also to others. In this sense, a good citizen is pulling his own weight as opposed to relying on others, or government, to provide for him. Work, to Roosevelt, is a moral imperative for good citizens—something they ought to do, for the betterment of themselves and the entirety of society. Roosevelt does not speak to the manner of employment or the virtue of any particular vocation—that is up to the individual in a free society within a free enterprise system. An honest day's work provides not only "material well-being" but also the foundation upon which good citizens can engage beyond themselves and their household.

This "earned success"—to use a phrase recently coined by the American Enterprise Institute's Arthur Brooks—is also central to the self-worth, dignity, and happiness of the individual. It makes someone independent; it affords options, opportunity, and ultimately, more happiness (as Brooks's studies attest). That is not to say that work is always enjoyable, but the alternative is dependency, which brings with it restrictions, limitations, and ultimately, limits on happiness. According to Roosevelt, it should also bring with it shame. He says,

> *The average man must earn his own livelihood. He should be trained to do so, and he should be trained to feel that he occupies a contemptible position if he does not do so; that he is not an object of envy if he is idle, at whichever end of the social scale he stands, but an object of contempt, an object of derision.*

Not only is idleness not okay; it ought be an object of "contempt" and "derision." Good citizens should earn their keep but also *shame* others who are capable but still choose not to work, earn, or strive. Of course, each of us has moments of dependency, either on other people or government; it's natural, and brings with it a measure of healthy humility. That is not what Roosevelt is referring to; his criticism is reserved for systemic and perpetual dependency that is anathema to both human development and good citizenship. My deployment to Guantanamo Bay, Cuba, in 2004–05 included long shifts, late nights, and many mundane days; but as I wrote in my journal then, "there is a small and subtle peace that goes with the daily grind." Hard work isn't always sexy and not always enjoyable—but it brings a rewarding peace that is ultimately healthy for the soul.

Good citizens should also have contempt for systems that don't afford workers the ability to work, earn, and achieve to their utmost potential. To this point, Roosevelt—who always battled the "moneyed interests" and was a populist champion of the little guy—is clear in the speech, saying, "The deadening effect on any race of the adoption of a logical and extreme socialistic system could not be overstated; it would spell sheer destruction; it would produce grosser wrong and outrage, fouler immortality, than any existing system."

Socialism and other forms of collectivism purport to support "workers" through greater government control of the economy and steeper forms of wealth redistribution, but the opposite plays out every time such a system is attempted. Socialism inherently restricts the competitive engine of any economy, creating less opportunity, and less wealth, for the entire society. Socialism shrinks the economic pie, puts a ceiling on earned success, and diminishes citizens. Only capitalism unleashes the potential of individuals, families, and companies to innovate, compete, and earn in ways that benefit themselves and the entire economy. Free-market capitalism, while never perfect, is by far the most moral, fair, and prosperous form of economic organization the world has ever seen. It seems like a simple point, but too many average citizens in America today are utterly unprepared to defend capitalism in the face of a seductive socialist onslaught.

FIGHT

Speaking of onslaughts, Teddy Roosevelt's second ingredient for citizenship is "the ability to fight at need." He says further, "the good man should be both a strong and a brave man; that is, he should be able to fight, he should be able to serve his country as a soldier, if the need arises." This point is made in two parts (physical and will) and on two levels (war and ideas). First, there is a very physical aspect to what Roosevelt describes. He believes the good citizen must possess the physical *ability* to fight when necessary—to be "strong," "brave," and physically fit—but always keeping in mind that "physical development is a means and not an end." Teddy Roosevelt was always a burly man, certainly not trim by modern standards, but he believed in a "strenuous life" that kept him prepared for life's eventualities—which, even in a white-collar world, could be physical. Good citizens need not be soldiers, but if necessary, they must be both able and willing to fight. Who knew the perpetuation of citizenship could be a motivation for hitting up CrossFit and buying your first firearm?

That is, however, the less important part of Roosevelt's fighting citizen; more important is the sheer will to fight. A cowardly bodybuilder is of no use in a fight, but even the most modest man or woman, given the will, courage, and ability to fight, is an asset. At this point in the speech, Roosevelt is subtly addressing his elite French audience, with words that ring equally true today:

> There are well-meaning philosophers who declaim against the unrighteousness of war. They are right only if they lay all their emphasis upon the unrighteousness. War is a dreadful thing, and unjust war is a crime against humanity. But it is such a crime because it is unjust, not because it is a war. The choice must ever be in favor of righteousness, and this is whether the alternative be peace or whether the alternative be war. The question must not be merely, Is there to be peace or war? The question must be, Is it right to prevail? Are the great laws of righteousness once more to be fulfilled? And the answer from a strong and virile people must be "Yes," whatever the cost. Every honorable effort should always be made to avoid war, just as every honorable effort should always be made by the individual in private life to keep out of a brawl, to keep out of trouble; but no self-respecting individual, no self-respecting nation, can or ought to submit to wrong.

A long quote, but a simple truth. War is bad, but injustice is worse. The question is not "war or no war"; the question is, if war is necessary—or thrust upon us—do we have the ability not just to fight, but also to fight to win, "whatever the cost" (a concept I explore later in this book)? Ask yourself, *Do I have that ability?* The willingness to physically fight for those things we hold dear—our freedom, our faith, our family—is what separates righteous people and civil society from those who eventually "submit to wrong" and become slaves, subjects, or serfs. The citizen who loves freedom so much he will fight for it is what ultimately keeps a republic free. This ethos is what sent volunteers to a green in Lexington and a bridge in Concord, to a field in Pennsylvania, to a hill in Cuba, to islands in the Pacific, and to the sands of Baghdad. It also sent draftees to Vietnam, men and women who bravely fought an honorable and hard-fought war against communists—while America spat on them.

The ability to fight in the arena belongs not only to the battlefield, but also the public square and the war of ideas. Cultivating this fighting spirit for both arenas, however, does not happen by accident and in making this point Roosevelt uses the phrase "a strong and virile people." The word *virile* means having or showing masculine spirit, strength, vigor, or power. It means manliness—a manliness that America is quickly losing among both our young men *and* women. From fifth-place trophies to ubiquitous bike helmets and safety equipment to obsessive antibullying efforts to helicopter parents and their hand sanitizers to gender neutrality, we are raising a society of entitled, coddled, sheltered, feeble, and emasculated future citizens. In today's safe, fair, and politically correct culture, we teach our men to be more like women, and our women to be more like men. The result is youth who enjoy their freedoms—and their own socially constructed sense of self—but have developed little constructive *ability* to fight for them. They believe their fifth-place trophy is special, and will wear bike helmets as dainty adults and shun the "violence" of tackle football (a sport Teddy Roosevelt literally saved from abolition during his presidency); they obsess over every "microaggression" and micromanage their kids, and refuse to acknowledge the physiological reality that boys and girls are very different. The wussification of America is in full effect.

It's not easy to fight, and it's no fun. I didn't get in fights as a kid and shied from confrontation because, frankly, I was scared of it. I didn't know how to fight ideologically or physically. My father was—and is—an incredible man, but confrontation isn't necessarily his forte. My rough-and-tumble days as publisher of a conservative campus publication taught me how to stomach ideological warfare, and the infantry taught me to channel nervous energy into physical confrontation—both learned skills that have served me well in life. For generations, American fathers especially but also mothers—in different forms and in different ways—taught their kids to be virile, to value strength, vigor, and victory. My dad taught me through basketball, and I will teach the same to my kids through any number of sports, activities, and arenas. Fifth-place trophies will meet the trash bin, bike helmets already gather dust and football helmets will be put to good use, bullies will be confronted, the woods will be open for free-range exploration, and their natural inclinations—male or female—will be encouraged and nurtured. At the same time, my kids will be taught to fight and compete hard, but that if they lose, to lose with grace; they will be taught to take risks, but also look both ways before they cross; they will be taught not just to confront the bully, but to defend the innocent, bullied kids without yelling for an adult "mediator"; they will be taught to enter the woods with a compass they know how to use; and they will be taught to treat everyone with kindness and respect regardless of gender, race, class, or sexual orientation. Being a virile people doesn't mean being brutes or barbarians—it means raising citizens physically and morally capable of defending the freedom they've inherited.

As Roosevelt forcefully states, shame on those who "profess that they would like to take action, if only the conditions of life were not exactly what they actually are." Our republic cannot afford to be creating an entire generation of kids unequipped to confront the harsh realities of a dangerous, unfair, and hotly contested world. Some of the things listed above may seem trivial—like helmets and hand sanitizer—but a society unwilling to embrace small risks and get dirty soon loses the ability to fight for larger things on a longer time horizon. Morality is useless without the ability to muster action, especially when something must be fought for—either on a battlefield of a great war or in the public square of a great republic. America needs men, just as they're going out of style.

CHILDREN

Just as important as the ability to work and the ability to fight at need is the third aspect of a good citizen—a family full of children. Said Roosevelt, "The first essential in any civilization is that the man and women shall be father and mother of healthy children, so that the race shall increase and not decrease." In this address Roosevelt is principally talking about having large families, remembering that "chief of blessings for any nations is that it shall leave its seed to inherit the land." Not only does having many kids—three, four, five, or more—ensure the growth of a people (and in America's case, a principle!), but it is also a check against the "self-indulgence" of peoples. Having children is difficult. It's expensive, exhausting, and utterly life altering. Kids change your plans, priorities, and ability to pursue certain forms of happiness. They humble you, teach you, and keep you grounded. Children, whether you are a billionaire or a bellhop, are a common experience in humanity. Parents want to provide for their kids, raise them to be good people, and give them every opportunity to succeed.

For some, not having kids is not a choice but instead a painful reality. Roosevelt is not talking about the physically barren; he is talking about the "willfully barren." Oftentimes, but certainly not always, couples who decide not to replace themselves—meaning they have only one child or none at all—are consciously or unconsciously prioritizing other, more seemingly sophisticated, endeavors. It is understandable that desires for career, leisure, and even convenience can take precedence over a large family, a trade-off made especially prevalent given the proliferation and permanence of women in the workplace. Men used to work and women stayed at home; that arrangement is increasingly scarce and will never return to its previous levels. As a result, even more intentionality—for parents and in policy—must be given to childrearing. The reason, as Roosevelt asserts, is that no amount of "refinement . . . delicacy . . . progress . . . riches . . . art and literature . . . can in any way compensate for the loss of the great fundamental virtues; and of these great fundamental virtues the greatest is the race's power to perpetuate the race." Large families are the lifeblood of healthy societies and, as I outlined in the previous chapter, they are growing scarcer in modern America.

Roosevelt doesn't just mention children; he specifically mentions *healthy* children—children of character who grow up to become good citizens. Healthy children don't happen without good parents and healthy families; in fact the number of kids is irrelevant, or even counterproductive, without it. Roosevelt specifically talks about the "good housewife and housemother" and the "good husband and father," without which good children are rarely raised. Roosevelt calls them the "homely virtues of the household" and holds them in high regard, even higher regard than the refined habits of the cultural elite. These formulations—which sound very old-fashioned to the modern ear—do not mean telling women they must stay at home, barefoot and pregnant. To the contrary, they are helpful in reminding women and men that even in a modern America where both parents often work, childbearing and childrearing must still be a priority, and need to be made viable. This means that women (or men) should not be stigmatized by society if they decide to stay at home with kids. If anything, where possible, full-time childrearing should be encouraged, praised, and incentivized. That said, mothers who do choose to work—or have no choice but to work—should be greeted by public policy that makes it possible to juggle having a career and having lots of healthy children. Working women are critical to America's economic engine, and our policies need to reflect that. Men don't get a free pass in either scenario and must be partners—in the workforce and at home—to ensure

healthy children, because healthy families and marriage are the building blocks of society. The family is, simply put, the greatest antipoverty
and equal opportunity tool in our arsenal, and is the key incubator of
future good citizens. This is not a socially conservative construct, but
instead a civic imperative. Strong families = healthy children = good
citizens.

Despite this truth, conservatives have lost a lot of ground in the area
of "family" through an obsession with preventing same-sex marriage—
a fight I was engaged in for quite some time, especially in college. A
principled stance against same-sex marriage remains a legitimate, personal choice and all sides of the issue should be tolerated openly in
the public debate. Christians and other religious adherents must be
afforded the religious liberty to continue their principled opposition
to same-sex marriage; however, I now believe that fight to be counterproductive. Opposition to same-sex marriage itself only undermines
our credibility to fight deeper problems facing American families and
children. My personal preference is for children to have a father and
a mother, as I believe that relationship brings the best mix of natural,
emotional, and psychological ingredients for young boys and girls. But
this belief does not mean same-sex couples cannot be good parents.
Many have been, and many are; just as many traditional families are
terrible, torn apart, and bad for children. The focus of family policy
should instead be on strengthening families and creating good citizens
by preventing divorce of parents with kids, encouraging large, productive families, and facilitating a work-life balance that allows for both
economic freedom and active parenting.

I've taken to calling myself a child of privilege simply because I was
raised by great parents who invested in my development. By measures
of American society, we were an average family—middle class, public schools, no connections, and no advantages—except the greatest
advantage of all. My two brothers and I were raised by God-fearing,
America-loving, and hardworking parents who took pride in the
"homely virtues of the household." My father was a teacher, basket-

ball coach, and eventually an athletic director at a local public school and my mother was an involved homemaker who worked various part-time jobs and was active in our lives and community, from rebounding basketballs in our driveway to watchdogging the curriculum of our schools. Both were full-time parents—again, hardworking, strong, and principled—who instilled values that have enriched every aspect and season of my life. This is not to say that every family has to do it the way Brian and Penny Hegseth did, only that investing in families—conventional, unconventional, traditional, or fractured—is absolutely fundamental to raising good citizens who will work, fight, and appreciate the exceptional country they have inherited.

CHARACTER

Underwriting all three previous ingredients—working, fighting, and raising children—are the "solid qualities" of character. Without character, and the perspective that comes with adhering to principles larger than yourself, hard work, the ability to fight, and raising healthy children become hollow and, in many cases, counterproductive. Character is the indispensable attribute of good citizenship. Says Roosevelt, "There is need of a sound body, and even more of a sound mind. But above mind and above body stands character—the sum of those qualities which we mean when we speak of a man's force and courage, of his good faith and sense of honor." Alongside the "homely virtues" of the household, Roosevelt further describes the "great solid qualities" of character as "self-restraint, self-mastery, common sense, the power of accepting individual responsibility and yet of acting in conjunction with others, courage and resolution." Courage, faith, honor, self-restraint, common sense, individual responsibility, and resolve—all are used by Roosevelt to describe character, and all are in shorter supply in today's America.

Of course, many other words inform character. Attributes like love, honesty, humility, and respect top the list, and Roosevelt would embrace those, too. However, the "solid qualities" he listed in the speech demonstrate a preference for civic and martial virtues over explicitly religious or "socially conservative" values. He lists "faith," front and center, because belief in God is a core tenet of character. America's founders cited faith—time and time again—as necessary for any republic to flourish; George Washington's farewell address called "religion and morality . . . indispensable supports" of political prosperity. Roosevelt would agree but does not dwell on religiosity as the only tenet of character. Not because religion isn't important, but because it is not in and of itself sufficient for good citizenship. In addition to faith, other secular values—like honor, hard work, courage, and common sense—must be instilled in citizens of a republic. Whereas the church and families are where religious values are mostly instilled, it is up to America's civic and public institutions (and families!) to instill the "solid qualities" of good citizens. From Boy Scout troops to athletic fields and the military to civic organizations, America must forge these attributes into future citizens. This is especially necessary given the postmodern emphasis on "soft qualities" of character like self-esteem, fairness, gentleness, sensitivity, and tolerance. America's youth are taught, ad nauseam, to "coexist" but not to confront real evil. These chickens, figuratively and literally, will eventually come home to roost when we need hawks and eagles instead.

Roosevelt's emphasis on the "solid qualities" of character mirror a hard-learned shift in my own life. Growing up in an earnest and observant Christian household, I made sure to zealously avoid all forms of sin—especially sex, alcohol, and cursing. I thought that as long as I avoided those vices I met the technical, biblical definition of a good person—and therefore *was* a good person. Even by that standard, I fell short, but I was still often insufferable (and hypocritical) about it. For those who knew only the pious caricature I had carefully crafted, this manufactured façade of goodness made a period of faith and life reevaluation in my midtwenties, following war and divorce, that much more puzzling. Today, while I am a believing Christian—saved only by the grace of Jesus Christ—I barely trust someone who doesn't enjoy a few drinks and won't drop a well-placed F-bomb. Not because I think drinking and swearing are good things—but because I think moral lines are better served elsewhere. War, like other struggles in life, will teach you that. Give me a cursing, drinking, and mistake-making sinner willing to fight for America over a self-important, insular, and irrelevant saint any day of the week. Some can do both, and God bless them. But many—including me for years—end up misplacing their moral energy toward smaller, self-righteous, and socially conservative causes rather than mustering the courage to fight the larger battles for goodness and truth. The arena is not about scoring moral points, but instead about fighting—imperfectly, passionately, and with principle—for our shared cause of human freedom.

There is another reason Roosevelt emphasizes civic and martial values: because, without them, "occasional crises which call for the heroic virtues" will fall on deaf ears. Most of citizenship is about the day-to-day pursuit of freedom and flourishing, but inevitable crises will arise—horrors like 9/11 and the attack in San Bernardino—that require an unwavering and courageous citizenry. At those moments, progressive holy grails like self-esteem, fairness, and gender neutrality are of no use. These moments require leaders and heroes who will sustain their commitment to a difficult cause; ordinary citizens willing to dare in pursuit of extraordinary things.

Heroic virtues are forged, not found—republics must instill them each day, or they will find them lacking when the hour of truth arrives. After a decade of overseas wars and domestic dysfunction, Americans of all political persuasions must be reequipped to be resolute in purpose, tough in battle, and vicious against enemies of freedom. This demands a shared and proud civic narrative, leading to a reservoir of vigilance, that must be bolstered by a reeducation—in classrooms, churches, communities, and kitchen tables—undertaken with intentionality, self-awareness, and evenhandedness. *Reeducation* is not a word I use lightly, as it has a terrible historic connotation. By reeducation, I mean rehabilitation of the civic, martial, and heroic virtues—duty, honor, patriotism, courage, guts, "manliness"—needed to muster a robust, sustained, and victorious defense of freedom on all fronts, foreign and domestic. To fight for victory, as Roosevelt said, "whatever the cost." Families must be intentional about instilling it, communities must be intentional about affirming it, and—if done properly—our educational system should be intentional about reinforcing it.

Beyond the ability to muster heroic virtues, a lack of character in the citizenry is an invitation to both bad ideas and misplaced priorities. Plain and simple, said Roosevelt, "If a man's efficiency is not guided and regulated by a moral sense, then the more efficient he is the worse he is, the more dangerous to the body politic." Without character, no cause—working, fighting, childrearing, or otherwise—will long be a good cause, and eventually, due to human nature and failed institutions, good causes can soon become the wrong causes.

Roosevelt goes even further, saying of citizens, "if they grow to condone wickedness because the wicked man triumphs, they show their inability to understand that in the last analysis free institutions rest upon the character of citizenship, and that by such admiration of evil they prove themselves unfit for liberty." Save for unassimilated Muslims who seek to join the Islamic State, I'm not talking about the type of evil that stands atop a Humvee clutching an AK-47 and a Quran. It's rarely sheer and unabashed evil that undermines citizenship—most enemies of freedom don't fly airliners into skyscrapers or blow themselves up in concert halls. Instead, it is far more likely that average citizens become susceptible to more subtle cultural erosions. Poisoned and seduced by "blame America first" progressivism, the view of average citizens can shift from duties to rights, utopia can sound attainable, the lines between right and wrong can be blurred, and class warfare can start to look really attractive. Too many Americans have become anti-citizens, and good citizenship—informed by character—is the only real antidote to these seductions.

Seduced or not, people still want to fight for *something*. As social animals born with a conscience, we inherently feel the need to be a part of a group or show support to a cause. Inevitably, a citizenry slight of civic and martial virtue (the "solid qualities") is overwhelmingly attracted to noncontroversial causes—causes without moral valuations and without evil human faces. Two prominent examples, among many others, are breast cancer awareness and climate change zealotry.

While the cause is worthy, it takes no special *moral* or *civic* virtue to join a cause that fights a physiological disease that is, by definition, amoral. Cancer causes harm, anguish, pain, and death—but cancer victims are chosen in a ruthlessly random manner. There is no evil person or evil cause seeking to kill humans with cancer—the evil is an arbitrary scourge that has no ideology and no rhyme or reason. Yes, we should fight cancer! Yes, we should seek to eradicate it! Yes, we should have organizations dedicated to a cure! But—except for the sheer courage of those who battle cancer themselves and the families and friends who support them—it takes minimal courage to put on a pink ribbon or participate in a walk (and then post it to Facebook so everyone can congratulate you). There is no pro-cancer lobby—hence the solidarity fight is inherently riskless. I've witnessed family members fight breast cancer, and other forms of cancer, with toughness, courage, and sheer determination—their fight is hard, but joining the anticancer cause is not. The fact that the National Football League spends a month wearing pink, and only one week wearing camouflage—for Veterans Day— is emblematic of how far this ethos has permeated American culture.

Much of the same can be said of citizens who choose to champion climate change—propagating doomsday rhetoric about rising tides and weather patterns. Postmodern climate crusaders cling to meteorological prophesies like skinny-jean Spartans, spewing warrior-like rhetoric against a faceless, nameless, and soulless enemy. Climate change is the perfect enemy for postmodern leftists because, unlike cancer, there is no good or bad. With cancer, progress is at least discernable and measurable, but, for climate change evangelists, no matter if the weather is hotter or colder, calmer or stormier, dryer or wetter, it is all evidence that our climate is changing for the worse. They're always right, and never wrong. And if they had to put a face to the enemy? It is *all* of us. It is modernity. The enemy is the modern world that brought about the computers, jets, and cars that every climate change activist relies upon to condemn . . . the modern world. Like most of the students I went to school with at Harvard University's public policy school, the modern Left believes what Obama often says: "No challenge poses a greater threat to future generations than climate change."

Breast cancer awareness activists (all) and climate change adherents (most) are wonderful and dedicated people. The problem is that many of those same activists are *simultaneously incapable* of confronting human evil that *has a face* and is therefore scarier and messier. From human sex trafficking to the subjugation of Middle Eastern women to the horrors of abortion, good citizens of solid character are required to confront the human evils of our day. The solace of uncontroversial causes absorbs the sole focus of too many potential good citizens—who must *also* have the ability and character to fight human evil, to fight for the contentious causes. I'm not saying people should stop fighting for good and personal causes like eradicating cancer, only that they should also fight for civic and selfless causes. Think less focus on bike helmets and more on preventing the Iranian bomb; less focus on endangered species and more on stopping the slaughter of Christians; less focus on weather and more awareness of Wahhabi Islam. Not helping the matter is the full-scale proliferation of political correctness, and pressure to meet every socially acceptable litmus test that comes with it. Tough fights that ruffle feathers and draw distinctions are deemed divisive, dirty, and dangerous—and therefore frowned upon, even attacked. All the more reason for those who seek the arena and understand the stakes of the American experiment to ensure character is "reeducated" as a central tenet of citizenship.

Earlier I said that good citizens are the only antidote to bad and big government; Roosevelt made a similar observation about character, saying, "Without [the everyday qualities and virtues] no people can control itself, or save itself from being controlled from the outside." In one manner or another, our freedoms are never truly secure if our citizenry has rejected the core virtues that constitute character. Absent grounding in the homely, civic, and martial values of the good citizen, the misguided pursuit of other values—with different emphasis—emerges. In many cases, good principles that had always been means to a better end now represent ends in and of themselves. While useful guideposts for any republic, treating principles like diversity, equality, mutual understanding, and tolerance as the lifeblood of civic society—as modern progressives do—has unintended and negative consequences. The obsessive pursuit of diversity devolves into divisive racial balkanization (think #BlackLivesMatter), equal opportunity is replaced with equal outcomes (think socialist Bernie Sanders), mutual understanding without a moral compass becomes blind "coexistence" with dangerous ideas (think the Council on American-Islamic Relations), and rudderless tolerance is exploited by those who actually practice intolerance.

This last point is exemplified on modern American campuses. Politically correct rhetoric (that is, progressive, postmodern, or anticonservative) is applauded, whereas "intolerant" rhetoric (that is, conservative, religious, or antiprogressive) is vilified and instead, silenced. Speech codes and safe zones, which mandate what can and cannot be said on campus, are enforced to ensure only certain forms of speech are tolerated—imposing a stifling intolerance for dissenting speech, intolerance that is unconstitutional anywhere else in America. I saw it firsthand at both Princeton and Harvard, but it's even worse today. I would probably be expelled today for the things we wrote in our conservative campus publication. This mood is no longer emanating just from professors and administrators, but students as well, leading one professor to pen an op-ed in 2015 titled: "I'm a Liberal Professor, and My Liberal Students Terrify Me." The professor wrote, "The problem [is] a simplistic, unworkable, and ultimately stifling conception of social justice" where the feelings of students are paramount and are shielded from offense, discomfort, and challenge. Those who disrupt their coddled ideological cocoon are punished, not protected. This tyranny of so-called tolerance was something Roosevelt warned against, saying,

> *In a republic, to be successful we must learn to combine intensity of conviction with a broad tolerance of difference of conviction. Wide differences of opinion in matters of religious, political, and social belief must exist if conscience and intellect alike are not to be stunted, if there is to be room for healthy growth. Bitter internecine hatreds, based on such differences, are signs, not of earnestness of belief, but of that fanaticism which, whether religious or antireligious, democratic or antidemocratic, is itself but a manifestation of the gloomy bigotry which has been the chief factor in the downfall of so many, many nations.*

This tyranny of tolerance is used not just to silence conservatives on campus, but also as a bludgeon by those who seek to advance their own form of "fanaticism." Just as they have in France and throughout Europe, Islamists—and even mainstream Muslims—exploit American "tolerance" in order to achieve accommodations that would never otherwise be tolerated. Simply put, their sheer insistence, the specter of agitation and violence (even if remote), and resulting perceived "earnestness of belief," as Roosevelt observed, lead many average citizens to retreat on demands for assimilation to American life and principles, a reality we have seen powerfully in my home state of Minnesota among a large Somali Muslim refugee population. For fear of public reprisal, including cries of "intolerance" from Muslims against anyone who questions their religious demands, most of Minnesota's leaders simply cave to the forceful demands of a stubbornly insular Muslim community. Worse, many are apologists for nonassimilation, including Minnesota's Democratic governor, Mark Dayton, who angrily said, "if you don't like our Somali refugees [and their demands], get out of

Minnesota!" From schools to language to policing, Somali Muslims in Minneapolis frequently leverage the undying "tolerance" of Minnesotans to avoid assimilation and maintain a separate form of civil society. A good number of Somali Muslims are great people who contribute to the fabric of Minnesota, but a multitude of others simply do not—and have no desire to assimilate in the future. This is a serious problem, not just of assimilation, but also of national security—as dozens of young Muslims have left Minneapolis to join Islamic armies in Somali, Syria, Iraq, and elsewhere in the Middle East.

Worse, the problem is not limited just to insular and homogeneous communities; it also affects suburban communities of mixed race, religion, and class. Recently at a prominent public school in suburban Minnesota, after an aggressive and forceful Muslim father pushed school administrators, his children were given special accommodation to have a designated prayer space and prayer time during school hours. I wouldn't necessarily have a problem with this accommodation if other religious students—Christian, Jew, or otherwise—were afforded the same accommodation on school grounds and during school hours, except they are not. God was completely and wrongly stripped from our public schools years ago—from the Ten Commandments, to school prayer, to in some places the pledge of allegiance (we long since forgot that it's freedom *of* religion, not freedom *from* religion). But at this *public* high school, because the school's soft administrators want to look "tolerant" of a minority faith, they make a special exception, an accommodation that would never be granted Christian students.

Moreover, the same insistent Muslim father refused to look female school administrators in the eye during meetings, believing females unworthy of even his gaze. But rather than confront his sexist behavior—an action that would never be otherwise tolerated—school administrators capitulated, choosing the path of short-term least resistance. In other Minnesota public schools—rural, suburban, and urban—small Muslim populations are making demands for footbaths, prayer spaces, and forms of male-female segregation. In each instance, creeping Islamism—a movement dedicated to the supremacy and imposition of Islam both nonviolently and violently—advances, and American equality retreats. Where and when does it end? Not until, and unless, good citizens stand up. Unapologetic fellow American citizens—good citizens, Christian, Muslim, or any other creed—must call out instances like this and demand equal treatment for all citizens in order to maintain the distinctly American ethos that has served since our founding. They must demand, as we always have, full assimilation—of schooling, language, and most important, ideas. Critics will call it bigotry, as did the Muslim family at the public school, but good citizens in the arena know it has nothing to do with bigotry, and everything to do with preserving the principles and lifeblood of our fragile republic. It has *only* to do with America.

Make no mistake about it, sheer guts, courage, and principle are needed to confront forms of anti-American intolerance—whether it's closed-minded college campuses or intolerant Muslim ideologies. Taking on threats to our freedom and way of life—subtle or otherwise—is a sticky business. The arena can be a difficult and lonely place, where mistakes are made, critics are many, and any combination of "dust and sweat and blood" is likely. In large ways and small ways, the arena is available to each of us, in our everyday lives, schools, neighborhoods, and workplaces; and only citizens who encompass the attributes of good citizenship will muster the ability to enter the arena—to fight for the basic principles that have made America free, prosperous, and great for the past 240 years. Do you have it in you? If not, why not?

As you consider those questions, don't get hung up on the specific examples—pink ribbons, climate change, campus codes, or Islamist intolerance. In channeling Roosevelt, the first key to good citizenship is not the specific cause you pursue, but instead your ability to "hold your own." Roosevelt's point is that being a good citizen is not something that happens in a vacuum, or simply because of the cause you champion. Before fighting for the public good, the first step in being a good citizen is, as Roosevelt said, "self-mastery." Before championing the causes of others, or seeking fights on foreign battlefields, the first task of a good citizen is to simply understand what it takes to be a good citizen, and then to do it. It's not enough to know what the right thing is, and it is not enough to do something—a good citizen must both have the character to know what is right and the courage to do it. This includes knowing both yourself and our country—understanding our history, our form of government, our economic system, and the moral fabric of our civic society.

Most people miss these points, assuming that good citizenship is defined by activism, discourse, protesting, or even voting. Those activities can, of course, be important; but in terms of citizenship, they are secondary. Roosevelt poignantly goes even further, saying, "contempt is what we feel for the being whose enthusiasm to benefit mankind is such that he is a burden to those nearest him; who wishes to do great things for humanity in the abstract, but who cannot keep his wife in comfort or educate his children." Activists without jobs, discourse without comprehension, protesting without character, and voting without knowledge are all civic actions that actually *undermine* citizenship. Citizens who do "great things for humanity in the abstract" but cannot "hold their own" or "keep his wife [or husband] in comfort or educate his children" are no citizens at all. Someone who protests, activates, debates, or votes without first addressing the baseline virtues of good citizenship ultimately contributes very little to our republic, and actually detracts from it. In this way, a single mother raising good kids of character who works hard and holds her own is a much more meaningful citizen than a middle-age activist for [insert cause here] who can't hold down a job, depends on government benefits, and would never think of physically fighting for the freedom he enjoys.

In this way, the health of American civic life also cannot be judged simply against the amount of activism or apathy for civic causes. In fact, if anything, a lack of activism from good, hardworking people—who are adding value to their lives and, by extension, society—can also be indicative of a healthy citizenry. When freedom abounds, apathy from the right people means the political and economic climate is healthy enough to be ignored. More activists and voters, especially uninformed and entitled ones, is not a good thing; their civic participation will not bring about fruitful outcomes. However, we live in a time when freedom is eroding, and therefore civic apathy from good citizens is detrimental and will eventually be fatal. Call it a silent majority that has been silent too long, and if we don't take action soon, we will no longer be a majority. Instead, for too long, professional activist classes on the left have dominated the discourse—defining a "public good" that is antithetical to traditional American principles. American freedom today is facing death by a thousand causes.

America today requires good citizens who, as Roosevelt said, are prepared to "[act] in conjunction with others" for causes of "public good." My father, Brian, is a perfect example of the type of citizen America needs in the arena today. Working hard and toiling silently for a year on day and night shift, I wrote this about my father in my Guantanamo Bay journal in 2004: "My father has the good-old-fashioned Scandinavian work ethic. If I were ever to start a business, my father would be my first hire. He is smart. He works extremely hard. He is a man of integrity. He loves his family. He is fair and honest. I admire him." I could have written the same thing about my mother, Penny. They are good citizens: God-fearing, freedom-loving, and gun-toting American patriots. They ask for no favors, and make no excuses. They are models of Teddy Roosevelt's *efficiency*. Except we live in a different country, and a different world, than we did when I wrote that in 2004. The trajectory of America is headed in a scary direction, and therefore it is no longer enough for my father or my mother—good citizens by every aspect of Roosevelt's definition—to merely continue "holding their own." The future of America will require each of them (as they have already) and other good citizens of all ages, genders, races, and stations in life to band together, enter the arena (or stay in the arena), and fight for the freedoms, opportunities, and virtues that made America great in the first place. Brian, Penny, me, *you,* and millions of "good citizens" must be willing to fight the big fights and the small fights—in private and public—if we hope to perpetuate the American experiment our forefathers passed to us. Teddy Roosevelt summed it up best: "Good citizenship is not good citizenship if exhibited only in the home."

Why does this ultimately matter? Because other nations and other peoples have flirted with abandoning their civic duties and ended up with a very clear and consistent result—decline. Teddy Roosevelt knew this when he addressed his French audience in 1910, and we would be well served to study the prospect of the decline of great powers in order to get a preview of what our world would look like with a weakened America. France fell; what if America fell as well?

TWO

★ ★ ★

Great Republics: Why France Fell and Why America Could

A democratic republic such as ours—an effort to realize [in] its full sense government by, of, and for the people—represents the most gigantic of all possible social experiments, the one fraught with great responsibilities alike for good and evil. The success of republics like yours and like ours means the glory, and our failure of despair, of mankind. In the seething turmoil of the history of humanity certain nations stand out as possessing a peculiar power or charm, some special gift of beauty or wisdom of strength, which puts them among the immortals, which makes them rank forever with the leaders of mankind. France is one of these nations. For her to sink would be a loss to all the world.
—TEDDY ROOSEVELT, 1910

We men of the Western Culture are, with our historical sense, an exception and not a rule.
—OSWALD SPENGLER, *THE DECLINE OF THE WEST*, 1918

Inscribed on massive marble pillars bookending the hardwood stage at the Sorbonne is the official French motto: *Liberté, Égalité, Fraternité.* The backdrop for the sprawling and raised stage is a massive and ornate canvas—more than eighty feet in length—depicting living scenes of French literature, the sciences, and art. Five large viewing galleries, each with two levels and its own beautifully lit dome, surround a grandiose amphitheater filled with benches and individual seats, each upholstered in plush shades of green, the color of knowledge. Built just twenty years before Colonel Teddy Roosevelt's historic trip to Europe, the ornate venue was designed to represent the historic splendor and grand history of France. The beautifully intimate amphitheater normally holds roughly one thousand people, but on the Saturday afternoon of April 23, 1910, more than three thousand crowded into that same space to hear former president Roosevelt take the podium and deliver his "Citizenship in a Republic" lecture. Fittingly, he delivered his famous "Man in the Arena" statement in one of the world's most storied academic arenas.

It was a day of great excitement in the French capital, a day that came a week later than originally expected, due to delays in Roosevelt's far flung travels. Nonetheless, as Roosevelt made his way along the brief route from the American embassy to the Sorbonne that morning, more than twenty-five thousand Frenchmen and Americans lined streets, waving French and American flags alike. The former American president tipped his hat and waved eagerly to the adoring crowds. When he reached the famous university, the *New York Times* reported, "an enormous crowd was assembled and frantic cheering and waving of hats greeted the arrival of the ex-President."

Thousands had to be turned away, and university officials were "besieged by impatient throngs" clamoring to get inside for a glimpse of the celebrity American president. The energy was palpable outside, but even more so inside, where, the *Times* reported, "enthusiasm was unbounded." France was receiving Colonel Roosevelt fresh off a famed African safari and at the height of his postpresidential popularity. He was American royalty, and was treated as such—even if Roosevelt had asked his hosts in advance to minimize the pageantry.

Roosevelt's mere presence on the stage that afternoon brought "storms of applause" from both common Parisians and academics alike. Not alone on the stage, Colonel Roosevelt was surrounded by "many of the leading men of France." One of those leading men, Louis Liard, the vice rector of the University of Paris, did not mince words in his introduction of Roosevelt, calling him "[t]he greatest voice of the New World, that of the man who speaks by action as well as words, giving to the world counsels of justice and energy—justice as the end, and energy as the means." Liard then turned to Roosevelt directly and said,

> *You denounce the idle and the useless, but you combat also the mischief maker and the selfish. You do not separate morality from politics nor right from force. You are a rough soldier and pacific thinker, and a man of action, preacher of high virtue and a living example of the virtues you preach.*

During the ensuing speech, the colonel did not disappoint, delivering a "long and aggressive address" punctuated by "sweeping and impressive gestures" so vigorous that, as one reporter noted, a "rebellious shirt cuff" kept slipping over his hand. He further endeared himself to the audience by sprinkling rudimentary French language phrases throughout the lecture. Roosevelt's lecture was interrupted "again and again" by applause and ovations from the overflow crowd. As the *New York Times* reported the next day, "when he resumed his seat, after *speaking an hour and a half,* tumultuous applause burst from the vast audience," but also from the leading men of France standing around him, who "were evidently quite as much impressed as the students and other auditors in front."

The reaction in the press—both across the Atlantic in America and there in France—was also abundant and positive. The *New York Times* headline the next morning read "Acclaim Roosevelt at Paris Lecture.

Storms of Applause Punctuate His Talk on Republican Citizenship at Sorbonne," with their above-the-fold coverage deeming Roosevelt's talk "a triumph." The *Times* even devoted two full pages—nine and ten—to reprint the entire text of the address. More significantly, they reported that French newspapers "devote[d] an immense amount of space to it" and that the "lecture at the Sorbonne has created a tremendous impression in France," with "papers of all shades of opinion ring[ing] with approval of the doctrines of civic morality expounded by the ex-President."

Le Temps, one of Paris's most important daily newspapers at the time, appealed to France to take "the advice of an honest man whose deeds and life during thirty-years qualify him to speak." One French paper captioned his speech "A Magnificent Lesson," and still another unabashedly asserted, "No nobler lesson of civic duty ever fell from human lips." *Journal des Débats*—another French newspaper of the day—said of the speech and Roosevelt's visit to France, "Our great democracies are experiments. From the beginning they lean toward corruption. Roosevelt's simple and energetic language is that of Hercules, armed, not with a club, but with a broom, at the door of the Augean stable."

The reference to the Augean Stable—a scene in Greek mythology where Hercules accomplishes an impossibly huge and dirty task using not just brawn, but also brains—describes a condition marked by great accumulation of filth or corruption. In 1910, France was a power with global reach and colonies in Africa and Asia. It was a nation that took great pride in its history, culture, and revolutionary spirit. But, as mentioned in the introduction, France was also a fragile and uncertain culture that was on its third republic since the revolution. Two previous efforts at republican governance had descended into chaos, violence, and the return of absolute rule. Behind the great pride of France, the dawning twentieth century brought internal problems, and soon external threats, to the door of the French stable. For all the grandeur of Paris and flowing robes of the Sorbonne, France was a country—like

America today—as much in need of Roosevelt's Herculean "broom" as a big stick.

We also know that much of France heard his speech. A historic lecture like Roosevelt's—reprinted and commented on, at length, in nearly every major paper in Paris and across France—had far more impact than speeches in today's saturated, sound bite media environment. Newspapers were the major media of the day, and this speech was "breaking news" in France for weeks. While only thousands personally witnessed the address, glowing media coverage across the French political and media spectrum ensured millions of French citizens heard, digested, and discussed Roosevelt's remarks. They heard his argument for intentional and active citizenship, for the bold and strenuous life, for vigorous work and necessary fights, for raising large and patriotic families, for justice first and peace later, for serving the greater good rather than narrow self-interest. Roosevelt's address, as with the entirety of this book, was an attempt to articulate an antidote to civilizational decline by inspiring an active, informed, and patriotic citizenry.

France heard Roosevelt but couldn't take his advice. Roosevelt's raucous reception was sincere, but it was also sentimental. The *Journal des Débats* summed up the underlying romanticized French response well, saying, "Mr. Roosevelt's words are the echo of the old Puritan spirit . . . and common sense to those who are seeking after Utopia." Almost like an energetic younger brother—or an "echo" of a former self—Colonel Roosevelt stood at the academic lectern as a living reminder of what a younger, trimmer, tougher, and freer republic looked like. Looking at Roosevelt, France was looking into a mirror and wanting to see a glimpse of its former self. They wanted what he articulated, clapped for it, and clamored for it—but also still sought after the utopia their younger brother warned against and they had sought since their own revolution. They wanted both the puritan spirit and utopia, but Roosevelt's message was—in part—that the French, or any free people, cannot have both. In many ways, Roosevelt's argument was a corollary of what differentiated the American and French republics from the beginning.

In making this point, Roosevelt was generous and complimentary to his audience. He heaped praise on the many lessons France had taught other nations, lauding France's long and historic "leadership in arms and letters" and emphasizing the "ancient friendship" between France and the United States. He then closed his speech:

> *In the seething turmoil of the history of humanity certain nations stand out as possessing a peculiar power or charm, some special gift of beauty or wisdom of strength, which puts them among the immortals, which makes them rank forever with the leaders of mankind. France is one of these nations. For her to sink would be a loss to all the world. . . . You have had a great past. I believe you will have a great future. Long may you carry yourselves proudly as citizens of a nation which bears a leading part in the teaching and uplifting of mankind.*

Powerful rhetoric, no doubt. Sincere, certainly. But, upon examination, mostly hyperbolic. "Peculiar power," "charm," "beauty," and "uplifting" all ring of high praise, but also of superficial treatment. Roosevelt was a man of intentional verbiage, but also an astute student of history. He respected the French immensely, but understood the fundamental differences between our allied republics.

The American and French revolutions occurred just thirteen years apart but represented very different views of republican revolution, human nature, and self-governance. American-style republican revolution, as articulated by the founding generation, was seen as fulfilling true human freedom, self-government, and free enterprise. The American founders did not reject the church or even the British government, but instead rejected the prescription of religion and the imposition of government mandates without redress and representation. A quote apocryphally attributed to de Tocqueville sums up the American revolutionary position well: "*The American is an Englishman*

who wants to be left alone." This simple observation explains why the
American Declaration of Independence is split in two parts: the first
half an eloquent and lofty appeal to liberty, the second half a specific
list of grievances against the British Crown. American revolutionaries
were ultimately trying to improve their republican politics, not radically alter them. De Tocqueville, author of *Democracy in America,* writing sixty years after the American Revolution—and directly following
the *second* French Revolution—agreed, saying, "where [American constitutional principles] are not found the republic will soon have ceased
to exist." America's founders were conservative in their revolutionary
desires. They were Burkeans.

The first French Revolution, on the other hand, was much different.
Rather than basing their revolution on the proper orientation of long-
established institutions, French revolutionaries rejected them outright.
French revolutionaries were, at heart, radicals. They were disciples of
Thomas Paine. They rejected all forms of feudalism, persecuted and
expelled religious clergy, redrew land boundaries, established a new
(antichurch) calendar, imposed price controls, and publicly executed
the king. French revolutionaries tore down nearly every tradition, convention, and system that had existed in France prior to the revolution.
It was a purge, and a complete remaking of French society. The purge
eventually turned violent, including a "reign of terror" against opponents of the revolution and the eventual rise of Napoleonic dictator-
ship and civil wars. (Americans would, of course, fight our own civil
war eighty-five years after the revolution. But unlike the French Revolution, President Abraham Lincoln's Civil War aims were to fulfill the
founding promise of human freedom, not radically alter it.)

Roosevelt knew better than to tread on this core difference on
this occasion and with this audience, but certainly understood it—
having once called Thomas Paine, a revolutionary instigator of both
the American and French revolutions, a "dirty little atheist." In many
ways Roosevelt's insult neatly described the difference between the
American and French revolutions—one steadfastly religious, the other

violently secular. But rather than dwell on the glaring and foundational differences between the republican origins of France and America, he instead turned his gaze on the things both America and France could impact in the immediate future: citizenship, birthrates, patriotism, and hard work. A *New York Times* subheadline even more succinctly described the topic of his Sorbonne lecture as "Must Work, Fight, and Raise Healthy Children." Roosevelt was gazing toward the future, giving the best common advice he could to two very different republics that were both standard-bearers of Western civilization—and both grappling with the trajectory of their power in an uncertain and unknowable world.

Teddy Roosevelt spoke his inspiring words looking out at an expansive new century with limitless potential for America. Today we face another young century, except, if you're like me, you have a more conflicted and concerned view about the trajectory of America than Roosevelt had one hundred years ago. You're worried about the long-term viability of America's experiment in human freedom, because our government grows larger each year; our national debt continues to skyrocket; our economy is being strangled by regulations; our higher education system has been captured by intolerant progressives; our military is being gutted from within; and we are "leading from behind" on the world stage. These are not ingredients for dynamism, growth, and strength. Not only does it feel like America is no longer headed in the right direction; it feels like America is headed for decline. If America declines, that means by default, and as a matter of fact, the entire Western civilization declines. Other powerful, ambitious, and ideological civilizations are waiting in the wings.

Roosevelt closed his Sorbonne speech by saying, "For [France] to sink would be a loss to all the world." Today, Roosevelt would surely say, "For *America* to sink would be to lose the entire free world." America is—as a military and economic point of fact—the only remaining guarantor of Western civilization, and by extension, the only guarantor of freedom and free peoples in the world. Other countries may have strong militaries, but they are either not free or not prosperous. Some countries may have free and growing economies, but not the ability to project military power. Most Western countries today—saddled with massive welfare states and limited by anemic militaries—have neither. Others rely solely on the so-called international community. This means that the rise and fall of America is completely and inextricably linked to the rise and fall of human freedom. The two cannot be separated. America is the last and only linchpin of the free world. Only a restoration of American values and power will keep the world from sliding toward collectivism and stagnation.

The study of how and why great powers and civilizations rise and fall is a massive and inexact science, filling millennia of events and volumes of academic study. These pages won't remotely attempt to enter that expansive debate, but instead will briefly illuminate developments in France since Teddy Roosevelt took the lectern at the Sorbonne in order to tease out the contours of why modern Western "great republics" decline. Dozens of other countries could be dissected in these pages—our close cousin Great Britain, or the modern case of the moribund and debt-ridden Greece—but given Roosevelt's remarks, France provides a natural and telling case study.

WHY FRANCE FELL

In August 2013, 103 years after the *New York Times* hailed Teddy Roosevelt's historic trip to France, a headline from the same paper read "A Proud Nation [France] Ponders How to Halt Its Slow Decline." Once a far-flung empire, a global power in Roosevelt's time, then a European leader, and now on the verge of "slipping permanently into Europe's second tier," the French Republic has seen grander days. France today ranks 28th out of the 60 most competitive economies in the world, has seen more than a thousand factories closed since 2009, and has record-high unemployment. Its public debt recently surpassed its entire economy, the central government accounts for more than half of the country's gross domestic product, and they have serious demographic challenges in their midst. The active French military ranks 25th in size in the world—making it the largest standing military in Europe, but at 2 percent of its budget, still just one-sixth the size of the active U.S. military. France's ability to project military power is so minimal that in order to commence its 2013 intervention in its former colony of Mali, U.S. military cargo planes literally had to transport French troops and equipment. Like all of Europe, France's sovereignty is ultimately guaranteed by America.

The decline of great powers like France—and so many others throughout history—is not a historical happenstance, but instead the result of individual and collective choices. Some choices are conscious, many unconscious, and others uncontrollable. The weight and trajectory of history have, in fact, not been kind to great powers—and certainly have not been kind to France. As broadly outlined by German historian Oswald Spengler in his contemporaneous 1918 book *Decline of the West*, great civilizations—like great countries—go through identifiable seasons of maturation: from infancy (spring) to growth (summer) to peak (fall) and ultimately, and almost inevitably, to decline (winter). The history of France stretches back thousands of years, encompassing umpteen seasons. Even when applied *only* to France's postrevolutionary history, the seasons develop in fits and starts; but no matter how one breaks up the progression of postrevolutionary France from spring to fall, there is little dispute the former great power is stuck in a prolonged winter of decline—with no spring in sight. From economics to governance to demographics to the military, France has seen its stature in the world slip, and slip rapidly. France ignored Teddy Roosevelt's exhortation, and has paid the price for it.

It's essential to note, when talking about great powers, that nothing happens in a vacuum. The rise and fall of countries can be taken only alongside the relative advances or degradations of other countries. It's not enough to build wealth, effective governance, and a strong and technologically advanced military; great powers must be able to grow faster, larger, and more durably than their competitors, rivals, and enemies. Otherwise, advances in peacetime can still beget defeats in wartime. No country exemplifies this better than France, especially during the lead-up to World War I and its aftermath. France before World War I was much more powerful than it had been fifty years earlier, making substantial economic and military advances in the later part of the nineteenth century. Between 1871 and 1900 alone, France added 3.5 million square miles to its colonial territories and made impressive domestic economic gains. But, by the time World War I broke out, Germany had caught up to and far surpassed France in economic and military might. Stifled by small-scale production, outdated technology, and protectionist local markets, France's economy was only half that of Germany's at the war's outset. Moreover, while Germany's population increased by roughly 18 million in the twenty-five years before the war, France's population crept up by only one million. France was growing, but Germany was exploding.

Nonetheless, with a skewed impression of the power balance with Germany, the French believed they could win the war. France was a nation that took great pride in its fighting spirit, the tricolored flag, and its long military tradition. In fact, as the drumbeat of the approaching Great War grew louder, there was talk about changing the French uniform. Most other countries were adopting less colorful uniforms—in recognition that bright colors and modern weapons were a bad combination. But not France. In the famous words of Minister of War Eugène Étienne to the French Parliament: *"Eliminate the red trousers? Never! The red pants are France!"* So French soldiers marched into the machine-gun fire of World War I wearing bright red pants, a fitting demonstration of their predicament.

As unprepared as they were for the horrors of modern combat, the French fought valiantly in World War I. With the Germans threatening Paris, the entire fleet of Parisian taxicabs joined in a massive twenty-four-hour effort to rush more and more French men to the front, saving the city. The stand against the Germans also may have saved the Allied war effort, as the fighting quickly settled into four years of trench warfare. So many young men died in the Great War that the French people felt they had "lost" an entire generation. They mobilized 8,410,000 citizens, and suffered 1.3 million dead and more than 6 million casualties—more than 73 percent of those mobilized—the highest rate in the war except for Russia. Following that carnage, France was unable to maintain its martial spirit in time to fend off a vengeful and resurrected German Reich. The "global community" was unwilling to step in and stop the rebirth of the German war machine as it began to churn out tanks and planes, and the French were not able to muster a war effort capable of deterring or defeating Hitler.

In 1940, Hitler's Blitzkrieg forces of tanks and planes met little resistance from the French. The French Republic fell and was replaced by the collaborationist Vichy regime, and Paris was occupied for the duration of the war. The French fighting spirit was not totally dead, with Charles de Gaulle and his hardy band of resisters keeping it alive. The French took to the mountains, trying to make life difficult for the German occupiers and passing crucial intelligence to the British and Americans who were preparing for D-Day. World War II may have been won by the Allied powers, but the conflict confirmed—without a shadow of a doubt—that France, and even Britain, had been fully eclipsed as world powers. The United States and Soviet Union, with their competing ideological worldview and economic engines, set the terms of global power for the next fifty years.

Following World War II, the French people felt the agony of a nation divided between the pride in those who had actively resisted and the shame of citizens who had passively collaborated with the Nazis. Through the 1950s and '60s, de Gaulle was determined to re-build French power and insisted on France having a nuclear weap-ons capability   its own independent "force de frappe" (military strike force) to deter future external threats. The return of that martial spirit, even absent the economic and military base to support it, led to an effort to maintain select colonial interests, most prominently in French Indochina—or Vietnam. French military forces took horrific losses at the battle of Dien Bien Phu, eroding support for the conflict in Vietnam as well as French military action around the world. The French withdrew from Vietnam humiliated. In the 1960s, as leftist pacifism and opposition to the American war in Vietnam grew around the world, Paris became a hotbed of student protest—a moment in time from which France has never recovered.

Following World War II, France may have rejected Soviet-style communism, but it still succumbed to other, more subtle forms of collectivism. "Socially democratic" political parties—tracing their roots back to the workers' rights movements of the 1830s—championed a hybrid of socialism and capitalism, ultimately manifesting in an advanced welfare state. France's democratically elected representatives voted for more extensive state regulation, and full-spectrum government social programs, intended to provide both economic security and equality of outcome. As French influence around the globe shrank, generous social welfare spending, restrictive business regulations, and class-based stratification established increasingly deeper roots in France (and, for that matter, across Europe). Over the course of decades, France exchanged economic dynamism, global relevance, and organic military might for economic security, the pursuit of domestic utopia, and the American military's security umbrella.

Gutting its military capability to pay for it, France built a social welfare system predicated on providing a comfortable standard of living for its citizenry. But at the turn of this century that system ran headlong into a combination of globalization, domestic demographic problems, and fiscal pressures the likes of which France had never seen. As the French economy stagnated and public debt grew, protestors—mostly disenchanted youth—filled the streets to protect the generous benefits French citizens have accrued over decades. Meanwhile, an anticompetitive business environment drove companies out of the country, limiting the opportunities available to French young people. There never was a Ronald Reagan restoration in France; instead France pulled back from the world in order to serve the demands of a war-weary, increasingly insular, and risk-averse public.

Today the French don't protest for more freedom, but instead against the very reforms needed to keep their social model sustainable. They protest *for* the status quo. Most retirees in France enjoy government-funded and controlled health care and pensions, made even more costly by the fact that—after careers with six weeks of vacation, a fiercely guarded thirty-five-hour workweek, and ironclad restrictions against layoffs and firings—many French workers retire before they're sixty years old. As the state-run, command economy has shrunk, the French government has continued to grow, with fully one in five French workers employed by the government. France's decline touches all strata of society, with youth unemployment at historic highs (and 80 percent of new jobs temporary), wage growth outpacing productivity for current businesses and workers, and massively generous entitlement benefits coming due for an aging generation of retirees. France is getting older at the same time it is declining in wealth, with no sign that organic population growth and economic dynamism will return.

These realities belie underlying cultural, civic, and political erosions that have taken deep root in France and were forewarned against by Roosevelt. The supremacy of "rights over duties" has permeated all aspects of French society. The relationship between the French people and their government has always been different than that of America, but the result of the country's leftward lurch is much the same: a generation of youth (a growing number of them Muslim youth) without good jobs and many lacking pride in French identity, and raised to demand rather than earn. Powerful strands of secular humanism, globalism, relativism, socialism, and Islamism have infected the French Republic, creating a societal sclerosis, a lack of will to restore France's scrappy republican roots. Most dangerously, as Roosevelt forewarned, class warfare has become a permanent fixture of French politics—with political and economic cronyism rampant among an elite and self-perpetuating government class. There exists only a theoretical path to wealth and privilege for those in the lower class, with an entire generation of immigrants and children of immigrants growing up in ghettolike suburbs outside major French cities. In fact, from the podium at the Sorbonne, Roosevelt proclaimed that a republic predicated on class—with the wealthy at perpetual odds with the lower class—was doomed:

> *There have been many republics in the past, both in what we call antiquity and in what we call the Middle Ages. They fell, and the prime factor in their fall was the fact that the parties tended to divide along the wealth that separates wealth from poverty. It made no difference which side was successful; it made no difference whether the republic fell under the rule of an oligarchy or the rule of a mob. In either case, when once loyalty to a class had been substituted for loyalty to the republic, the end of the republic was at hand.*

A detached elite and a permanent French underclass—unassimilated and uninterested in traditional notions of French society—represent a ticking demographic time bomb that France still has not figured out. Following a baby boom after World War II, the birthrates of French families stayed high for decades until slowly declining in the mid-1970s and reaching an all-time low in the mid-1990s. At that point French families were consistently having fewer than two kids. Birthrates then increased, and today they are the strongest in Europe, with a total fertility rate just above two—meaning, taken alongside immigration, the population is growing. But where is that growth coming from? Rough estimates place the non-Muslim French-born-parent birthrate barely above one child per family, far lower than the overall all-time low of the mid-1990s. However, the birthrate of first or second-generation immigrant Muslims remains very high—with between three to four children per family. By some estimates, fully one-third, or at least a quarter, of newborns in France today are born to Muslim parents. French birthrates may be the highest in Europe, but only because of growing Muslim populations.

This fact is not a bad thing if large Muslim families in France are raising their kids in the French tradition, speaking French, and joining republican institutions. But the evidence suggests otherwise. Whereas America has traditionally been a melting pot (if less so today), France remains a tossed salad of separated communities. France is, at its core, a secular republic—grounded in an agnostic and atheist tradition, whereas Islam, and especially Islamism, is grounded in a closed and rigid religious tradition. As you might imagine, the two mix like oil and water. France's ability, or so far its inability, to assimilate a growing Muslim population (currently around 10 percent and growing) will have lasting systemic and existential ramifications for the republic.

A powerful personal anecdote is helpful here. While serving in Afghanistan, I befriended a young Afghan interpreter named Esmat. He was smart and Westernized, coming from an average family from the capital city of Kabul. We spent a great deal of time together and had many long conversations about life, family, marriage, religion, and Islam. He was a Muslim, but not particularly devout. One evening, when discussing Christianity, Islam, and the future of both, he casually said, "Of course Islam will rule the world someday—the prophet [Muhammad] foretold it. We are having ten kids, and you are having one." Esmat was not radical. He was not an Islamist. I trusted him with my life, and helped him get to the United States because of threats against his family and because of his service to our shared cause. But even peaceful and educated Muslims believe that Islam's destiny is to control the world—and by having many children, they are contributing to that cause. These moderate Muslims don't want to cut off heads or subjugate nonbelievers. However, radicals—of which there are many in France—seek to exploit the growing number of Muslims in order to challenge French values and tradition. Militant and political Islam, known as Islamism, is growing in France, and simple demographic math is its most powerful tool. The recent refugee crisis—with Muslims fleeing the Middle East and flooding Europe—will strongly and quickly exacerbate this existential problem.

Without significant structural changes, especially with tax rates, welfare benefits, pensions, worker protections, and Muslim immigration, France as we know it cannot continue. Nervous French politicians talk about the need for reform but prove incapable of delivering it—even after the Islamic State infiltrated their capital and killed 132 innocent civilians in November of 2015. Pervasive in French culture and elite circles is the wistful belief that France is a socialist paradise, if only religion would fade away and the international market system would, too (France has always had a tepid relationship with free trade and free markets). Or if the rest of the world would stop working so hard. France is not yet in complete fiscal collapse, but Greece provides a powerful glimpse of the kind of future in store for France should it not enact meaningful pro-market and pro-assimilation reforms.

Save for a momentary surge of patriotism following the Paris terror attacks, France is a textbook example of a great power that no longer lives in history. By virtue of its inability to heed the words of Teddy Roosevelt—to "work, fight and have plenty of children"—France is, at best, managing its steady decline. At worst it is headed for societal upheaval, violence, and eventual subjugation to Islamism. The power it currently maintains on the world stage is a vestige of earlier eras when it had the work ethic, civic pride, and military might necessary to grow and prosper. It remains the fifth-largest economy in the world today but will only drop lower by virtue of the simple fact that government outlays and obligations are gobbling up France's economy faster than it can produce jobs and levy taxes. An inevitable result of economic decline is that France's military power—despite recent reactionary increases in spending—continues to decline relative to other global powers. Meanwhile, below the surface, the entire demography of France is changing; in fifty years, an up-for-grabs Muslim population in France will be a powerful bloc, if not the most powerful. The trend lines are all heading in the wrong direction for France, and for that matter, are doing so across almost all of Europe.

France today may still be a republic, but it is far from a "great republic." Rather, it serves as a powerful and damning preview of what America will become if we don't heed Roosevelt's lessons. De Tocqueville once said of America, "America is great because she is good. If America ceases to be good, America will cease to be great." What if America stopped producing good citizens? What would happen to our great republic?

AMERICA FALLING?

It's important to remember that, beyond their respective revolutions, France and America are very different in origin and circumstance, with most differences playing decisively to America's advantage. First and foremost, as mentioned earlier in the chapter, America was founded on a more durable set of revolutionary principles—ordered liberty, religious faith, and real free markets—that made its institutions ("laws not men!") more elastic and enduring. But that founding difference is only just the beginning. Whereas France has a long and contested religious and political history that eventually included a free society, America— the land and later the country—was always a magnet for religious pluralists and freedom-seeking people. Whereas being "French" has traditionally been understood as an ethnicity, being "American" means subscribing to a set of principles—regardless of ethnicity or land of origin. Whereas France is without naturally occurring defenses, America's geography is immensely fortuitous—buffered on both sides by massive oceans. Whereas historic enemies surround France, America is situated between two largely benign and friendly countries. Whereas modern France is limited in land and resources, America is blessed with an abundance of natural resources (most recently with America's energy renaissance) that allow for nearly endless entrepreneurial, energy, and economic possibilities. Whereas France has repeatedly faced threats to its very existence, there is no immediate and existential territorial threat to America's existence. Whereas, despite the egalitarian zeal of the revolution, issues of class and privilege have unavoidable historical relevance in France, America was founded largely on a rejection of patronage and the elevation of meritocracy.

Of course these advantages were not inevitable, and certainly not without controversy. America's revolution was the ultimate long shot, with a band of colonial misfits—many times on the verge of ruin—ultimately defeating the world's most powerful empire. Moreover, just two decades later, that same British Empire—still powerful and with America still vulnerable—burned America's capitol to the ground during America's "Second War of Independence." A great deal of blood was shed to ensure victory in both cases. Fifty years later, under President Abraham Lincoln, Americans would turn on each other, waging a civil war that cost three-quarters of a million lives and fully exposed—and finally confronted—the scourge of slavery. Even today, despite decades of progress, the legacy of American racism and injustice remains. Native Americans faced mistreatment and subjugation as the American territory expanded, an unfortunate casualty of frontier life. Each new wave of immigrants—no matter the skin color—was also greeted with difficult cultural transitions, yet the American melting pot has (thus far) integrated every race, gender, and creed. America's oceans and shipping lanes have long been seen as a strategic advantage, but if we had not invested in a powerful Navy, they could have been easy avenues of approach for enemies and the sea-lanes for American goods left precariously dependent on Pacific and Atlantic trading partners. Finally, America today benefits from an international system that we—as the victors of World War II and crafters of the Bretton Woods monetary system—established and still dominate. Only winning the most vicious wars of the twentieth century brought about this geopolitical reality.

Understanding and acknowledging her imperfections, America has been, and remains, a blessed country. From sea to shining sea, it has more than a million square miles of arable land (the most in the world), the world's largest reserve of natural gas and energy resources, a healthy, diverse, and growing population of over 325 million, a stable form of government, and the world's largest and most advanced economy and military. The combination of these factors—founded on a set of republican ideals in 1776—has enabled America to do more than any other country in human history to provide freedom, prosperity, and well-being to its citizens and the entire human race.

From planes to Pepsi, televisions to telephones, lightbulbs to liberating continents, microwaves to machine guns, laptops to lunar landers, refrigerators to remote controls, independence to, of course, the Internet—the modern world is an American world. Our inventions, innovations, corporations, soldiers, and values permeate the world. But these developments were not inevitable, and not accidental. They were carefully incubated, cultivated, and protected. They are the result of painstaking republican politics, efficient, free, and sometimes ruthless markets, unyielding and decisive military power, and piercing cultural and moral clarity. The American way of life is truly exceptional, for all the right reasons.

Without taking any of this for granted and fully appreciating America's earned exceptionalism, it still feels like America is merely fifty years behind France and the rest of Europe—slowly bending (or slouching, as Robert Bork warned) toward the postmodern, socialist, and stagnant ways of the Old World. Whereas the French Republic is inarguably in the middle of Spengler's long and cold season of winter, America's republic—our Tree of Liberty—is at a seasonal pivot point. America's fall colors—bright and beautiful leaves of orange, red, and brown—may have been on full display for the past few decades, but many believe our leaves are falling, that America's inevitable and permanent winter is hastening. In fact, most Americans polled today believe America is in some stage of decline. Others, including myself, believe a renewed American spring is possible—for generations to come. America's bold colors are exceptional, but permafrost is forming below the tree. Many of the complications and ailments that beset France, Europe, and other advanced countries are on the horizon for America.

America's decline starts with civic erosion and cultural seduction outlined in the next chapter, an erosion quickened by the presidency of Barack Obama but the result of a much deeper cultural crisis gripping America. Our education system is dominated by political correctness, mediocrity, self-esteem, and speech codes; America's families are fractured, especially in vulnerable communities; and religion and morality have been replaced by relativism and "feelings." When you lose that cultural battle—from higher education to religious tradition to civic patriotism to strong families to the virtue of work—even massive and in some cases *former* advantages like geography, economics, energy, governance, military, and demographics are not sufficient to sustain freedom and greatness. It's all downhill from civic society, and the view at the bottom is not pretty. As Roosevelt said in his speech, echoing de Tocqueville's observation about the centrality of American goodness, "The average citizen must be a *good* citizen if our [great] republics are to succeed."

Geographically, our frontier—our westward march and expansion—has long been a driver of the American ethos. Today America has a massive landmass but tenuous control over its own border. Illegal immigration, Islamic terrorists, and the illicit drug trade—which is only growing—threaten to undermine American sovereignty, identity, and security. Moreover, developments like high-speed transport, laser-guided long-range missiles, electromagnetic-pulse weapons, and the sheer power of cyberwarfare are rendering certain forms of geographic advantage obsolete. America's Navy is now the smallest it's been since World War II, calling into question our previously unquestioned maritime advantage.

Economically, America may have the world's largest economy, but it also has the world's largest debt burden ($19 trillion)—a sum that is nearing the same size as the entire U.S. economy. Foreign countries now own more than 50 percent of our debt. Debt service and unfunded liabilities, especially when interest rates hover near zero, are a massive and looming fiscal crisis crying out for long-overdue budget reform and debt relief, both nowhere in sight. America's economic growth potential is also limited by the world's highest corporate tax rates, burdensome (and ideological) regulations, massive social welfare programs, and the failure of political reforms. America's energy renaissance in the past decade—which has effectively made America energy independent—is a bright spot, breathing life and long-term vitality into the American economy. However, America's energy boom happened *in spite of* government policies and regulations intended to limit energy exploration. The Left's obsession with climate change regulation puts the future of America's energy in great doubt.

In terms of governance, FDR's New Deal–era government programs, later expanded by LBJ's Great Society, started a slow march toward a more expansive American welfare state. The federal government grows larger and larger each year (legislatively and through executive order), pulling more people and resources from the productive sector of the economy (private) to the unproductive sector (public). The sheer size and scope of the federal government hang like a wet blanket on America's free enterprise system. The sprawling federal bureaucracy has become America's "fourth branch of government," to quote Mark Levin—free from oversight, unaccountable to the people, and centralizing power with bureaucrats and central planners. Making matters worse, larger government almost never means better outcomes—with the failing Department of Veterans Affairs being a signature example. Armed with 340,000 employees (twice the size of the Marine Corps!) and a $160 billion budget (second largest in government), the VA bureaucracy still cannot provide timely or quality care to America's veterans. The same goes for almost every other federal agency.

Militarily, we remain the world's most powerful nation and the global order still hinges on our capabilities. But those capabilities are shrinking, and aging. Thanks to shortsighted policies like defense sequestration, America's Army, Marine Corps, Navy, and Air Force have all seen steep and dangerous budget and personnel cuts. Moreover, due to antiquated personnel and acquisition processes, the bulk of Pentagon dollars go to the maintenance of aging weapons systems and facilities—instead of rapidly investing in next-generation technology needed to maintain America's decisive edge. The concern is not only the weight of America's power, but also a shrinking gap in technological capabilities with rival powers in an increasingly interconnected world.

Roosevelt described the last factor—demographics—as "more important than ability to work, even more important than ability to fight." He argued that a strong, young, and growing population is essential to the perpetuation, economy, and power of any nation, but especially a republic. Today, on the surface it appears the United States is generally in good shape demographically, with a fertility rate above two—meaning just over two kids are born to a woman over her lifetime. While the U.S. fertility rate has been declining since 2007, it is not yet upside down like much of Europe's (meaning less than two). For now America is having "plenty of children" but America must be on guard against the silent stranglehold that Roosevelt aptly named "willful sterility." Choosing to have smaller families—as Europe has done—is not just about fewer kids, but also demonstrates an "ease and self-indulgence, of shrinking from pain and effort and risk" that is a key indicator of a culture's decline. A society that cannot maintain strong, healthy, and *large* families eventually shrinks into selfish irrelevance and risks being surpassed by stronger, younger, and healthier nations.

America is not there yet, but preventing demographic decline is directly tied to preventing the decline of America. Like France, much of America's demographic growth comes from immigrant populations—as has always been the case for America. America is a land of immigrants, and proudly so. The key ingredient to productive immigration for a country, but especially America, is assimilation. Whether it's my family of Norwegian heritage, or a Hispanic family who immigrated legally, large families must be *American* families that are invested in our language, laws, and history of pluralism. Americans need to have more kids, and those coming to America for the first time need to raise *American* kids; they need to get into the American melting pot, not the tossed salad of "coexistence." Muslims can still be Muslims, and Hispanics still Hispanics—just as Puritans were Puritans, and Catholics were Catholics—but, for the sake of our survival, their civic allegiance and identity need to be distinctly American. This fact ensures that no matter how America grows, we control our own destiny instead of our destiny being controlled by demographics.

Ten years ago, as a soldier in Iraq—deep in the heart of the Sunni Triangle—I found myself with a stomach full of Pizza Hut while getting a massage from a Pilipino lady. It was my first afternoon off in months, and we had driven to sprawling Camp Speicher, outside Tikrit, to stock up on supplies and take in a movie at the MWR (Morale, Welfare, and Recreation) center. After months of patrolling the contentious city of Samarra, it was a surreal day. As I noted in my journal that rare June day, "America really is an *empire*. Not a conquering empire, but an empire of freedom and opportunity. As we work to free the Iraqis and give them a better life, we import, supply, and pay professional massage artists to serve soldiers. Who else does this? While it may sound pretentious to outsiders, it is quite impressive." Maybe it was pretentious, and surely excessive. But it was American power on full display.

As of last year, the Islamic State controlled Camp Speicher. No Pizza Hut, no movie theater, no Iraqi allies, no massages (just sexual slavery), and definitely no freedom. What seemed so powerful to me—so immovable—no longer exists. Setting aside the merits of the Iraq War, which I will talk about later in this book, this scene, and this reality, is a powerful reminder. What was, will not always be. Power declines. Economies stagnate. Militaries lose. And, in the case of great powers, they are replaced. The French Empire two hundred years ago looked powerful and felt immutable, but today it no longer exists. In fact, contemporary France—thanks to self-inflicted wounds and battlefield losses—is no longer a great power at all. America, if we're not careful—at home and abroad—could see the same fate, or worse. The path of decline for America is not inevitable, but it is certainly possible—and way too close for comfort.

How then do we prevent that decline? Rejuvenating the American republic—ensuring it remains the free world's linchpin—does not require charismatic politicians, conquering armies, or new government programs. We do not need, or seek, our own Napoleon. The solution is far more powerful, far more difficult, and was poignantly articulated by Teddy Roosevelt inside that Grand Amphitheatre at the Sorbonne in 1910. As outlined in the first chapter, the essential antidote for republic decline is the virtue of the *individual citizen*. "The success of republics like [America] means the glory, and our failure of despair, of mankind," said Roosevelt, and "the average citizen must be a good citizen if our republics are to succeed." I'm no mathematician, but I do understand the transitive principle: if the fate of mankind is tied to the fate of republics *and* the fate of republics is tied to the average citizen, *then* the fate of mankind is tied to the average citizen of those republics. Meaning, the fate of freedom in the world today is tied—directly and literally—to the collective ability of individual American citizens to perpetuate their American experiment.

The future of freedom in the world hangs in the balance . . . and we, America's citizenry, are the solution.

If we are not seduced first . . .

THREE

★ ★ ★

The Orator: The Left's Cultural Seduction

Unless oratory does represent genuine conviction based on good common sense and [is] able to be translated into efficient performance, then the better the oratory the greater the damage to the public it deceives. Indeed, it is a sign of marked political weakness in any commonwealth if the people tend to be carried away by mere oratory, if they tend to value words in and for themselves, as divorced from the deeds for which they are supposed to stand. The phrase-maker, the phrase-monger, the ready talker, however great his power, whose speech does not make for courage, sobriety, and right understanding, is simply a noxious element in the body politic, and it speaks ill for the public if he has influence over them. To admire the gift of oratory without regard to the moral quality behind the gift is to do wrong to the republic.

—TEDDY ROOSEVELT, 1910

Generations from now, we will be able to look back and tell our children that this was the moment when we began to provide care for the

sick and good jobs to the jobless; this was the moment when the rise of
the oceans began to slow and our planet began to heal. . . .
                   —BARACK OBAMA, ST. PAUL, MINNESOTA, JUNE 2008

S peechmaking has always interested me. As a kid, I remember
watching my father confidently address his high school basketball
team. The sermons our Baptist minister delivered when I was growing
up (and he still delivers them today) were always poignant and powerful. When I was a teenager, Billy Graham's crusades were like nothing
I'd ever seen. So, as an undergraduate at Princeton University, I sought
the academic study of rhetoric—devouring courses like "Behind the
Bully Pulpit" and "Political Rhetoric." My senior thesis was titled
"Modern Presidential Rhetoric and the Cold War Context" (it's not
worth reading), and my research led me to Teddy Roosevelt's "Citizenship in a Republic"—spawning, in many ways, this book. I have always
been drawn to leaders who can turn a phrase.

   A quick study of the literature on rhetoric reveals a central question: how effective is rhetoric if it is not grounded in life experience?
The ancient Greeks wrestled with both sides. Plato looked down on
the orator and criticized rhetoric: "It doesn't involve expertise; all you
need is a mind which is good at guessing, some courage, and a natural
talent." Aristotle, Plato's protégé, took a more utilitarian view: "it is
necessary to be also acquainted with the elements of the question . . .
in each case, to see the available means of persuasion."

   But it is the Roman citizen and godfather of oratory, Cicero, who
remains the gold standard of ancient analysis. As a gifted orator and
political statesman, Cicero used his persuasive rhetoric in defense of
the Roman Republic, even at the cost of his own life—he was brutally
murdered in 43 BC for his oratory and writings. Stated Cicero, "I hold
that eloquence is dependent upon the trained skill of highly educated
men . . . and made to depend on a sort of natural talent and on practice." Cicero believed talent and practice, mixed with experience and

education, created the best orator; otherwise "oratory is but an empty and ridiculous swirl of verbiage."

Cicero was right. He just didn't see the teleprompter coming.

But Teddy Roosevelt did. He understood the same thing Cicero did, but with a better grasp of the devastating modern consequences of misused rhetoric. A student of Western philosophy, young Teddy read the ancient Greeks. He understood the timeless debates about nature, duties, and oratory—and took them into account. Like America's founding generation, Teddy understood that speechmaking was a very powerful tool, capable of swaying the hearts and minds of average citizens. In the hands of a Cicero—a "defender of the Republic"—rhetoric was a powerful tool for good. But, as Teddy Roosevelt warned, in the hands of a "phrase-monger," oratory is a "noxious element in the body politic" and will "do wrong to the republic."

Enter Greek columns, two teleprompters, and a presidential candidate with "the gift of oratory." I remember watching Senator Barack Obama deliver his acceptance speech at the Democratic National Convention in August 2008. Watching on television from a friend's apartment in Denver, I was awestruck by his ability. He was at the top of his rhetorical game. An entire nation was captivated. As it was during the entire campaign, Barack Obama's rhetoric was lofty—even by the standards of Greek gods. He extolled the American electorate with aspirational visions of hope, change, and healing. After eight years of George W. Bush and difficult wars, Americans wanted something different and projected that desire on a young, inexperienced, but very articulate candidate who promised to *fundamentally transform* the United States of America."

The substance of his lofty rhetoric—*fundamental transformation*—raises a key question. Have you ever looked at your husband or wife, your boyfriend or girlfriend—or anyone you loved—and said: "I love you so much. You are so beautiful, wonderful, and talented. But there's just this one thing, I need to *fundamentally transform* you." It sounds absurd, right? Best-case scenario, they look at you sideways with a sad look, tears in their eyes. Worst-case scenario, they stand up, slap you in the face, and tell you to go to hell!

But what if you said it charmingly, with a smooth smile? And while you said it, you made big promises and cast grand visions about what your relationship would look like after the transition? What if you told them they would be more perfect, and so would *you*? That everything would be easier, fairer, and more equitable for both of you. That nobody would judge them, and everyone would love you both. And that if there were still problems in the relationship after the transformation, it would be somebody else's fault.

On a personal level, it sounds absurd. But behind a podium, armed with a Harvard degree and a silver tongue, the words sound like a vision for a new future. So, rather than look at him sideways or slap him in the face, Americans enthusiastically embraced Barack Obama. They embraced his rhetoric, in the manner Teddy Roosevelt warned against. Most voters projected their view of "hope" and "change" onto the Obama candidacy, a basic desire for a better life (and/or to make history). What they didn't know at the time, because his speeches were delivered so eloquently, was that their vote for Obama was a vote for a radical—if very seductive—vision for "transforming" America's future. His words were soothing to America's ears, but as Teddy Roosevelt warned, they were "divorced from the deeds for which they are supposed to stand." Obama's rhetoric sold a vision for America divorced from what made us great in the first place.

I'm not saying Barack Obama is a terrible person. By all accounts he's a kind man, a loving husband, and a good father. He's arrogant and I disagree with him on almost everything, but I respect his ability to navigate our political system. That said, he does want to "fundamentally transform" America. Not because he's a Muslim sleeper agent or secretly seeks America's utter destruction, but because he has a fundamentally different view of our country than most Americans—and our founders. One of his first actions upon entering the White House was to send back to Great Britain a bust of Winston Churchill that was gifted to the United States during his predecessor's term—setting the tone for his administration. Many insightful books have been written, and films produced, that convincingly confirm Obama's anti-Western and anticolonial worldview and demonstrate how his upbringing, education, and associations forged a man with radical leftist views who does not believe America is an exceptional nation. They are all correct.

But Obama is not the problem. He is merely a symptom of much larger problems—two problems, really. The first problem is a citizenry easily seduced by his rhetoric. Even the most dangerous views can be beaten back by an informed and invested citizenry; but if citizens of a republic are asleep at the wheel, they can be "carried away by mere oratory" (which, for the record, happens on both sides of the aisle!). The second problem, however, is even deeper. I call it the Left's cultural seduction of America's citizens. The Left has managed to engineer an incremental, but fundamental, reexamination of America's core tenets—and, by extension, the core tenets of Western civilization and citizenship. From human nature to political and economic freedom to American virtues, the Left's misunderstanding—then distortion—of what made America great and free is the *root cause* of America's cultural, civic, and ultimately political erosion. Barack Obama and his rhetoric just happened to be in the right place at the right time.

When I served in Afghanistan, I was a senior counterinsurgency instructor. My job was to train American, allied, and Afghan troops and leaders on our strategy in various parts of the country. We taught military leaders to look for *root causes*—the real reasons—for the insurgency in their area. It was far from a perfect science, and some root causes ran much deeper than anything a local military authority could address. But the general thrust was to ensure that military, diplomatic, or economic efforts were not wasted on superficial "symptoms" of the insurgency. If Afghan or NATO units could address root causes in an area—like killing bad guys, providing swift dispute resolution, or irrigating crops—it could help dry up population support for Al Qaeda and the Taliban.

If Obama is just a symptom of a larger problem, then what are the root causes of America's leftward lurch? What is the real reason for the Left's seduction of America's citizens and culture? Steeped in history and freed from true partisan allegiance, Teddy Roosevelt's "Citizenship in a Republic" leads the way—getting to the heart of what is missing in American citizenship today. His speech, and my experience, reveal four core root causes.

Roosevelt opens his speech by describing to his "Old World" French audience America's ongoing "New World" transition. From "stump-dotted clearings" to "fertile farm land," from "log cabins" to larger towns—America in 1910 was slowly moving from "pioneer days" to an "industrial civilization." But his imagery had little to do with material progress on American soil, and everything to do with the impact that progress has on the land's people. Teddy recognizes the inevitable progress of the young American nation, and in doing so, tips his cap to a sophisticated European audience that—for better or for worse—provides a preview of America's future. Teddy then delivers an overarching prophecy to a progressing America: Material progress does not equal moral or civic progress. If anything, "progress" exacerbates the best and worst attributes of citizenship.

RIGHTS, NOT DUTIES

Specifically, Teddy warns against a "self-centered" citizenry that is "far more conscious of its rights than of its duties." That is Roosevelt's *first root cause* for what undermines the bedrock of any great republic—her citizenry. When individuals are raised, educated, socialized, or governed to *expect* rather than *earn*, it creates a social disease that is incredibly difficult to cure. When duties or obligations of the individual become either the mandate of the state or an immutable "right" to that individual, the foundations of citizenship—and thereby the American experiment—are fundamentally threatened.

I'm not referring only to the expansive modern welfare and entitlement state. Many observers of the "self-centered" trend point only to the economic manifestation, but this point is not just about the 47 percent of Americans who Mitt Romney famously said were "dependent upon government." Economic dependency, as bad as it is, is not the worst manifestation of rights usurping duties. Economic policies—like "workfare" or wage subsidies, for example—can be enacted to shift citizens off government payrolls and into self-sufficiency. During his two terms in office, Barack Obama moved millions of Americans onto some form of government assistance, but the next president could roll that back. Not easily, but it could be done.

The more dangerous manifestation is societal—not economic. Replacing duties with rights produces a much different type of citizen, and eventually a much different kind of society—a "fundamentally transformed" one. Morally, the state regulates and "incentivizes" a wider variety of direct and indirect actions, replacing responsible individuals, robust families, friendly neighbors, tight-knit communities, and conservative churches in the process. Quietly, the government usurps sound individual decision making as well as the collective moral centers of gravity. Big government slowly gobbles up civil society. Civically, the average citizen gets more cynical about, and detached from, the process—less proactively engaged, less proud of his or her country, and more concerned with fleeting "feelings" than steadfast "duties." In short, replacing duties with entitlements leads to a society that is less free, less driven, less responsible, and less civic-minded. Less *American*.

America's founders understood the proper role of rights and made that understanding central to their founding premise. The "unalienable rights" of American citizens—per the Declaration of Independence, enshrined in the Constitution, and codified in the Bill of Rights—are endowed on us not by the government, but by a Creator. The government is instituted to "secure these rights," not create an ever-expanding list of new rights that it must also manage and secure.

The rights our founders laid out, and Teddy Roosevelt spoke of often, were grounded in core principles and liberties ("negative rights," in political science speak). "Life, liberty, and the pursuit of happiness" are opportunities afforded each American, and the government exists to protect these basic principles. The same holds for basic rights like the freedom of speech, religion, and assembly. With these rights, the duty—the choice—lies with the individual to act on them, and the government exists to ensure the individual has an equal opportunity to exercise those rights (with powers not enumerated reserved for the people and the states). These negative rights are not the ones Teddy Roosevelt was worried about.

His warning was grounded in the type of "rights" his fifth cousin, President Franklin Delano Roosevelt, introduced thirty years later through his New Deal legislative packages. While FDR was not the first president to introduce "positive rights" to the political debate, he was the first to fully institutionalize them. Alongside rights of "freedom of speech" and "freedom of worship," FDR introduced a new right— "freedom from want"—that shifted America's collective perception of rights. Positive rights like the right to economic security, health care, or housing create a duty on others—usually the government—to act. As such, the duty to *ensure*—not just secure—these rights and responsibilities shifts from the individual to the government. Phrased differently, positive rights are entitlements.

Following the Great Depression, what started as an earnest attempt by FDR to care for the downtrodden in a time of need eventually morphed and metastasized into an expansive set of government programs, regulations, and mandates that have elevated the "rights" of consumers, taxpayers, and the less fortunate above the "duties" of all citizens. Where the government steps in, citizens and communities are crowded out. Again, our temptation is to indict only the most obvious manifestation of this trend—the modern welfare state. But as bad as economic dependency is, the deeper cultural rot is worse: a citizenry blinded by a selfish attachment to new government-bestowed rights and allergic to duties and obligations to family, neighbors, faith, and, ultimately, country.

Citizens who don't work never actually earn. Citizens (and corporations!) who rely on government—and therefore never fail—never actually achieve. Citizens who have no faith or allegiance greater than themselves never understand the shared sacrifice that led men to pledge their lives, fortunes, and sacred honor for their freedom. Citizens who lack the "great solid qualities" Teddy Roosevelt outlined are not citizens, they are subjects, answering to a system that perpetuates a larger government, smaller citizens, and broken families. Teddy knew this, saying, "Self-restraint, self-mastery, common sense, the power of accepting individual responsibility and yet of acting in conjunction with others, courage and resolution—these are the qualities which mark a masterful people. *Without them no people can control itself, or save itself from being controlled from the outside.*" What good is a "right" if, once obtained, you give away your founding premise—your citizenship—in the process?

MAN, PERFECTED

This brings me to the *second root cause*. Completing his thought about replacing duties with rights, Teddy ends the sentence by saying that material progress can breed a citizenry "blind to its own shortcomings." Teddy goes on to state multiple times throughout the speech that a man of progress—a man of "refinement"—may also believe himself to be a more perfected person; thereby blinded to the fallen human nature within each of us. But Teddy Roosevelt, a student of Western civilization, the American founding, and his own shortcomings, understands that human nature is not perfectible. There are limits to progress, starting with the human soul.

Like generations before, I've experienced this on the battlefield, and in the shortfalls of my own life. Human beings are capable of wonderful things, but also terrible cruelty. Humans build beautiful museums, but also dig mass graves. We build shrines to great democrats, but also dictators. We'll fight civil wars to set men free, but also to enslave them. Men and women are not angels, not even close. Not in 1776, not in 1910, and not in 2016. No amount of regulations, policies, agreements, forums, or social experiments will remove the deceptive, devious, and destructive tendencies of our sinful nature. We may be able to hide, hinder, or temporarily suppress the inner demons of human nature—but they never go away. We can build systems and structures that mask our raw human tendencies, but we will never heal them. The line between civilization and savagery will always be thin.

Ultimately, Christian, Muslim, or Jew—religious or not—the recognition of our own sins, failures, and fallen nature reminds us to take a humble, constrained, and realistic view of the world we live in. Our shortcomings should remind us of the thin threshold between society and its breakdown. Citizens with a healthy sense of their own imperfections are less likely to believe in the perfection of man, and thereby less likely to devise government structures dependent on perfected citizens. From communism to socialism—to every form of utopian statism in between—leaders who ignore human nature will always tinker with power structures that, in theory, end in hypothetical utopia. Except, as history teaches, visions of utopia never end well in practice—promising heaven, but delivering hell. This fundamental detachment from human nature today, seductively posited by modern progressives, is the second root cause of America's cultural seduction.

NO RIGHT OR WRONG

When moral duty and civic obligation are no longer valued, a *third root cause* emerges that is a manifestation of the second. If you believe man to be perfectible through societal progress, that means the big questions of our day—right and wrong, good and evil—become subjective, and largely moot. Good and bad—absent any religious or civic core—become old-fashioned and passé formulations perpetuated by conservatives, or "enemies of progress." If everyone is right according to his or her own moral compass, then the founding premise of America is wrong and the trajectory of history inevitable. In that case the ideas and institutions of the West—and America—are obsolete.

This third root cause—the end of right and wrong, good and bad—ripples through every aspect of modern American society, underwriting the Left's grip on the levers of influence. In higher education, as I experienced at both Princeton University and Harvard's public policy school, every moral and civic question is up for grabs and deconstructed. Nothing is sacred, nobody is "right," and there is no home team. Everything is morally *relative*. In government-run grade schools, God has been removed and American history is taught politically correctly and selectively, if at all. Across our society, grounded religious tradition is replaced by a rudderless but militant secularism. America's youth are taught, as my younger brother was, their Native American "spirit names," but not the names of their American founders. Earth Day is a huge deal, D-Day not so much.

In our media, alternative families are celebrated as the new norm, veterans are damaged goods in need of pity, and celebrating America is limited to politically correct formulations of racial diversity, environmental consciousness, and gender empowerment. In wartime, American actions are impugned, to the benefit of our enemies—like when the *New York Times* splashed the 2004 Abu Ghraib prison scandal in Iraq on their front page for thirty-two straight days. For contrast, the attack on America's consulate in Benghazi in 2012—which killed our ambassador and three other brave Americans—received *one* front-page story from the so-called paper of record. Our politics are no better, mostly a lagging indicator of a society divorced from the heavy lifting of citizenship. And on the foreign stage, America is no longer considered exceptional—instead merely one among a community of coequal nations. When right and wrong are subjective, who is America to wage war in defense of our own interests? Or, for that matter, other free peoples'?

Teddy warned, "let the man of learning, the man of lettered leisure, beware of that . . . cheap temptation to pose to himself and to others as a cynic, as the man who has outgrown emotions and beliefs, the man to whom good and evil are as one." A graduate of Harvard College who attended Columbia Law School for a time, Teddy Roosevelt was not against higher education. And neither am I. Yet Teddy understood that more "higher learning" and book knowledge does not necessarily equate to greater insight or understanding of human nature—or of the way the world is, not the way we want it to be. Instead, as he told his French audience in 1910, and I've observed in America's so-called elite institutions, more learning—more belief in one's personal perfection— often leads instead to personal arrogance and ideological intolerance. This is especially true when knowledge is divorced from any sort of larger moral framework. For Christians that framework is the Bible; for Muslims, the Quran; Jews, the Torah; atheists, any number of con- structs. But for all Americans—regardless of religion—it should be the shared sense of civic duty and core tenets that bond together diverse peoples to a single American experiment, under God. *E pluribus unum.* Out of many, one.

Teddy, himself a believing Christian, understood this larger con- text, saying, "If a man's efficiency is not guided and regulated by a moral sense, then the more efficient he is the worse he is, the more dangerous to the body politic." And, I might add—more dangerous to the trajectory of the world. To a man, America's founders echoed the same sentiment, recognizing that free peoples cannot govern them- selves without individual citizens tending to their own actions and moral character. This is why, in real time, the rhetoric and reality of the Barack Obama presidency have been so damaging to the fabric of America. At every turn, with every well-crafted speech, and with a smile—he has subtly advanced a fundamentally different formulation of the West, and America. Obama's faith, religious or secular, is invested in something different than America's original social contract.

Barack Obama's rhetoric exudes a shift from duties and obligations to rights and "wants," a belief in the eventual perfection of man, and a blurring of the lines of right and wrong, good and bad. In a postmodern world, his formulation is seductive and goes down easily in carefully crafted sound bites. But the manifestation leads to self-absorbed, shortsighted, and myopic citizens who believe, incrementally, that the good, safe, peaceful life of modern America is the *inevitable* life. And with big fights of a free society no longer necessary, a drifting citizenry—still saddled with debt, working for low wages, and stripped of pride in America—is left searching for the point of all the hard work, and tough warfare, that created modern America.

CLASS WARFARE

At that point, the modern Left—and Barack Obama specifically—have a vulnerable electorate right where they want them. *Why is life still so hard?* people ask. The Left's answer is ready, and powerful: *It's not your fault. It's somebody else's fault!* Enter class warfare, the *fourth and final root cause* of a fledgling citizenry—and the nail in the coffin for a republic according to Roosevelt. Class warfare, expressed forcefully on the campaign and from the presidential bully pulpit, is a defining characteristic of Barack Obama's rhetoric. If his transformation of America doesn't transform the lives of individuals for the better, then it's not his fault—it's the fault of a failed American system of governance, economics, and culture. Class warfare can be very effective on the campaign trail, but the result—as Teddy Roosevelt saw—is devastating to a citizenry.

The Left today preaches diversity, tolerance, and equality in all ways—and then uses those principles as a bludgeon. Of course, as conservatives we should embrace—and do embrace—diversity, tolerance, and equality as *means* to a better end; the Left, however, treats them as fundamental ends. For the Left, we are good because we are diverse; we are at our best when we tolerate everything; and everything is better when we are all equal. Teddy Roosevelt's conception of citizenship in 1910 would beg to differ. Instead, when we are diverse, yet united in purpose, we are good; when we tolerate divergent views even when we disagree with them, we are good; and when we give people real "equality of opportunity," we are good. The latter conception unites; the former divides . . . but makes for good politics.

The class-based blame game is the approach of the modern American Left, and Teddy Roosevelt saw it coming: "The citizens of a republic should beware, and that is of the man who appeals to them to support him on the ground that he is hostile to other citizens of the republic, that he will secure for those who elect him, in one shape or another, profit at the expense of other citizens of the republic." Obama has mastered this rhetorical and policy device and America has suffered accordingly. Whether it's America's wealthiest citizens, the cops who police our streets, our campus "safe spaces," or the war on women, Obama pits rich against poor, old against young, black against white, and male against female in a way that has exacerbated the differences of individual Americans, undermining the social contract our founders set out to establish. His straw men are many, and well worn. Starting with his 2004 speech at the Democratic convention in Boston, Barack Obama pledged not to see red states or blue states, but instead our *United* States; in reality he has done the exact opposite—emphasizing America's class, racial, and gender differences. In effect, he has reversed America's de facto national motto. Today, we are *Ex uno, multis*. Out of one, many. Teddy Roosevelt foreshadows, quite clearly, that these developments mean "the end of the republic [is] at hand." I fear he could eventually be proved right.

• • •

While there are other critical factors at play, this combination of *four root causes*—rights overtaking duties, the destructive pursuit of utopia, pervasive moral relativism, and class warfare—erodes the basic tenets of what made our imperfect country the last, best hope for free peoples and free markets. The "fundamental transformation" of America is under way, but it didn't just begin within the past seven years. While Barack Obama has hastened America's transformation, the ingredients were set in motion long ago—in academia, media, culture, and politics. American traditionalists have attempted to fight back, but in many ways our counterattacks have been mostly counterproductive—only accelerating the pace of the Left's cultural seduction.

Reflexively defensive, traditional advocates for America and her exceptional ingredients have walked into the Left's trap, and we have been easily framed by politically correct zealots as "anti-everything"— anti-woman, anti-gay, anti-immigrant, anti-caring, anti-environment, and anti-progress. These labels are unfair, but they are powerful from the podium. They also push the debate into a sphere weighted toward social conservatism, where frustrated traditionalists dig in their heels: *Transgendered rights . . . what? White privilege . . . really? Earned amnesty . . . never! Climate change . . . prove it!* Taken alongside shifting cultural sands, and hastened by the four root causes listed above, the ideological terrain slants in favor of the Left's narrative. American traditionalists, relying on beliefs they have long held, are made to look like they don't care, whereas the Left does. They're made to look cruel, the Left compassionate. They're made to look backward, the Left progressive. They're made out to be cranky old white men, the Left young and multicultural. They're made out to be tired; the Left looks fresh and futuristic. And as the terrain slants more and more against American traditionalists, they fight back harder with the same tactics—only exacerbating the contrast the Left hopes to exploit.

This is not just an observation, but something I've learned personally. When I showed up at Princeton University as a freshman in the summer of 1999, I was largely nonideological and laser-focused on trying to make the varsity basketball team. I wasn't very political, and considered myself a Republican only because my dad was one. I was a Christian, but more out of diligent habit than deep conviction. I came from a strong family and a safe and supportive community. I believed America was a great country, that faith was critically important (even if I lived it poorly), and that family was the foundation of success in life—regardless of race, class, or gender. My parents were squarely middle class, yet I was a child of privilege because I had a family that loved me, a God who forgave my sins, and a country that had given everything to me.

But none of that seemed to matter at Princeton, and from the first week I arrived on campus, I was confronted with a very alternate belief system. My preparatory summer session was largely sorted by race and socioeconomic class. Our first week, the school promoted and cosponsored an event called "The Joys and Toys of Gay Sex." Liberal professors outnumbered their moderately conservative counterparts 30:1 in the politics and history departments. The chapel had a Christian edifice that only preached a gospel of moral relativism. And after 9/11, "mutual understanding" peace protests were more prevalent than condemnations of Islamic terrorism.

I felt compelled to respond, and respond we did. As the publisher of the *Princeton Tory*—the freewheeling campus conservative publication—we confronted the biggest issues head-on. Bombastic cover stories (and headlines) splashed the front page of every issue, confronting topics like homosexuality ("Coming out of the Closet"), abortion ("Abortion at Princeton"), feminism ("Killing Feminism"), atheism ("God and Politics"), and Islamists ("Dig in and Fight"). We pulled no punches, and made the full-throated case for traditional values. In most ways I'm proud of the stances we took and the arguments we made. I was not in the business of making friends, but wanted to hold the line—and represent a viewpoint I believed was sorely lacking on campus. As a social conservative warrior, I waged an aggressive, if lonely, "culture war" on campus.

But, in retrospect and with the distance of time and experience, I fear we did as much harm to our overall cause as we did good. We fought the good fight—*in the arena*—but did not cogently or convincingly address the root causes of the Left's cultural seduction. We dwelled on a handful of counterproductive cultural battles—like unfairly demonizing homosexuality—while failing to address actual reasons for American civic decline. Rather than a socially conservative focus, we should have challenged what Teddy addressed in his speech—an upside-down civic culture that unilaterally disarms our citizenry's ability to muster the duties, virtues, and responsibilities necessary to restore American citizenship, freedom, and prosperity. We did a lot of good things, but we also missed the mark—and they used it against us. I'm quite certain the Left will try to use it against me for the rest of my life.

There is an excuse for our bombastic, if principled, behavior: we were undergraduates, letting arguments fly, in what used to be an open campus discussion. But we cannot afford to make the same mistakes in the larger public square today. If we don't refocus our efforts on the civic realm of the next generation, we will keep losing ground to the Left. What once infected only our elite institutions today infects a broader swath of our country. The Left's cultural seduction has sallied forth far beyond the Ivory Tower and permeated America's cultural consciousness. In many ways, this reality is the reason for this book. Teddy Roosevelt understood the fights worth having, and the principles worth fighting for—like work, citizenship, family, and character. Unapologetic believers in America must undertake a similar education—pointing our immediate and finite firepower at problems we can actually address, rather than flailing away at cultural trends we cannot reverse (save for abortion, an issue we should never relent on). Until we do this, we will never address the root causes driving America's decline.

The 2016 presidential election has already featured soaring and testy rhetoric . . . and even more teleprompters. But America would do well to remember Cicero's advice—that without grounding in education and real-life experience, "oratory is but an empty and ridiculous swirl of verbiage." Again, Obama is a great example of this. As good as he was with a teleprompter in 2008, he has shown himself to be quite inarticulate without the aid of the technology. His awkward pauses and constant "ums" and "ahs" without digital assistance reveal his real speechmaking skills—and would make ancient Greek orators shudder. They are also an apt personification of the Left's cultural seduction. Their ideas sound good, but those ideas are merely a smoke screen for failed and recycled ideas of human nature and class warfare. Ideas that rot America's core and undercut her ability to be a beacon of freedom in a hotly contested world.

PART II

★ ★ ★

The Good Patriot | Our War and America in the World

FOUR

★ ★ ★

Citizen of the World:
The World the Left Wrought

I believe that a man must be a good patriot before he can be, and as the only possible way of being, a good citizen of the world. Experience teaches us that the average man who protests that his international feeling swamps his national feeling, that he does not care for his country because he cares so much for mankind, in actual practice proves himself the foe of mankind; that the man who says that he does not care to be a citizen of any one country, because he is the citizen of the world, is in fact usually an exceedingly undesirable citizen of whatever corner of the world he happens at the moment to be in. . . . If a man can view his own country and all other countries from the same level with tepid indifference, it is wise to distrust him.

It is war-worn Hotspur, spent with hard fighting, he of the many errors and valiant end, over whose memory we love to linger, not over the memory of the young lord who "but for the vile guns would have been a valiant soldier."

—Teddy Roosevelt, 1910

The burdens of global citizenship continue to bind us together. . . .
Now is the time to join together, through constant cooperation, strong
institutions, shared sacrifice, and a global commitment to progress, to
meet the challenges of the 21st century.

—Senator Barack Obama,
Berlin, Germany, July 24, 2008

September 17, 2001, was the first day of class my junior year at Princeton University. I still remember casually stepping over the Monday edition of the *Daily Princetonian* at our doorstep that morning, but then pausing to pick it up. I didn't always read our campus newspaper, but given the times we were in, I was curious. Standing outside our Gothic dorm room, I thumbed through the paper, eventually landing on the editorial section, where a headline and op-ed caught my eye: "A Time for Restraint," by Dan Wachtell, a Princeton student I had never met. As I read his piece, fully engrossed and never looking up, I wandered back into the room—my blood pressure rising in real time. Shoving the paper in my roommate's face, I grumbled: "Read this horseshit! Who the hell is Dan Wachtell? We need to respond today." He agreed.

Forty-five miles from the comfy confines of our Ivy League campus, smoke was still billowing from two massive holes in lower Manhattan. Six days earlier—using airliners as human-filled missiles—violent Islamists had attacked America in broad daylight. More than three thousand Americans were dead in New York, Washington, D.C., and Pennsylvania, the illusion of our security rocked. On the morning of September 11, war was declared on America, and less than a week later a range of emotions—shock, pain, grief, anger, and anxiousness among them—were still very raw inside most American souls. But, as we read that morning, clearly not *all* American souls.

Having been at Princeton for two years already, I was certainly familiar with the liberal arguments of rank-and-file students like Dan

Wachtell. I'd heard their arguments in class, read them in print, and attended countless campus events reinforcing their views. By the time I read Wachtell's article, I had a good sense of the modern Left's worldview. But following such a brutal and cowardly attack on fellow Americans—innocent civilians, no less—I anticipated that the campus Left would, at the very least, soften their approach. But I was wrong. Worse, Dan Wachtell was not a progressive leader or outspoken College Democrat on campus. He had written two editorial pieces earlier, both largely nonpolitical in nature. But there he was, a normal guy, making a full-throated and unambiguously "blame America" case six days after the worst terrorist attack in American history.

According to Dan Wachtell—and the reflexive, elite, left-wing view he gave voice to—America was mostly to blame for the attacks. He wrote in the *Daily Princetonian* that day:

> *Tuesday's terrorists felt that such monumental wrongdoing had been inflicted upon them, their families and their way of life by the United States that such calamitous action was the only remedy . . . at this moment in which emotions are understandably running wild, the question we must ask is not "Who?" but "Why?" . . . What has America done to lead these people to the conclusion that murderous terrorism is the only appropriate action?*

America's blame didn't stop there, but instead extended to retaliatory attacks that hadn't even happened yet. To Dan Wachtell, America's soon-to-be military response was racist, outdated, and no more moral than the actions of Al Qaeda terrorists. He continued:

> *[T]o attack large groups of people or entire nations makes us no more just or moral or right than were the 19 who attacked humanity on Tuesday. . . . The conflation by this country's leadership of the "terrorists who commit such acts and the nations that harbor them" is dangerous, illogical, unacceptable and, in fact, nothing short of a prejudiced and racist*

statement. [America's leaders] only want to arouse the anger and hatred
of the American people to justify their rash, outdated and hawkish mili-
tary action.

But the argument Dan Wachtell concluded with reveals the Left's underlying worldview, to wit: not only was—and is—America on the wrong side of the 9/11 attacks, but the very idea of America is wrong. He concludes:

Nothing pains me more than to hear people who live in this country an-
nounce, as one woman did on yesterday's news, that she is, in light of this
tragedy, "not Yankee, not Southern, not Black, not White, but above all
else, American." Is she not, above all else, Human? Would she—would our
political and military leaders—rather be called Inhuman than be called
Arab?

His final point—that America is not worthy of fundamental allegiance—brings the entire argument into focus. Dan Wachtell does not see himself as an American, but instead as a global citizen. It's not that he is an apologist for terrorists or anti-American, per se. He's a perfectly nice guy. He is just *over* America. As Teddy Roosevelt foreshadowed in his speech, his "international feeling swamps his national feeling" and "he does not care for his country because he cares so much for mankind." To Wachtell, and to the modern Left, patriotism is outdated, exceptionalism passé, and America too flawed to merit allegiance. Instead the cause of naked humanity—regardless of flag, freedom, or creed—is the future.

Our response to Dan Wachtell the next day in the *Daily Princetonian* was not Pulitzer worthy, but at least it didn't pull any punches. We summed up his argument with a phrase: "cowardice masquerading as conscience." We zeroed in on his blame-America-first argument, answering his *why?* question and laying out the so-called grievances used to justify mass murder—support for Israel, defense of Kuwait, and the promotion of human rights and freedom around the world. Like the rest of America, we echoed the need for unity, for patriotism, for justice, and for prayer. Finally, we pointed out the ultimate irony to the likes of Dan Wachtell: "American soldiers will die to give you . . . the privilege to sit safely in your dorm room and criticize your own country . . . [and] we hope you would be ashamed to send your article to the families of [the] victims." With bodies still being pulled out of the wreckage, our response was more *'Merica!* than anything else—but at an Ivy League campus we felt it needed to be said. It may have only been a student publication, but it was the most consequential rebuke we had at our disposal. It was what we could do, where we were. As Roosevelt might say, "We held our own."

It's not that Dan Wachtell was, or is, a coward. It's that he and a generation of rank-and-file liberal "elites" like him have been educated and socialized to unilaterally disarm themselves, and thereby disarm America. His argument was dangerously naïve and ungrateful for the sacrifices of all those who have fought and died on the battlefield to preserve America. Worst of all, he is far from alone. In fact, he is typical of a growing American elite who, as Roosevelt put it, "but for the vile guns would have been a valiant soldier." To them, America is not special and therefore America should not act; and when America does act, we're usually the real problem. In their mind America *is the problem,* not a part of the solution. To them, if we can all just coexist and mutually understand, the ills facing humanity will eventually wash away. Those pesky "vile guns" have turned generations of citizen soldiers into cynics and cowards, prospective "good patriots" into detached global observers.

Two days after our exchange in the Princeton newspaper, another "citizen of the world" gave his take on the 9/11 attacks. Writing in the *Hyde Park Herald,* a state senator from Illinois named Barack Obama gave his first public statement on the attacks. Page four of the *Herald* provides reaction from multiple local Chicago officials, most hitting familiar tunes: calling for a "heroic spirit . . . against evil forces," call-

ing out the "arrogance and cowardice" of the attackers, and quoting
Churchill's words at the dawn of World War II. Barack Obama's first
instinct, on the other hand, was none of those things. He started out his
brief post by saying that he hopes America "draw[s] some measure of
wisdom from this tragedy." He compels America to "understand" the
source of terrorism, and blames the attack on "a fundamental lack of
empathy" from the attackers. Ultimately, to Barack Obama, the nineteen hijackers were motivated by "a climate of poverty and ignorance,
hopelessness and despair." He concludes by chiding the U.S. military
to "take into account the lives of innocent civilians abroad."

Dan Wachtell eventually became a lawyer in New York City, but
Barack Obama became a two-term president of the United States.
Both—along with an entire generation of young Americans—are the
"citizens of the world" that Teddy Roosevelt warned about a century
earlier. Swamped by layers of education and cultural reinforcement,
even the attacks of 9/11—the worst single act of terrorist violence in
American history—motivate them only to introspective empathy, mutual understanding, and a restrained response. To both, military action
is "outdated." Even simple facts—like the fact that the 9/11 terrorists
all came from intact families, most were upper-middle-class, and none
came from the fringes of society—seemed to have little to no impact
on the worldview of global citizens hell-bent on "coexisting" with even
the most poisonous ideologies. The resulting common thread between
Wachtell and Obama—as forewarned by Teddy Roosevelt—is cowardice masquerading as conscience. Their self-emasculation unwittingly turns them into foes of freedom, foes of American values, and
ultimately, "foes of mankind." It unknowingly turns them into cowards,
and it weakens the resolve of our American experiment.

Early in his speech at the Sorbonne, Teddy Roosevelt cites the "war-
worn Hotspur"—one of Shakespeare's best-known characters. Sir
Henry Percy, nicknamed Hotspur, was one of the most valiant knights

of the fourteenth century, who, after helping to bring King Henry IV back from exile, ultimately rebelled and took up arms against the king—citing a long list of grievances, among them "tyrannical government." Hotspur ultimately fell on the battlefield, but rumors spread that he was not really dead. King Henry, eager to squash any talk of further rebellion, had Hotspur's body exhumed, impaled, and displayed throughout the land. Said Teddy Roosevelt, "It is war-worn Hotspur, spent with hard fighting, he of the many errors and valiant end, over whose memory we love to linger . . . not over the memory of the young lord who 'but for the vile guns would have been a valiant soldier.'" For the past seven years, America has been led by the type of "young lord"—Barack Obama—that Roosevelt warned about. But for the vile guns, but for the founding principles, but for fanatical enemies, Obama and his fellow global citizens are valiant soldiers . . . against climate change! Prior to the era of Obama, both Republicans and Democrats, if at times reluctantly, embraced a life "spent with hard fighting," filled with "many errors," but ultimately tending toward "valiant ends." Such lives—and such countries—are "over whose memory we love to linger." In a dangerous world, we don't have the luxury to sit back and simply remember the days when America *was* a great power, *was* the world's beacon of freedom, and ultimately *was* the guarantor of free peoples from Krakow to Kalamazoo. Defending freedom has always required vile guns and good patriots willing to use them, and the twenty-first century will be no exception.

The manifestation of our "young lord's" worldview—I call it a "coexist" foreign policy—has been laid bare before America, and the world, since Obama's inauguration on January 20, 2009. On that date a "citizen of the world" became president of the United States. Of course Barack Obama considers himself an American, and mountains of his rhetoric underscore that, but unlike any of his forty-three predecessors, there is very real reason to confidently posit that at his core, Barack Obama's "international feeling swamps his national feeling." Teddy Roosevelt once again diagnoses the manifestation of this shift;

it creates an "exceedingly undesirable citizen of whatever corner of the world." Once again it comes back to citizenship, but this time it applies to America's interaction with the world—a relationship that is currently off the rails.

To be clear, Teddy Roosevelt does not believe being some form of a "citizen of the world" is inherently a bad thing, and neither do I. Seeking strong international alliances, being good stewards of shared natural resources, and humanitarian relief are all things America—as a citizen of the world—has done, and should do. We live in a more interconnected and international world than ever, and retreating behind Fortress America, or unilaterally withdrawing from our alliances, is not an option. But there is a necessary precursor to constructive global engagement that Teddy Roosevelt identified clearly, which is even more necessary in today's international world: "a man must be a *good patriot* before he can be, and as the only possible way of being, a good citizen of the world." Note the certainty in his voice—*must be* a good patriot as the *only possible way* to be a good citizen of the world.

"The Good Patriot" was the original title for this book, as I felt it succinctly encompassed the sentiment that America, and her leaders, need in the twenty-first century. Loving a free and prosperous America—warts and all—is the best way to constructively engage an equally fallen world. Teddy Roosevelt believed it, presidents since have believed it, but Barack Obama (and his fellow coexist adherents) does not. His upbringing, education, and career track reinforced a deeply held belief that America—and the West generally—have not been a force for good in the world, and therefore being a "patriot" is passé and fully subjective.

But Obama is not the problem; he is once again merely a symptom. A new generation of elitist leftists fundamentally misunderstands human nature, thereby underestimating the threats to America and undermining American power. Like the "foolish cosmopolitans" of Teddy's time, modern progressive elites—perched in their Ivory Towers and insulated government orbits—see nothing exceptional about America, believing instead that the "global family" can simply "coexist," "mutually understand," and be made more "culturally aware." As such, they minimize their American allegiance and maximize their global orientation. They seek to neuter American power for the sake of leveling the global playing field. Obama may have been the first American to go on a post-inauguration global apology tour, but he did so with the adoring approval of the mainstream media, foreign policy establishment, and Ivy League professoriate—his fellow global citizens. I went to school with the next generation of "coexist" leftists at Princeton and Harvard; armies of Little Obamas ready to legislatively save the world from climate change, income inequality, and . . . America.

But not every action taken by the Obama administration on the world stage has been driven by a core "coexist" ideology. A second pitfall of Barack Obama's foreign policy orientation centers on another elite group, whom Teddy dubs "perpetual pragmatists" in his speech. Less ideologically committed than their progressive brethren, these modern pragmatic elites take soft solace in shades of gray that perpetually prohibit them from decisive, contentious—and necessary—actions. This group of squinting, "thoughtful," and on-the-one-hand-and-on-the-other-hand elites emphasizes their conflicted nature at every turn—only thinly veiling their sheer lack of fortitude. In the minds of left-of-center foreign policy pragmatists, because every U.S. action has a potential reaction or unintended consequence, every raid the potential for civilian casualties, and every piece of strong rhetoric a potential offense, they default to consensus, capitulation, and the lowest common denominator.

Whereas ideological progressives believe America *is the problem,* America's modern "perpetual pragmatists" still believe in America—they're just ashamed of it, beaten down by leftists, internationalists, and elite institutions. They believe in principles like advancing freedom and free markets, defending our allies, and defeating Islamism. They're just intellectually timid, their instincts and beliefs blunted by

leftist pressure and the inevitably messy nature of foreign affairs. As
the world grows more complex, solutions more difficult, and stark con-
trasts more passé, modern pragmatic elites hide behind international
institutions and faux causes. They believe in a strong America, but
they're more worried about getting an invitation to the next Council
on Foreign Relations luncheon (of which I'm a term member, I will
note), so they hedge every bet, caveat every stance, and slap "coexist"
bumper stickers on their Volvos. They look thoughtful and nuanced,
but they actually lack the fortitude to fight the real fights. More cowardice masquerading as conscience.

Modern pragmatic elites are, as a result of their conflicted and
timid nature, seduced into advancing causes favored by committed
leftists. Perpetual pragmatists still believe in America's role as freedom's guarantor, but they are coaxed into advancing a much narrower
leftist agenda that neither believes in America nor confronts the big
problems of our time. Instead of fighting hard threats, they join the
self-congratulatory chorus of leftists combatting soft threats—most
especially radical environmentalism, but also many forms of political incorrectness and historical reparations. They vow to defeat faceless enemies but cower and equivocate when asked to defeat—or
even confront—enemies with faces. They rally against global climate
change using apocalyptic and militaristic rhetoric but stretch the
limits of imagination to understand and "coexist" with committed
Islamists.

The two camps of elites—ideologically progressive and obsessively
pragmatic—differ in their roots but reinforce the same pitfalls. The
former believe American interests, unilaterally or aggressively applied,
are actually the cause of the world's problems. The latter are so consumed with consensus, collaboration, and context that they are often
paralyzed in confronting real threats. Both undermine America, both
live inside the mind of Barack Obama and his national security staff,
and both contribute to the "coexist" foreign policy disaster that has
unfolded since 2009.

• • •

The world Barack Obama inherited in 2009 was much more stable than today, but still far from a perfect place. Between his election and inauguration alone, Pakistani-based Islamists killed nearly two hundred people in a brazen terrorist attack in Mumbai, India, Israel launched an air and ground offensive in the Gaza Strip in response to rocket fire from Hamas, and Vladimir Putin shut off all Russian gas supplies to Europe through Ukraine. All a preview of things to come. At the same time, on the battlefield of the war Obama was elected to "end," U.S. war casualties in Iraq plummeted to an all-time low between his election and inauguration. And just ten days after Barack Obama assumed office, Iraq held critical provincial elections with very minimal violence. The world was not perfect in 2009, but Iraq was stable, the world relatively secure, and America at least respected.

Yet, in Barack Obama's mind—and in the mind of progressive elites, foreign policy intelligentsia, and millions of voters—George W. Bush's response to the 9/11 attacks was fundamentally wrong. To them Bush was a cowboy, a bumbling idiot, a simpleton, whereas Obama was the opposite—a peacemaker, a smooth sage, an international man of nuance. George Bush spoke loudly and carried a big stick, while Barack Obama spoke apologetically and was willing to set the stick down and talk to anyone.

But what would Obama actually do? His foreign policy platform in both elections centered on slogans—first *I'm not George W. Bush* and then, in 2012, *Osama bin Laden Is Dead*. Both were popular with voters, but neither constituted anything resembling a strategy. As a result, since his first day in the Oval Office, a great deal of ink has been spilled attempting to decipher what an "Obama Doctrine" actually looks like. Speeches have been analyzed, interviews given, and books written— yet nobody, including this author, actually knows what the real Obama Doctrine is. If George W. Bush's foreign policy was defined by bold, unilateral action, Barack Obama's is defined by incoherence.

But why? The answer is simple, and again rooted in the flawed left-ist view of human nature and history. Progressive elitists like Barack Obama—and the so-called elites I went to school with at Princeton and Harvard—are eventually forced to emerge from their utopian ideological cocoons, only to find that there are still lots of people in the world who don't want to coexist with even a "progressive" America led by someone as culturally sensitive as President Barack Obama. But what do progressives like Obama do when—instead of coexisting—enemies of freedom saw off the heads of our journalists, savagely mas-sacre thousands of innocent civilians (and Christians) in their own lands, and target our military veterans at home for attack? What hap-pens when, instead of coexisting, enemies of freedom want to expand their sphere of influence in the South China Sea or threaten Eastern Europe? What happens when, instead of coexisting, enemies of free-dom want to accumulate permanent nuclear capabilities while deny-ing the Holocaust and reiterating their desire to wipe our allies off the map? What happens when, instead of coexisting, the Islamic State throws four gay men off the top of a five-story building in Iraq at the same time the president is lighting up the White House in rain-bow hues? At that point, Barack Obama's brain—and the brain of the American Left—reads: DOES. NOT. COMPUTE. Unilaterally disarmed by decades of a "coexist" moral equivalency, the modern American Left is incapable of confronting such unspeakable evil—the real threats to America and the West.

Instead, they retreat to warm places and familiar causes. Rather than calling out real threats and abject evil—or, heaven forbid, con-fronting them—the Left looks around for the mutual understanding mediation groups and global climate change solidarity marches they so eagerly and self-righteously facilitated as graduate students and com-munity organizers. Except this time, they're in charge; they're the pol-icy makers, the negotiators, the commander in chief. As such, they lunge for the international equivalents of their campus comforts. They seek an impossible global consensus. They work for peace agreements that are untenably detached from military realities. They declare the need to negotiate without preconditions. They unilaterally withdraw from tough wars. They dismiss growing threats as the "JV team." They close wartime detention facilities like Guantanamo Bay with no plan to replace them. They apologize profusely for past sins. They provide "nonlethal" aid when the lethal stuff is what is actually needed. They seek moral high ground by "leading from behind," and they declare the very use of violence a "nineteenth-century behavior." They secretly and sheepishly hope Iran will defeat the Islamic State for us, so we don't have to confront the group ourselves. They try to "coexist" with a dangerous, backward, fallen, chaotic world and—surprise, surprise— it doesn't work.

The result over the past seven years has been an incoherent maze of American interventions, noninterventions, surges, withdrawals, negotiations, high-stakes raids, and plenty of drone attacks. A few different labels have been used to describe the schizophrenic Obama foreign policy, namely "Leading from Behind," "Don't Do Stupid Shit," and "Strategic Patience." Each phrase pertains to one aspect ("patience") of their approach, one intervention ("leading from behind" in Libya), or an ongoing obsession with not being "stupid" like their caricatured George W. Bush. But taken together, they are fundamentally incoherent. Hence, America gets intervention in Libya, but no red-line enforcement in Syria; a surge in Afghanistan, but full withdrawal in Iraq; negotiations with Iran, but a worse relationship with Israel; a supposed pivot to China, but only nonlethal aid to Ukraine; the bin Laden raid, and the Bowe Bergdahl swap. What America actually stands for today is unknowable, because America's leadership doesn't know what it stands for.

But it wasn't supposed to be this way. As a candidate, Senator Barack Obama wrote a *Foreign Affairs* piece titled "Renewing American Leadership," followed by a very similar speech in July 2008 that laid out five strategic goals for his foreign policy: ending the Iraq War responsibly, finishing the fight against Al Qaeda and the Taliban, securing nuclear weapons from terrorists and rogue states, achieving energy security, and rebuilding America's alliances. Except for energy security—which happened *in spite* of his policies—the other four have been utter failures. Iraq is in chaos, the Islamic State has usurped Al Qaeda, the Taliban are swarming Kabul, the Islamic State is actively seeking dirty bomb capabilities and Iran has secured a dangerous nuclear future, and our allies don't trust America's word. By any measure, Barack Obama has utterly failed to meet his strategic goals.

But why? Because the list above is neither a plan nor a doctrine; it's a list of tasks. A doctrine is the lens through which the merits of action—or inaction—are evaluated. Almost all presidents have had one, and all previous forty-three presidents have premised their foreign policy plans on the rightness of American values and virtue of decisive American action. There have been shades of gray in all directions—more engagement, less engagement—but never before a belief that America was *the* problem and her role should be constrained. That is, until Barack Obama and his coexist foreign policy took the helm.

When asked in April 2015, Barack Obama finally encapsulated six years of incoherence, saying, "You asked about an Obama doctrine. The doctrine is: *We will engage, but we preserve all our capabilities.*" The first, and central, part of the doctrine is engagement. This three-word phrase represents the naked supremacy of his "coexist" worldview. For most, engagement is a *means*, but for the modern Left, it is an *end* in and of itself. Engagement seems to work well in the carefully crafted, warm purple spaces of modern academia, so why couldn't it work with dictators, religious zealots, and international institutions? Even seven years into his presidency, as the world spirals out of control, Obama cites engagement—even with those who hate us, undermine us, and lie to us—as the key to bettering American security and a more peaceful world.

Except the rest of the world didn't get the memo. The Islamic State doesn't want to coexist, they want to dominate, subjugate, and terrorize. Al Qaeda doesn't want to coexist, they still seek to strike the American homeland. China, while a robust trading partner, doesn't want to merely coexist, they want to take advantage of our equivocation to crack down on internal dissent, expand their sphere of influence, and undermine American hegemony. Vladimir Putin's Russia doesn't want to coexist—or hit Hillary's reset button; they want to assert military and economic dominance over former Soviet satellite states. And, yes, Europe may want to coexist, but they have neither the will—nor the military might—to assert themselves against real threats. Polls taken in June 2015 by the Pew Research Center show that many European countries are much *less* willing to go to war to save a NATO ally like Poland from a Russian invasion than are American citizens, who are thousands of miles away and across an ocean. Thanks to expensive welfare states, minuscule militaries, and massive demographic complications, European countries have no choice but to coexist . . . and ride the wave of history, *hoping* that despots like Putin choose to attack someone else.

The second aspect of Obama's doctrine ("we preserve all our capabilities") is a rhetorical bluff, and ultimately a sham—both morally and materially. Morally, if America's leaders are not capable of naming our enemies and standing by our allies, then physical capabilities are at best rudderless, and at worst useless. Obama all but banned use of the phrase "Islamic terrorism," replacing the "Global War on Terrorism" with "Overseas Contingency Operations" and declaring the Islamic State "not Islamic." Domestic terrorism became "workplace violence" and battlefield deserters were welcomed home with Rose Garden ceremonies. Red-line ultimatums on genocide and the use of chemical weapons were declared on the international stage, and then completely ignored. All the while, America's closest Middle Eastern ally, Israel, watched as the Obama administration fell over itself to strike a nuclear deal with Iran, yet repeatedly snubbed Israel's overtures and preferences. As the Obama administration used engagement as an *end* instead of a means, the moral bottom fell out of American leadership.

Materially, there is little dispute that the past seven years have undercut America's core military capabilities. One of Obama's first executive actions was to close the Guantanamo Bay detention facility,
with no plan to replace it. He quickly abandoned missile defense systems in Europe in order to appease an assertive Vladimir Putin. He
precipitously removed troops from Iraq with no consideration for conditions on the ground. He tepidly surged in Afghanistan while simultaneously declaring a political timeline for a withdrawal. He allowed
sequestration to take effect, leading to dramatic reductions in military
manpower and dangerous cuts to defense modernization. He increased
drone strikes and used more special operators to paper over these strategic shortfalls, in a failed attempt to stem the global chaos his policies
accelerated. But, to be fair, Obama did increase some capabilities at the
Pentagon: fairness and tolerance. Combat positions are now open to
all women and the era of Don't Ask, Don't Tell is over. Regardless of
the merits of both changes, these changes have no material bearing on
America's ability to better fight and win wars. I'm certain, eventually,
the Pentagon will (be forced to) lower physical standards in pursuit of
a "gender neutral" force—weakening our military from within.

There is no better example of Obama's "coexist" foreign policy than
his Iranian nuclear deal, which also happens to be the issue context
in which the president articulated his "Obama Doctrine." Under the
guise of reducing the Iranian nuclear threat, Obama feverishly engaged
an avowed enemy in the hopes of curbing its appetite for a bomb and
affirming its desire for peaceful nuclear power. From the beginning,
the administration engaged with Tehran's narrative, without preconditions, and slowly caved to their demand in pursuit of a deal—any
deal. But when the deal does not hold together and Iran inevitably and
wantonly cheats on the deal, the administration will say, "We preserve
all our capabilities!" Except, they don't. When Obama gives tepid lip
service to a military option, the entire world—most especially Iran—
knows he would never use it. It is just not in his leadership DNA.

Worse, Israel truly wonders if America would have its back. Following his articulation of the Obama Doctrine, and in the context of Iranian nuclear negotiations, Obama said, "If anyone messes with Israel, America will be there." But what does "America will be there" *really* mean? Does it mean military action in conjunction with, or in support of, Israel? If Obama's track record is any indication, then Israel has cause to seriously question whether his America would take decisive action to either confront Iran or defend Israel. The lessons of Ukraine are apt here. In exchange for tacit security commitments after the Soviet Union collapsed, the United States encouraged Ukraine to give up not only its nuclear arsenal in 1994, but also its long-range bombers and missiles. Then Russia invaded sovereign Ukrainian territory and we did nothing—except send them military Meals, Ready to Eat (MREs). Iran saw this unfold before their eyes and took note.

More likely, Israel could count on America to "be there" at the United Nations, sponsoring a strongly worded (and unenforceable) memorandum. The credible threat of military action against Iran's nuclear program, while complicated and messy, actually has teeth to it; whereas the United Nations resolutions and "red line" rhetoric this administration sheepishly pursues are meaningless. As a Marine Corps veteran friend often says, "Everyone wants to be a gangster—until it's time to do gangster shit." Robust military capabilities are critically important, but the willingness to use them, or your enemies believing you would use them, is even more important. Barack Obama is a wannabe geopolitical gangster—and the world knows it.

This gulf between rhetoric and reality creates an ideologically induced incoherence that impacts every other aspect of U.S. foreign policy and national security. The Obama Doctrine—which perfectly sums up the Left's coexist foreign policy—is a sham because it's meaningless. Obama thinks he's being progressive, yet tough; instead the world sees naïveté and weakness. Of course Obama doesn't believe his policy is weak, as evidenced by his out-of-character and hawkish Nobel Peace Prize speech from 2009. But the inevitable result of his so-called doctrine is both real and perceived weakness, relegating America to spectator status on the world stage. If America doesn't have the moral and military conviction to lead, then nefarious international powers with very different values and priorities have freedom of action. The result is exactly what we have seen over the past seven years—enemies of freedom, of which there are many, racing to fill the power vacuum America leaves behind. As it turns out, "leading from behind" is simply following, and we're reaping the outcome of American followership.

Setting aside the diminished credibility and capabilities of America, the threats created by Barack Obama's ideological naïveté have sowed the seeds of international chaos and American vulnerability. In a matter of seven years, Iraq went from a fragile but stable success story to an Islamic State caliphate with international ambitions. Syria is even worse, an Islamist and humanitarian disaster of biblical proportions. America hastened Libyan revolution with no investment in the aftermath, creating a vacuum that vicious Islamists, including the Islamic State, have filled. Rinse and repeat strategic failure in Yemen. Afghanistan has slowly and steadily slid back into the hands of the Taliban, following a halfhearted surge. An emboldened Russia invaded Ukraine and militarily propped up Syria's ruling dictator, "resetting" only one thing: the Cold War. China is rapidly expanding its military reach and ambitions, taking provocative—and unchallenged—actions in the Pacific. Worst of all, Iran is now on the fast track to nuclear weapons capabilities, triggering a fast-paced Middle East arms race. Their pursuit of nuclear weapons, whether we officially recognize it or not, has set off a spiraling Sunni-Shia civil war of game-changing proportions, as America's (former) Sunni allies start to fend for themselves and eventually get their own nuclear weapons.

Turns out, weakness really is dangerous, and a threat to the American way of life—and the free world—in the twenty-first century.

In the eyes of Roosevelt's critics, at the time of his speech Teddy was a bellicose American cowboy wielding an unnecessarily large stick. But for Roosevelt, whose views were forged on the battlefield and grounded in a proper understanding of America's exceptionalism, strength was the foundational ingredient for securing freedom. Following his personal exploits on San Juan Hill, and after America's resounding triumph in the Spanish-American War, President Roosevelt continued to project U.S. strength and influence by extending the Monroe Doctrine (via his "Roosevelt Corollary") to the Western Hemisphere, taking the Panama Canal by force, and sending U.S. Navy warships—the "Great White Fleet"—to circumvent the globe. Teddy Roosevelt was proud of a young, free, and increasingly powerful America—and was unabashed in his belief that projecting that power would both serve the interests of Americans and lead to a safer, and freer, world.

Roosevelt carried a big stick not because he was an arrogant warmonger, but because he understood that looking tough—and yes, being tough when required—goes a long way in a dangerous world. It both deters threats and, if necessary, defeats them. Like presidents before and after him, that did not mean Teddy was "pro-war." Nobody seeks to instigate war; least of all those who have experienced it like Teddy Roosevelt.

Beyond that big stick, Teddy Roosevelt understood an even more central truth that is lost on America's current "coexist" leadership: that in order to be a good global citizen, you must first be a good patriot. A big stick in the hands of the wrong cause—communism, Nazism, Islamism—is horrific; conversely, a big stick in the hands of a "global citizen" stays on the shoulder even in the face of the worst threats. But a big stick in the hands of a good patriot serves not just the interests of America, but also of the free world. A good patriot does what is necessary—by force of arms, and alone, if required—to defend the freedoms we hold so dear.

To the ears of Barack Obama, Dan Wachtell, and the modern Left, these words—like the editorial response we wrote in the *Daily Princetonian* a week after 9/11—sound outdated and militaristic (insert "trigger warning" here). To the coexist crowd, defending America by force of arms, and doing so alone without the permission of international arbitrators, is *so nineteenth century*—as Secretary of State John Kerry asserted. Secretary Kerry, a textbook "perpetual pragmatist" who has seen both sides of every big foreign policy issue, also recently declared the Monroe Doctrine "dead"—and along with it, the Roosevelt Corollary to that doctrine. In effect, the Obama administration ended nearly two centuries of American leadership in the Western Hemisphere. This unilateral declaration, made to level the playing field of international politics—to better "coexist"—underscores how right Teddy Roosevelt (a man forged in the nineteenth century, I might add) was about the consequences of "citizens of the world."

Large threats—some new, some old, and some self-made—loom large both in the present day and on the horizon. How America confronts those threats will determine whether the next century is an American century, or is instead one marred by chaos, indiscriminate violence, and the rise of anti-freedom ideologies and institutions. America is going to need a big stick, because the future—the arena—remains as dangerous, disputed, and uncertain as it has always been.

This also means learning the right lessons from the wars that we fight, a subject I've been immersed in—abroad and at home—since the towers fell in 2001. While others might be "war weary," those who have faced America's enemies over the past fifteen years realize that our generation's fight is far from over. We may be tired of conflict, but our zealous enemies remain committed to their apocalyptic cause. Our ability to prevail in our fight against Islamism—like we did against Nazism and communism—will require learning the right lessons from the wars we fight and having the courage to apply those lessons to future fronts in a long and difficult war we cannot afford to quit . . . or lose.

FIVE

★ ★ ★

Is It Right to Prevail?:
Our Fight for Iraq

War is a dreadful thing, and unjust war is a crime against humanity. But it is such a crime because it is unjust, not because it is a war. The choice must ever be in favor of righteousness, and this is whether the alternative be peace or whether the alternative be war. The question must not be merely, Is there to be peace or war? The question must be, Is it right to prevail? Are the great laws of righteousness once more to be fulfilled? And the answer from a strong and virile people must be "Yes," whatever the cost.

—TEDDY ROOSEVELT, 1910

Where is the urgency to win, at all costs?

—MY IRAQ JOURNAL, MAY 7, 2006

SPRING/SUMMER 2006 | SAMARRA, IRAQ

"Zero–Seven–Seven–Zero. Three–Seven–Three. Six–Six–Nine–Five."

As we approached the front gate of the sprawling Camp Speicher base outside of Tikrit, I yelled at my driver to cut the noisy engine of our up-armored Humvee. I could barely hear the voice on the other end of the line, thanks in large part to the typically spotty Iraqi cell phone service. The voice was excitable, and I asked him to relay the phone number again. He did so in broken Iraqi English.

"Zero–Seven–Seven–Zero. Three–Seven–Three. Six–Six–Nine–Five."

I passed the phone to our interpreter to make sure I had it right. I then made sure it was written correctly in my Army-issue green book, and immediately relayed it to my boss, Captain Chris Brawley, who quickly sent it up the chain of command. Later that night, the word came. Hamadi Al Tahki—the Al Qaeda "Emir" of Samarra—was dead, along with his cadre of heavily armed bodyguards. Iraqi men I would never meet had obtained his new cell phone number and shared it with a trusted Iraqi ally—and the signal the emir's new phone gave off was his undoing.

Our unit had been looking for Al Tahki since we arrived in Samarra, just as previous units had. More a violent thug and profiteer than Islamist, Al Tahki was nonetheless responsible for numerous dead Americans, scores of dead Iraqis, and ongoing intimidation of anyone associated with U.S. forces or the Iraqi government. He was the Keyser Söze of Samarra—more a myth than a man—leaving a few of us to doubt whether he existed at all. Now he was dead as a doornail, killed by another set of men we never met.

Acting on signals from that cell phone number, Taskforce 77—an elite hunter-killer special operations unit—were the final arbiters of justice for Al Qaeda's prince of Samarra. Operating swiftly and precisely above the bureaucracy and acting on highly sensitive intelligence, they not only killed Al Tahki that night, but also tracked the vehicles that picked up the bodies, lay in baited ambushes, and even raided his funeral. They didn't just kill an Al Qaeda emir, they dismantled the core of his cell—killing those who resisted and detaining those who did not. That night, Team America delivered a gut punch to Al Qaeda insurgents in Samarra that would eventually lead to a precipitous drop in violence in that city. From the perspective of a rank-and-file infantryman, Taskforce 77 was by far the most feared element in Iraq. Arriving in the dead of night, with liberated rules of engagement, they knew how to kill with precision from the air and ground. While they sometimes created messes that land-owning units had to clean up, their impact was overwhelmingly positive—sowing fear in the hearts of flip-flop-wearing insurgents throughout Iraq. They had, and will always have, my unwavering admiration and respect. They were killers.

But that day, and in the months preceding and following it, the most potent weapon I carried was my Iraqi cell phone and the contacts it contained. Without those eleven digits of Al Tahki's phone number, Team America never arrives on his Al Qaeda doorstep to deliver justice. The painstaking process that led to those eleven digits—and the cooperation that came with it—was an intensely human one, built on trust that was established over many months, many risks, and many late nights. Unless America is willing to level entire cities with bombs from the sky—which is an option we should never foreclose—ruthlessly killing an enemy that hides in the shadows and among women and children is not possible without the human relationships and resulting human intelligence that come from having boots on the ground. As any military or intelligence professional will attest, there are serious limits to what can be accomplished through drones, data, and signals intelligence alone. Ultimately, guys with guns alongside allies on the ground—properly supported and resourced—can build relationships, and dismantle an enemy, in a way drones simply cannot. As Roosevelt said, "war is a dreadful thing" but its effective execution will always be necessary—usually in dangerous places, at night, alongside a shady mix of characters.

One of those nights came on April 22, 2006, in the heart of Samarra, just six days prior to the killing of Al Tahki. That evening I received a frantic phone call from the same person who called with Al Tahki's phone number—the eldest son of Samarra's city council president and strong American ally, Assad Ali Yasseen (we affectionately called him "Haji Assad" or "Mr. Assad"). Two of Mr. Assad's bodyguards had just been killed, shot execution-style in the head, while waiting in line to get a haircut. As we had on multiple other occasions when he and his family were under attack, our mishmash civil-military operations team geared up, grabbed a pile of AK-47s and crates of ammunition, and headed into the restive city. We dubbed our team "Taskforce 5-0," after the "Iron 5" call sign of our fearless leader and battalion executive officer, Major Steve Delvaux.

Like Major Delvaux, Mr. Assad was—and is—a special human being. A soft-spoken businessman and devout Sunni Muslim, he and his family were forced to leave Iraq and flee to Dubai under Saddam Hussein—under suspicion of attempting to assassinate Saddam's oldest son, Uday. Pro-Western, and pro-American, Mr. Assad and his family returned to Samarra after the 2003 U.S. invasion, in the hopes of a better life and building a business. As chaos grew around him, so did his recognition that a man of his stature could either succumb to it—or fight back. He did the later, in dramatic fashion. Declaring he would fight Al Qaeda "to the death," he frequently called his men—and Taskforce 5-0—the "true mujahideen, fighting the real jihad."

In his role as the Samarra city council president—and because of the bold manner in which he wielded it—he soon became a threat to, and therefore central target of, Al Qaeda and antigovernment forces. While other so-called leaders in Samarra stayed home or played double games, Mr. Assad traveled the city, worked on projects, met with tribal leaders and security forces, funded a newspaper, and eventually formed an extragovernmental intelligence network that temporarily became our battalion's primary source for dismantling enemy elements in Samarra. As a result, Al Qaeda ruthlessly targeted him, his family, and his bodyguards—as they did that night.

While his leadership was natural, his boldness was also born of the earnest and active support of Taskforce 5-0. We worked to establish a baseline of trust that cut both ways. When he called for support, we came; when he provided us intelligence, we rolled out and picked up his ski-mask-wearing, AK-47-toting informants; when one of our soldiers was killed, he was the only Iraqi civilian at the ceremony paying his respects. This trust was established because our small civil-military element had been working with him closely, and mostly covertly, since the bombing of the Golden Mosque two months earlier, after which the city's tribal leaders appointed him the new city council president. That bombing, which was a very negative, sectarian pivot point for the larger war, actually created a massive opportunity for renewed collaboration inside Samarra. As it turns out, the late Democratic Speaker of the House Tip O'Neill was right—all politics really is local.

Our humble Taskforce 5-0, often heading out on our own into the sprawling city of Samarra, held lengthy meeting after lengthy meeting, ate local meal after local meal, and initiated broad-daylight mission after late-night mission—forging a reservoir of trust with Mr. Assad, his family, his bodyguards—and, by extension, core elements of his Al Abassi tribe. We met with other city officials as well, but none of them remotely showed the same level of initiative, leadership, and sheer courage. He was fighting for his city, and we were fighting with him—side by side.

It all came to a head on that April night when his bodyguards were assassinated. When we arrived at Mr. Assad's compound, it was no longer time to talk—they had decided it was time to act. His house was a frenzy of activity, with dozens of armed men crisscrossing the dimly lit courtyard as we approached. We knew his core bodyguards well, and they were there; but that night, as men came out to grab the weapons and ammunition we delivered, it was clear that reinforcements had arrived. These were not the regular bodyguards; these were the quasi-shady guys who knew a bit too much about the bad guys to not be involved in the insurgency at some level. Mr. Assad was clean, but there was no way these guys were. Two of their own had been killed in murderous fashion. The gloves were off.

When we entered the couch-lined, carpet-covered, vaulted-ceiling living area we knew well, his dinner table didn't have the normal spread of lamb, bread, vegetables, and orange soda. This time it was covered with a city map and surrounded by armed men. By the time we arrived, he already had six informants and thirty targets picked out. For the next few hours, as night settled in and the neighborhood went to sleep, we worked through multiple interpreters to refine the target set. At one point, smoking a cigarette myself and feeling a bit like a cowboy, I stepped back and counted fifteen men poring over the maps—a mixture of AK-47s and M-4s slung amid a room filled with smoke . . . and purpose.

After passionate discussion, interpretation, and refinement, the targets' locations were narrowed to eight, with three informants se-lected to accompany the raids. Pining for revenge, Mr. Assad's body-guards made the case for more targets, many of which didn't meet our stricter sourcing criteria. Some of the newer bodyguards also appealed to Mr. Assad to execute the raids themselves—for all the extrajudi-cial reasons you might suspect. But Mr. Assad stepped in, saying, "Let the Americans handle it. That is the right way to do it." When a few continued to push back, he quietly and definitively declared, "They are with us. They are Al Abassi." With that, it was settled.

With targets and informants selected, we left all but a few overwatch vehicles behind and headed out on foot—doing our best to maintain the element of surprise in the back alleyways and dusty streets. In clas-sic Taskforce 5-0 form, we utilized a *Star Wars* cantina-scene mix of characters that night, as we would many subsequent nights—a rank-heavy mixture of civil affairs elements, Bravo Company infantrymen, bodyguards, interpreters, and local informants. And on this particular night, we were also toting a Russian-born *Wall Street Journal* foreign affairs reporter who was brave enough to walk the streets with us. Any screwups could make front-page U.S. news in short order.

It was one of those moments you never forget. We stepped off that night, into an unknown and eerie Samarra night, led by three skinny informants in ski masks, flip-flops, and AK-47s. Looking back on it, we were leading with our guts; no Army school ever taught the planning process and motley formations we maintained. Our movements were not always precise, but they were decisive. With dogs howling, and daylight still hours away, our elements hit all eight of our targets in succession over the course of the night. Only two were dry holes; in the other six we found our men—stuffing detainees into the back of crammed Humvees as we rolled along.

At the last target house, purportedly an Al Qaeda–linked target, a nearby minaret alerted the neighborhood to our presence with rhythmic Arabic chanting—the most ominous sound I'd ever heard, a call to prayer—or call to action—of some sort. As we approached the house, it was clear there was movement inside the perimeter walls—which accelerated the pace of our actions. Normally our breach and assault elements waited for our perimeter to be set up, to make sure nobody squirted off the objective. But at this house, with our element of surprise blown, it wasn't possible. Speed was our security, so we moved. As the lead element rammed the perimeter gate with a Humvee, I moved along the perimeter wall to cover the backside of the house. In my haste, I got ahead of my counterpart.

As I moved alongside a high perimeter wall, I could hear rustling in the back portion of the house. Because of the ambient moonlight and a smattering of dim lights in the area, my night-vision reticle was flipped up. The naked eye seemed the best way to go. As I tactically rounded the corner, I briefly caught a glimpse of two men sprinting through the rear street and around an adjacent corner. Not sure if we had an element on the other side yet, I gave chase to regain line of sight. But as I crossed some rubble and then the empty street with the typical open sewer gutters, I heard—and then saw—something on the rooftop next door. Unsure what to do—and frozen in the middle of the street—I first swung my head, and then my weapon. Two men in ski masks with AK-47s trained in my general direction popped up.

For a few of the longest seconds in my life, I trained my weapon on them—and they pointed theirs at me. It was dark enough that neither could fully recognize the other. Not knowing what else to do in such a vulnerable position, I yelled out to them, "Amriki!"—Arabic for American. They slowly lowered their weapons. They were allied bodyguards who, in zealous haste, had hopped onto the adjoining rooftop to overwatch our assault. Wanting to shit my pants, and with my heartbeat sky-high, I kept running across the alleyway. But I had lost valuable seconds, and by the time I hit the corner the men had rounded, they were long gone—lost in a maze of corridors and alleyways.

Frozen on that corner, and not looking to further overextend myself off that objective, I took a knee and faced back toward the house, in case more insurgents tried to squirt off the backside. By that time our elements were clearing the house. I was kicking myself, for multiple reasons—not getting there faster, shoddy tactics, and not being able to chase those guys down. It was not the first time a few runners had gotten away during my tour, and it irked me—as it did the other times. What if they went on to kill Americans? Or other members of Mr. Assad's family? Or now they belong to Abu Bakr Al Baghdadi's Islamic State army? (Al Baghdadi, the leader of the Islamic State, hails from Samarra, after all.) I will never know, but will always contemplate.

Like my first firefight—an event that every soldier remembers—these moments are seared into my brain. And, ironically, most of them happened not while I was an infantry platoon leader on patrol, but instead during my six months as a civil-military operations officer. The majority of the tactical successes our Taskforce 5-0 element had, and in many ways our companies and battalion had, came through consistent interaction with the city council president, other city leaders, and regular citizens. When we patrolled the streets on foot—and took the time to take off our body armor and break bread with the local population—our interaction with the people was vital to our success.

This recipe—local interaction, constant presence, and rolling up lots of bad guys—was the secret sauce that all of Iraq needed, we just didn't know it yet. And to think that, in Samarra at least, it pretty much happened by accident. As my platoon leader time came to a close halfway through our tour, our battalion commander pulled me aside and said, "You studied politics at Princeton, right?" I answered yes. With that I was reassigned from the great soldiers of Charlie Company to Captain Brawley's civil-military operations element at battalion headquarters—charged with helping to revive the moribund governance in Samarra. We had no special training, and no manual, but because I had studied the likes of Cicero and Machiavelli in college (note, sarcasm), I was on the team. Taskforce 5-0 was soon born, and we made it up as we went along.

On the second day of that new job, I woke up to the Al Qaeda–backed bombing of the Golden Mosque. In many ways, this bombing was the ground zero—the 9/11—of the Iraq War, during which we had a front-row seat. I'll never forget hearing the massive explosion and running into the tactical operation center, just in time to catch a live feed of a hollowed-out—in fact completely gone—Golden Dome. That night, after angling to join the patrol into the city, I was one of three Americans in the Samarra mayor's office when the tribal sheiks designated Mr. Assad as the new city council president—a very positive development we didn't fully understand at the time. I could spend a chapter recounting the back-and-forth that night between our battalion commander, the Golden Mosque imam (who was rarely seen), and all of the tribal sheiks. The room was full of anger, sorrow, and suspicion. In many ways, that is where my wider lens on the war in Iraq started—along with the lessons that came with it. Mr. Assad's courage, our outreach (good and bad) in Samarra, and the realities of combat all forged a firsthand view of war that informed, and still informs, every aspect of my postwar life. I saw what was possible, what was impossible, and what it takes—and what it means—to both win and lose. In nearly every way, the city of Samarra taught me more than Princeton and Harvard ever could.

Samarra, like all of Iraq, was a confusing product of historic and immediate circumstances. The redheaded stepchild of Saddam's hometown of Tikrit, Samarra lives with an inferiority complex, part of which comes from the overwhelmingly Sunni town hosting one of the most holy sites in Shia Islam; a point of pride, and contention. Like so many Iraqi cities, the town is controlled by a patchwork of tribes that fight like siblings. The town had been invaded and abandoned multiple times since 2003, with insurgents gaining control, losing it again, and waging a low-level insurgency throughout. Both urban and rural, an example of both Sunni-Shia cooperation and division, and skeptical of central governance—Samarra was a difficult problem set, and one that could head in any direction. If Samarra was hopeless, all of Iraq was hopeless. If Samarra could be won, so could Iraq.

The year 2006 was also a microcosm for the confusion of the entire Iraq War. The initial invasion had been swift and decisive, with Saddam's capture in December 2003 wrapping up a hopeful year. The next year saw clashes with Sunni radicals in Fallujah and Shia Sadrists in the south, but also the transfer of authority to Iraqis. Violence continued in 2005, but two national elections and a constitutional referendum provided a glimpse of a post-American future. By 2006, the United States was ready to put Iraq in the rearview mirror . . . but Iraq was not done with us.

The bombing of the Golden Mosque, while a moment of opportunity in Samarra, ripped the seams off America's extraction plans. Sectarian violence, and violence against U.S. forces, increased and Iraqi forces were not capable of handling it. Nonetheless, in the middle of a deteriorating situation in 2006, we continued to doggedly transfer responsibility to Iraqi forces. We held transfer ceremonies, but they were nothing but ceremonies and did not reflect real Iraqi capabilities. The Iraqis could not control the areas we were giving to them, and we all knew it. In 2006 we had one foot out the door of Iraq, which is what the insurgents wanted. The rest of the population—a silent majority—was still clinging to our other leg, hoping that we wouldn't quit and leave them the resulting shit storm.

That was the view from my small foxhole in a plywood shack in Samarra, with that black frame containing Teddy Roosevelt's "Man in the Arena" quote hanging inside. By the end of our tour, after a ruthlessly effective insurgent-hunting approach led by courageous infantry companies (Bravo and Charlie Company especially) in our battalion—aided by months of cooperation with Mr. Assad and interaction with the population—what looked like a hopeless situation was actually blossoming with promise. Amid the chaos were the seeds of success. Yes, our battalion was caught between a conventional approach and a population-centric approach, but with more troops, realistic rules of engagement, and a clearer mission set, we could execute a more successful, and even more deadly, counterinsurgency fight. Yes, Samarra was a restive town, but through careful study of atmospheric data our unit collected, we knew it had a "swing voter" population that was ripe for persuasion, or at least strategic alignment. And yes, 2006 held some of the deepest, darkest days of the war, but that darkness created the opportunity for a dawn that we had the ability to shape. The war was tough, but we could not afford to lose it.

Sometimes only those consumed in the darkest moments can see the tiny light at the end of the tunnel. And by the time I wrapped my arms around Iraq and started to see a faint light of hope, our rotation was over. A few weeks later I was home—where the view of the war was much different. When I came home from Iraq in the middle of 2006 and dropped my duffle bags in New York City, I picked up copies of a *New York Times* that on a daily basis dutifully trumpeted corrosive and entrenched myths about the fight. They said Iraq was descending into inevitable sectarian chaos, that the presence of U.S. troops only inflamed the situation, and that morale of U.S. troops was dangerously low and would soon break the military. Every myth has a grain of truth to it, as did these. Iraq was violent, but it wasn't inevitable; U.S. troops were targets, but didn't have to be; and the mission was tough, but the troops were far from broken. Right around this time, the *New Republic* quoted a Democratic campaign adviser as saying, "The war in Iraq is over except for the dying." That was the prevailing wisdom at the time, but it was dead wrong.

What do you do when you come home from war, as a small first lieutenant in a big army, and see that the domestic conversation is fundamentally divorced from the reality on the ground? I did the only thing I could, turning to my laptop and feverishly penning a thirteen-page after-action report titled "Lessons Learned in Samarra: How to Fix an Iraqi City." I circulated it with anyone who would read it, including—through the father of a friend's wife—members of the Iraq Study Group, a high-profile panel appointed by Congress to assess the situation in Iraq and make recommendations. I'm not sure if they ever read it, and judging by their recommendations, it didn't impact them either way. But I had to do something.

It was an empty, powerless, and ever-present feeling, fresh back from the battlefield and knowing we *could* win in Iraq, but wondering whether our leaders would ever have the stomach for it. Iraq was winnable, but were there enough leaders still around in America who believed that it was "right to prevail"? I believed, as Teddy did in 1910, that "the answer from a strong and virile people must be 'Yes,' whatever the cost." But I just didn't know. I had long thought President Bush had the ability to be the resolute leader needed for a long and difficult war, with my journal from Guantanamo Bay two years earlier reading, "Bush is a leader and will see Iraq through—will see the whole War on Terrorism through." But I now questioned that. All the tea leaves pointed to overwhelming public pressure and a midterm election pushing him toward the exits in Iraq. With the inside game feeling hopeless, I went public with my lonely fight—submitting an op-ed to the *Wall Street Journal* in September 2006. It ran on October 3:

More Troops, Please

I've heard President Bush repeatedly state he will send more troops to Iraq if the commanders on the ground ask for them. I think, having returned home from Iraq two months ago, that there must be a breakdown in communication somewhere along the line. Maybe units on the ground are painting too rosy a picture for the generals. Perhaps the generals aren't asking because it goes against the "can do" ethos of the Army. Possibly the military is being squeezed by the Pentagon to do more with less. Or maybe the White House doesn't want to admit more troops are needed. In any case, while I do not have the answers nor do I seek to place blame, it is painfully obvious there's a disconnect.

I volunteered to serve in Iraq because I believe in our mission there. I share the president's conviction about the Iraq war—we can and must win, for the Iraqi people, for the future of our country and for peace-loving people everywhere. But I'm frustrated. America is fighting with a hand tied behind its back. Soldiers have all the equipment we need—armored Humvees, body armor for every body part, superior technology, etc.—but we simply do not have enough troops in Iraq, and we need them now.

After witnessing two national elections during three months in Baghdad, my Army unit moved north to Samarra, where we spent eight months sowing the seeds of progress. While we had success in uprooting the insurgency and building the local government, it wasn't enough. We had just enough troops to control Samarra and secure ourselves, but not enough to bring lasting stability or security. "Not enough" became the story of my year in Iraq.

The future of Samarra, and Iraq as a whole, ultimately lies in the hands of her people—their sympathies are the ultimate prize in this war. No matter how many insurgents we kill, city leaders we meet or policemen we enlist, it is all for naught if we cannot provide security and stability. Tribal sheikhs told us that even within Samarra—deep in the Sunni triangle—a vast majority of people just want peace and order and will side with whoever can provide it. Right now Samarrans rightfully question who that will be.

The end goal in Samarra is for Iraqis to do everything for themselves. But their government and security forces are not ready. Insurgents use death threats and murder to assert power over anyone working with the City Council or joining the police force. This atmosphere forces moderate Samarrans to keep their mouths shut, and their silence abets the insurgents who live and fight in Samarra. Despite killing scores of insurgents, we are unable to provide lasting security, and so the Samarran street slips away.

Two things are to blame for our predicament, one a corollary of the other. The first reason is that we did not have enough troops in Samarra. The skill and courage of 150 American soldiers prevented chaos, but was never enough to fully secure a city of 120,000 people or maintain the rule of law. The soldiers in the city were preoccupied with defending themselves and conducting night raids, and were therefore largely unable to regularly patrol during the day—thus giving insurgents reign to move freely and intimidate the local population. A visitor in Samarra on an average day would be hard-pressed to point out a single American Humvee traversing local neighborhoods. The same is true for Baghdad.

Our four-vehicle civil-affairs patrol was often the only American presence deep inside the city and we were frequently greeted by locals with the question, "Where have you been?" Americans can't of course be omnipresent; but we should at least be there when it matters. When Americans are there, either the insurgents are not or they are on the losing side of a firefight.

Second, because of a lack of troops, American military leaders are forced to make a choice between mission objectives and self-preservation. Many of our leaders are opting to guard supply routes and coagulate on sprawling military bases, rather than consistently moving into danger-ous areas and fighting the insurgency. In our case, we had 500 soldiers stationed outside Samarra who made infrequent trips into the city cen-ter. There is little reason why most of these troops were not stationed in-side Samarra, canvassing every neighborhood with platoon-sized patrol bases and suffocating insurgent operations. Rather than take the risks necessary—like small patrol bases and frequent foot patrols—our unit opted to secure itself and its supply routes rather than commit resources inside the city. And while this approach is safer in the short run, it only prolongs mission accomplishment, ultimately endangering more troops. We often speculated our unit would be back next year, driving the same streets with even fewer guys.

In due time, the Iraqi Security Forces will take over Samarra, but they are not ready yet. If the Americans left today, the Iraqis would be co-opted by the insurgents—who are utterly ruthless, willing to kill fam-ily members of policemen or decapitate Iraqi soldiers to preserve disorder. It will take time. Both the Iraqi Army and Samarra Police need to get bloodied a bit and bounce back, proving their strength to the people. They will eventually be ready, but until then, security belongs to us.

I also understand calling for more troops is contrary to conven-tional thinking inside government and the military. Supporters of the current approach argue sending more troops would further inflame anti-American sentiment, incite more violence and retard independent progress. My experience suggests otherwise. American troops are tolerated, even welcomed when they effectively provide security; but their presence is cursed when it does not accompany progress. Violence persists not because American troops are present, but because our presence is futile. Many local leaders asked us, "How come the most powerful country in the world can-not defeat local criminals and thugs?" They suggested our failure was part of a larger conspiracy to keep the Iraqi people suffering.

I have not lost the optimism that sent me to Iraq. We did make gains. Our 10-man civil-affairs team established good relationships with brave Iraqi leaders and sat across from them as equals. I watched city lead-

*ers battle insurgents, not only with guns but with newspapers and eco-
nomic development. By the time we left, the City Council was meeting
on its own accord and with increasing legitimacy, forming committees
to oversee fuel allocation, new construction and security. Increased home
construction was evident and local markets were open.*

*Even the security situation inside the city improved. Previous sum-
mers in Samarra had been extremely violent, but the summer of 2006 was
different. Days passed without a significant attack inside the city. Less
than 150 Americans, along with Iraqi counterparts, controlled a town of
over 120,000 Sunni Arabs through targeted raids and sniper operations.
One local insurgent even begged city leaders for amnesty in exchange for
good conduct. Our unit killed or captured hundreds of insurgents, knocking the wind out of the local insurgency—but never crushing it.*

*I believe, as the president noted, that "the safety of America depends
on the outcome of the battle in the streets of Baghdad." Why then do we
have just enough troops in Iraq not to lose? Most of the people I've spoken
with since coming home—those both for and against the war—believe
we must finish the job in Iraq. Americans understand a defeat in Iraq
would have horrible consequences for America and its allies for decades to
come. America has the capacity to win and the will to support a winning
strategy.*

Why then are we pursuing a bare minimum approach?

Three months later President Bush rejected that bare-minimum
approach—announcing a 21,000-troop surge, putting General David
Petraeus in charge of it, and giving them a new counterinsurgency
mission. Although I've been told my op-ed was circulated inside the
White House in the fall of 2006, it was certainly not the impetus for
the new approach. Fortuitously and simultaneously, courageous military leaders and thinkers whom I hadn't met at that time—among
them former Army general Jack Keane, American Enterprise Institute
scholar Fred Kagan, and foreign policy savant Vance Serchuk—were
pushing for the same approach. They had seen what I had seen, as had

many others on the ground in Iraq: that the war was still winnable and that losing it would be a disastrous choice.

But our voice was the overwhelming minority. The Iraq Study Group called for gradual withdrawal. The Joint Chiefs pushed against more troops, and for "employment programs." The outgoing U.S. ground commander in Iraq, Peter Chiarelli, naïvely wanted to pull troops out of the city centers. White House hopefuls Hillary Clinton, Barack Obama, and Joe Biden all opposed the surge and fell over themselves in a de facto race to see who could oppose it the most adamantly. Each quarter echoed the same tired argument: "there is no military solution for Iraq."

As Teddy Roosevelt said, "War is a dreadful thing," but losing is worse—and President George W. Bush understood that, and did what courageous leaders do. He gathered all the facts—good, bad, and out-of-the-box—and made a tough call, for a course of action that would produce the best long-term outcome for America, a fragile Iraq, and the larger fight against violent Islamists. He did not put his finger in the wind. He did not consult his pollsters. And he did not stick his head in the sand and bow to the inevitability of conventional wisdom. He changed course, doubled down, and went for the win. He provided what every soldier wants from his or her commander in chief: moral clarity, resolve, and the resources to accomplish the mission. I've never been more proud of a president than when Bush announced the Iraq surge on January 10, 2007.

JULY 2007 | WASHINGTON, D.C.

Six months later, I found myself at the end of a stately hallway in the Russell Senate Office Building, as a young Senate intern fumbled for his key to room SR-289, eventually letting our motley crew of three dozen Iraq War veterans shuffle into the conference room. Our group's matching tan shirts and bad military haircuts gave us away as the Capitol Hill amateurs we were. For many, it was their first visit to Washington, D.C. For most, it was their first visit to Capitol Hill. For me—a first lieutenant, a fresh Iraq War veteran, and the leader of this misfit band of insurgents—it was my first official meeting with a U.S. senator. As *Politico* noted the next day, our small, nonprofit veterans organization—Vets for Freedom—had "scant money to spend and no contracts with professional public relations firms." Founded the year before by a combat-wounded Iraq War Marine to support the war effort, the founders and leadership of Vets for Freedom were feisty and focused. But make no mistake about it—we were rookies.

The vaulted ceilings and oversize conference table created a crammed and nervous energy in the standing-room-only confines. For a few minutes our group of young combat veterans, most who had met just the night before, sat alone and made standard military small talk. Army guys told the Marines not to grunt too much, asking if they could read the books on the table. The Marines asked the Army guys why they weren't wearing their signature reflective safety belts. And the Air Force guys stood proudly behind their signature, lavish military dining halls. The familiar banter revealed a confident, if unfamiliar and uncertain, sense that permeated the packed room.

We were fish out of water. But we were right where we needed to be.

Then in walked Senator Lindsay Graham. And with that, the room erupted into spontaneous and thunderous applause, something I had never witnessed before (and have never seen since). Veterans young and old rocketed to their feet, yelling "Hooah!" and "Oorah!"—shaking the senator's hand and slapping him on the back as he shuffled his way around the room. The response was unplanned, and Senator Graham's reaction was genuine; he was clearly surprised, heartened, and grateful.

The reaction was precipitated by a heated and high-stakes debate the senator had had two days before on NBC's *Meet the Press* with Democratic senator Jim Webb. With both sides interrupting each other and passions running very high, Senator Graham stuck to his guns, saying, "History will judge us, my friend, not by *when* we left, but by what we left behind." And when Senator Webb asserted that the troops no longer wanted to be in Iraq, our new favorite senator responded with a truism that resonated with all of us. "They [the troops in Iraq] want to win. Let them win," he said. "They go back [to Iraq] because they see the face of the enemy that we're fighting . . . they don't want their kids to go back, they don't want their grandkids to go back. Bin Laden said this is the 'third world war in Iraq.' They go back because they know the consequences of losing." A decade later, it's even more clear how tragically correct he was.

Senator Graham did not know any of us, and none of us had ever met him. *But we knew each other.* We didn't know where he stood on other issues, and we didn't care. There was an instant kinship on this critical issue at this precarious moment. There was a mutual respect and a mutual fortitude that had nothing to do with political parties, politics, or personal ego. This was about a complicated and controversial mission that was critically important for the future security and standing of the United States. We weren't here to lobby for a loophole, special interest, or preferential treatment. We were there for our war, and for America's future.

When the room finally settled, the senator sat at the head of the long conference table, and with a clear sense of the moment, spoke to our deepest passions. In a soft, feisty, South Carolina drawl and with a determined grin on his face, his first words to our group were, "Gentlemen, welcome to one of the last places in the United States Senate where you can still use the word . . . *victory*." And with that, the room erupted again.

Senator Graham, a colonel in the Air Force Reserve, was speaking for us. And we were in Washington, D.C., to have his back, and the backs of anyone else who would stand with us—Democrat or Republican. We had his back because he had the back of the warfighters currently on the battlefield in Iraq. But he was a rare breed. At that moment, the world and most in Congress were saying that the Iraq War was hopeless; some said we had already lost. We adamantly disagreed, and believed that winning the Iraq War was not only still possible, but in fact vital to the long-term security and credibility of America. In the words of Senator Graham that morning, "Al Qaeda wants us out of Iraq 'cause we're kicking their ass." It felt like us against the world; and in many ways, it was.

It was July 2007, I was twenty-seven years old, and it was my second Iraq summer.

After an exhaustive and spirited series of meetings that day, mostly with "on the fence" senators who were waffling in their war support (but also including an equally raucous and motivating meeting with Senator John McCain), our rookie crew of insurgents joined a core group of pro-victory senators—dubbed the "no surrender caucus"—at a podium just steps from the Senate floor in the Mansfield Room for a press conference. It was standing room only, with nearly as many cameras as people. Before the press conference, our group of veterans stood awkwardly behind the podium; then, already ten minutes behind schedule, I was tapped on the shoulder by a hasty staffer who asked me to step into a back hallway.

The staffer swung open the huge wooden doors, and I was immediately greeted, surrounded, and lavished with appreciation by a who's who of the U.S. Senate—including a half-dozen top Senate Republicans as well as former Democratic vice presidential hopeful Joe Lieberman—who was, in many ways, the heart, soul, and de facto ringleader of the newly minted "no surrender caucus." As the senators shook my hand and patted me on the back with words of encouragement, the only thought that passed through my mind was, *My dad would love this—I can't wait to tell him.* My dad was, and is, a voracious viewer of the Sunday political shows, which served as my initial (boring) introduction to politics. In my mind, these senators in their Senate chambers were titans from a far-off world that only the powerful—not a small-town kid from Minnesota—could access.

In eager and earnest tones, they thanked me and my "cavalry" for arriving in Washington "just in time." It felt like an alternate universe, and I'm certain the best I could do was babble out incoherent pleasantries in a rush to not look stupid. As the ad hoc "no surrender caucus" meeting wrapped up, Senate Republican leader Mitch McConnell turned to me and said, "You'll bat cleanup for us at the podium—giving the cameras the truth about what's going on in Iraq." I was honored, if terrified, as I clung to three pages of scribbled notes. The real honor came not from the compliments from senators, but from the opportunity—the privilege—to give voice to the warriors still slinging lead in the streets of Baghdad. This effort was never about me, or our group, or about senators—but about the men and women still fighting and the lasting legacy of our war.

This day on Capitol Hill, and our hastily arranged press conference, were necessary because Iraq War opponents had zeroed in on the summer of 2007 (dubbed by antiwar leaders as the "Iraq Summer"), this week, and this day to press for a Senate vote to mandate a withdrawal from Iraq. The big debate on the Iraq War was supposed to happen two months later, in September 2007, when the commanding general in Iraq, General David Petracus, came back to Washington, D.C., to testify about the progress of the troop surge. However, emboldened by a House vote in March that tied war funding to withdrawal, powerful outside groups that opposed the war sensed an advantage in July, and chose to push to end the war sooner by pressuring squishy senators to vote for a withdrawal deadline.

An amendment sponsored by Democratic senators Carl Levin and Jack Reed (the Levin-Reed Amendment) became their chosen legislation and, if passed with sixty votes, would set a certain date for withdrawal and effectively end the surge, and by extension, the unpopular Iraq War. Anticipating that General Petraeus's testimony in September could show signs of progress, they pressed ahead in dramatic fashion in July. Antiwar activists didn't yet have sixty votes in the Senate but thought a high-stakes, high-profile blitz might get them very close.

Squishy, finger-in-the-wind senators—especially those worried about their 2008 reelection campaigns—were targeted from all sides.

To raise the stakes, Democratic Majority Leader Harry Reid—who had already declared the war "lost" in April—scheduled an all-night Senate debate on the Levin-Reed Amendment, going so far as bringing sleeping cots just off the Senate floor. Antiwar groups like Iraq Veterans Against the War, MoveOn.org, and Americans Against Escalation in Iraq simultaneously swarmed Washington, with the latter group hosting 23 senators and 57 representatives at an antiwar candlelight vigil to coincide with the late-night Senate session.

Just as General Petraeus's surge forces were hitting the ground in Iraq, the antiwar movement was surging in Washington. Political and public opposition to the war had never been higher. Our small band of pro-victory veterans, alongside a tiny group of "no surrender" senators, were unpopular, outnumbered, and surrounded. They had the numbers and the momentum, but we had the moral high ground and the pulse of the battlefield.

We had them right where we wanted them.

I don't remember much of what was said at that press conference, nor does anyone else. In the arc of the Iraq War debate, this event is a mere footnote. The content of my remarks can be summarized as: *We can win the war in Iraq. Don't set a deadline for defeat. A hasty retreat will embolden Al Qaeda—and make the situation far worse.* Senator Lieberman also summed up our advocacy in one of the only clips from that press conference that still lives online, saying: "I'm so deeply grateful that the Vets for Freedom have chosen this day to come here, because what they are telling the Senate is—wake up. Wake up to what is actually happening in Iraq. . . . Now is not the time to legislate defeat by mandating a retreat of our troops. . . . The sad truth is that too many of my colleagues in the chambers are asleep when it comes to Iraq. The American military will never lose the war in Iraq. We'll only lose if we lose our political will." He was right then, and even more right today.

That moment on July 17, 2007—on a ninety-degree day in

Washington—was not about what was said, but instead about the stand that was taken. For those who stood there that day, it was a chance to stand in the breach of history during the darkest days of an unpopular war that we believed in then—and still believe in today. The three preceding months had been the most deadly of the Iraq War, as new surge forces pushed into contested areas. Regardless of what defeatists in Washington said, our warriors were fighting, from behind, for a victory in Iraq—in 102-degree heat. This was our chance to stand with them, guarding their exposed domestic flank. The troops in Iraq had reinforcements, a new strategy, a fortified commander in chief, and a courageous commanding general. Now all they needed was the time to see it through. That was our job.

And, there we stood. The political summer soldiers had long since gone home, shrinking from a bitter and unpopular fight, the outcome of which was far from certain; and many of my own politically savvy personal friends had pulled me aside to say, "Why are you carrying political water for a lost cause? For an unpopular president? This is going to hurt your reputation." *None* of this noise mattered. Antiwar groups had dubbed this the "Iraq Summer" in Washington, but the real Iraq summer was taking place six thousand miles away. We stood confident that we were doing the right thing for the soldiers in the field, consequences be damned. It was never—ever—about politics for us. It was about winning the war we were sent to fight.

There were more press conferences after the one in July 2007—and many were much more high profile. Vets for Freedom was back on the Hill in even greater numbers in both September 2007 and April 2008, when General Petraeus came back to testify before Congress. But by then our warfighters had already turned the tide. Progress on the ground—with violence dropping precipitously and progress becoming more evident by the day—eventually made our argument for us and fundamentally undercut domestic efforts to legislate defeat. But on that afternoon of July 17, the outcome was still in doubt—on the battlefield, on the Hill, and in the media.

That evening, as cots were ushered onto the Senate floor, I had an
opportunity to duke it out—Lindsey Graham–style—on *Hardball
with Chris Matthews* on MSNBC, as I would do many times that summer. The entire segment was heated, and Chris cut me off *twenty-
four times* after asking me if "the president's surge strategy had run
its course." It was one of my first television appearances and felt like
a slow-motion train wreck. With nothing resolved except the size of
Chris Matthews's ego, he ended the segment by telling me, "I wish this
government of ours had as much brainpower behind this war as your
passion for this war." A compliment, I guess.

Following that segment, I made the half-mile walk back to the
tiny American Legion post that served as our makeshift headquarters
for the day. Walking with one of Vets for Freedom's founders and my
good friend David Bellavia, a highly decorated Army veteran of Fallujah, I remember being in a daze and reflecting on the whirlwind of a
long day. David was reassuring, but I was nonetheless consumed with
whether or not my band of insurgents would approve of my train-
wreck television appearance. With a sigh, we walked into the small
hall of the Legion post. It was empty. We assumed folks had dispersed,
with our day over. I was disappointed, but unsurprised. So we swung
open the small door to the adjoining bar to grab a beer—only to find
it packed with our crew of tan-shirted misfits. The bar erupted just like
the conference room had for Senator Graham earlier in the day.

Chills went up my spine then, as they do each time I think about
it now. For us—as it had been on the Hill all day—it was not about
whether we got every word right or won every argument. It was the
fact that we were in the arena, and we understood—as Teddy Roosevelt understood based on the hills that he had fought for—that "it
is right to prevail." Showing up and fighting for what is right, when
the chips are down and everyone is counting you out, is the essence of
being in the arena. There we were, tan shirts and all.

The next day, two things happened nearly simultaneously. First, I
woke up in time to watch then-senator Barack Obama say on NBC's

Today show, "My assessment is that the surge has not worked and we will not see a different report eight weeks from now." His words foreshadowed a political battle—over a war that had nothing to do with politics for *us*—that would consume the next sixteen months of my life. Hours later, I received a phone call I didn't believe. President George W. Bush had seen the reports about our group of pro-victory insurgents and wanted to meet with us in the Oval Office . . . in two days.

In complete candor, when I first received the call—and consulted with other Vets for Freedom leaders—we thought about declining the White House invitation. It sounds weird now but made sense to us then. Even though we revered Bush's stance on the Iraq surge, and many of us were Republicans, we were worried about looking like merely pro-Bush and pro-Republican veterans. For us, the war was not about Bush, and was not about partisan politics—it was about America's security, reputation, and legacy. As recently returning veterans, we did not want to risk our credibility by looking like political props. But, after a quick discussion, we soon realized that in this case, reality was far more important than perception. Our wartime commander in chief was requesting support and a meeting; we would have been insubordinate idiots if we did not enthusiastically accept it.

Two days later, four Iraq War veterans—along with four military families—walked into the Oval Office for an hour-long private meeting with President Bush. The meeting was an incredible glimpse into the mind of a wartime president truly grappling with the best way to salvage—and win—a war. The conversation bounced from body counts to counterinsurgency theory to a comparison of General Petraeus and General Ulysses S. Grant, and everything in between. Reflections on the meeting could consume an entire chapter, but suffice it to say that I left that office—and the Rose Garden press conference that followed—confident that our president understood the stakes of the fight, recognized the nature of the enemy, and had the courage to see it through. His words that day underscore perfectly the stakes of the

cause we shared—and very much foreshadow the war we still see rag-
ing today: "Failure in Iraq would increase the probability that at some
later date, American troops would have to return to Iraq to confront
an enemy more dangerous and more entrenched. Failure in Iraq would
send an unmistakable signal to America's enemies that our country can
be bullied into retreat." Prophetic, to say the least.

A week earlier, I had never met a senator—let alone a president.
And, six weeks later, we were back in Washington with reinforcements
to amplify the success of our troops in the field—and back up General
Petraeus. As we believed it would, the surge was working—in dramatic
fashion. Our only job was to shout that fact from the rooftops. So,
standing at the same podium in the same room with a similar group of
senators and congressmen six weeks later, I couldn't resist laying out—
and rubbing in—how far the troops had come in just six weeks. The
confidence I felt at that podium in September was a far cry from July,
and an ever further cry from what I had felt in Iraq the year before.

> Six weeks ago members of Vets for Freedom stood with a similar group
> of senators and urged Congress to wait for the September assessment, at
> that moment—just six weeks ago—leaders in the United States Senate
> were loudly declaring that the war in Iraq was lost and they were calling
> for a timeline for withdrawal. Despite early signs of progress [in Iraq],
> the D.C. timeline was ticking—quickly—toward a hasty retreat.
>
> Simultaneously MoveOn.org and their puppet groups declared an
> "Iraq Summer" in which they would turn up the heat on members of Con-
> gress, and end the war in Iraq. In their words, this "historic summer"
> would "fracture critical elements of the Republican base of support for the
> war by early fall." Well, here we are, and I ask—did they succeed?
>
> Standing here with other veterans and this bipartisan group of sena-
> tors and representatives it is very clear that quite the opposite has hap-
> pened. Instead, since July, members of Congress, both Republicans and
> Democrats, have returned from Iraq and testified to the positive change
> that is happening there. And they've found common ground—the surge is

working and General Petraeus's testimony deserves to be considered with an open mind.

Why has this happened? Because facts about progress in Iraq always trump paid political operatives, spin machines, and ad campaigns. MoveOn, and other antiwar groups, did everything they could to convince the American people that "the war is lost" in Iraq.

But, while these folks spent the summer organizing sparsely attended rallies, chanting empty slogans, and running attack ads . . . on the other hand, our soldiers in Iraq, led by General Petraeus and his new counterinsurgency strategy, took the fight to the enemy. Putting Al Qaeda on the run, and sowing the seeds of stability throughout Iraq.

This is the true story of the Iraq Summer.

No two summers—the summer of 2007 in the swamps of Washington, D.C., and the preceding summer of 2006, in the sands of Samarra—taught me more about warfare, politics, and the high-stakes convergence of the two. No two summers will ever shape me more.

The rest of the story is well known—or at least should be. The Iraq surge was wildly successful. Violence plummeted, political progress started, and the Iraqi security forces were emboldened. Iraqi prime minister Nouri Al Maliki, far from perfect but with U.S. troops behind him and diplomats prodding him, even agreed to arm the Sunni tribes and proactively took the fight to Shia militias, all while initially giving the stiff-arm to Tehran. More troops, the right strategy, and strong leadership made the fundamental military and political difference we believed it would. Before Barack Obama's policies lost the war, we won it.

Along with other Iraq War veterans from Vets for Freedom, I saw it firsthand on two trips back to the front lines of the Iraq battlefield in 2008 as an embedded reporter with *National Review*. As I wrote about extensively during trips to Iraq in February and August 2008, the transformation on the ground was nothing short of stunning, especially for someone who had seen some of the worst places of the war at some of the worst times. As I wrote from Baghdad in February 2008, "It was then that I realized I had never really been to this place—I just thought I had. This is the real Al Doura, a neighborhood and a people reborn—thanks to the bravery and sacrifice of [American troops]. Today, I saw Al Doura for the first time." The Iraq I experienced as a soldier was war-torn and seemingly hopeless; the Iraq that existed after the surge was recovering and full of promise. It was only then that I saw the real Iraq, for the first time.

Yet, despite this overwhelming success, the Democratic nominee for president, Senator Barack Obama, remained committed to the narrative that the outcome in Iraq was inevitable failure (a narrative the Coexist Left—and right-leaning isolationists—will always be wedded to). In speeches, debates, and television commercials during the entire 2008 campaign, he simply insisted that Iraq was an inevitable failure, and a so-called war-weary public lapped it up—wishing away the difficult realities of what it would take to cement progress after a long and difficult war. He was anti–Iraq War, no matter what, and no matter the cost of a rapid withdrawal. He was, as he has remained since, fully and ideologically committed to his coexist foreign policy of retreat.

As a result, like a machine-gun position facing an enemy wave and locked on a final protective line of rapid fire, Vets for Freedom eventually raised and spent $8 million trying to prevent Barack Obama's disastrous Iraq policy—running national "I am the Surge" television ads throughout 2008. We also crisscrossed the country in a tour bus, a modern version of Teddy Roosevelt's effort to awaken the country before World War I, on a speaking tour to motivate the American public and highlight the success of the Iraq surge. The eventual Republican nominee, Senator John McCain, did the same, with his Iraq surge–focused "No Surrender" bus tour credited with reviving his presidential candidacy. (Little-known fact: I had the accidental good fortune of literally naming the "No Surrender Tour" during a private meeting with the senator and his team in 2007.) Whereas other groups pulled back in the final weeks of the campaign based on political calculation, Vets for Freedom internalized the battlefield stakes and did not hold back a penny. Our effort was wholly focused on exposing—thereby preventing—the terrible consequences of a commander in chief Obama. We knew that in Iraq and across the world, his policies would make a bad situation even worse.

Then, on November 4, 2008, Barack Obama was overwhelmingly elected our next president. And, over the course of two Obama administrations, our worst fears were realized. A Vets for Freedom radio ad we ran in 2008 foreshadowed this nightmare. As the pro-surge ad concluded, a young child—a daughter of an Iraq War veteran—left a chilling and prophetic message: "Please don't leave this fight for me...." That is precisely what Barack Obama and his coexist foreign policy have done. An unwillingness to finish an important war—for reasons of expediency, politics, and cowardice—has ensured, in terrible ways, that we have left the fight for the next generation. For your daughters and for our sons. George W. Bush and America's Iraq War veterans didn't leave the fight for the next generation—Barack Obama did.

Look where the Middle East is today. The rise of the Islamic State and the chaos spreading across the region are directly tied to President Obama's leave-at-any-cost strategy. Today we are sending more and more American military "advisers" back to Iraq and now Syria—countries and a region that are in infinitely worse shape than they were following the surge.

The biggest lesson of Iraq is resolve, when it matters most. With resolve, even in our deepest and darkest moments America cannot be defeated, militarily or politically. Without resolve, even with every technical advantage and employing advanced weaponry we will remain vulnerable to nimble, persistent, and ideological enemies. America's enemies, especially Islamists of all stripes, believe with great justification that America's weakest link is our resolve—both on the battlefield and in the court of public opinion. Osama bin Laden called us a "paper tiger," likely to flee from battles that got too messy or complicated. Bin Laden misjudged George W. Bush but had his successor pegged.

Through the lens of two summers—one on the battlefield and another in Washington—I saw the true character of America and our 9/11 generation. I saw what is possible, in both places, when men and women demonstrate resolve, courage, and intellectual integrity. I saw why, as Roosevelt said, "it is right to prevail." I've also seen what happens when political expediency and ideologically shallow arguments drive decision making. Unfortunately, the carnage that is Iraq and Syria today demonstrates that the latter group prevailed. We did not lose the war in Iraq, as some have suggested; we chose not to win, by handcuffing—and defeating—our warfighters and our country. It is a legacy the Coexist Left owns and ought to be utterly ashamed of.

SIX

★　★　★

Fight Hard:
Learning the Right
Lessons Since 9/11

The good citizen will demand liberty for himself, and as a matter of pride he will see to it that others receive liberty which he thus claims as his own. Probably the best test of true love of liberty in any country is the way in which minorities are treated in that country. Not only should there be complete liberty in matters of religion and opinion, but complete liberty for each man to lead his life as he desires, provided only that in so he does not wrong his neighbor. . . .

There is little place in active life for the timid good man. . . . The good citizen in a republic must first of all be able to hold his own. He is no good citizen unless he has the ability which will make him work hard and which at need will make him fight hard.

—TEDDY ROOSEVELT, 1910

How could I not work with people who came across the ocean to help save and rebuild my city?

—LITTLE OMAR, SAMARRA, IRAQ, 2006

The title of Teddy Roosevelt's 1910 speech, "Citizenship in a Republic," befits the content of his speech. The speech is largely about cultivating good and gutsy citizenship in order to maintain a robust and free republic. He alludes to foreign affairs only briefly, and mostly through the lens of domestic considerations. As such, nothing in the text is detailed—but instead based on principles that were evident during his presidency and colored his eventual agitation for American involvement in World War I. In the speech Teddy references, among other principles: patriotism, national sovereignty, international engagement, freedom promotion, military strength, and having the will to fight and win when necessary. The application of these principles is the difficult part—especially in challenging times.

Teddy Roosevelt lived in consequential times, as do we; times that challenge both the rigidity and elasticity of America's core principles. Everybody is a patriot when times are good, but allegiance can fade when outcomes are murky; places like Valley Forge and the Argonne Forest remind us that commitment can be sustained, provided the public and her military are invested. International engagement is important, but not when it erodes sovereignty—where is that line in an interconnected world? Promoting freedom sounds good but proves perplexing across continents and cultures. Military might and a strong posture can prevent wars, but once you're in them—fighting to win requires mustering finite national will, clear leadership, and a reticent citizenry. National security and foreign policy have always been more of an art than a science, requiring the "wise statesman" Teddy Roosevelt invoked. Roosevelt also understood that statesmen are often compelled to advocate for causes and positions that, in their time, are controversial, costly, or at cross-purposes with public opinion. Public opinion in a democracy, even with an engaged citizenry, is often shortsighted, fickle, and prone to advantageous political demagoguery. Foreign policy statesmen must cut through that, while making a compelling public case as to why certain enemies, certain engagements, and certain entanglements are necessary to advance American security and interest.

In Teddy Roosevelt's case, at the dawn of the twentieth century, his crucible was the rise of powerful American potential that was able to, for the first time, promote freedom in her neighborhood, block colonial meddling in the Western Hemisphere, and affect the outcome of a world war on the European continent. In the case of the 9/11 generation and the unfolding twenty-first century, the challenges are different: difficult wars and the growing threat of both violent and political Islamism, but also a rising China and the growth of international institutions that no longer serve Western interests and values. Confronting these threats will require the same principles that Teddy Roosevelt espoused, just in modern form. What should promoting American values, projecting American strength, cultivating free societies, and defeating determined enemies look like in the twenty-first century? Let's start with a series of controversial case studies: the intersection of the three recent wars that have thus far consumed the first fifteen years of this new century: the Iraq, Afghanistan, and Libya wars.

IRAQ: SURGING TO "PREVAIL"

When my mind goes back to Iraq—or anytime Gavin DeGraw's song "Belief" hits my iTunes playlist—I often think of an Iraqi teenager named Little Omar. His full name was Omar Hamid Al Abassi, but we called him "Little Omar." He was five foot two and maybe 120 pounds soaking wet. When the United States invaded in 2003, Little Omar's religious leaders told him the Americans were here to "convert Muslims to Christianity," "kill innocent civilians," and "rape Iraqi women." An impressionable and devout teenager, Little Omar said he was "brainwashed" to believe it was his Islamic duty to kill as many Americans as possible. So he joined the insurgency as a low-level fighter and attacked Americans when and where he could. Apparently and unfortunately he was aggressive and effective—which, after meeting him, did not surprise me. Shortly after my unit arrived in Samarra, his relative and tribal leader—Mr. Assad, whom I wrote about in the previous chapter—was fortuitously appointed the city council president. Little Omar reluctantly became one of his bodyguards, a position that brought him in proximity to U.S. forces. I'll never forget the first time we met him: still a teenager, his eyes were filled with both fear and hate. We didn't trust the new bodyguard, and the feeling was mutual. He was extremely hesitant to talk, selectively approaching our interpreters on the side to get the scoop on the Americans. After weeks of interactions—as he watched and listened quietly—he pulled aside our top interpreter and asked, "The Americans seem like such nice people. Are the Americans always like this?" A few personal conversations later—about family, religion, and America—Little Omar was soon our most courageous ally, and informant.

He reinfiltrated his former insurgent networks, this time with a GPS device. He handed over long lists of valuable information. He walked countless missions with us in a ski mask, pointing out insurgent hideouts and meeting places. One moment in particular sticks out when, in the early evening, my phone rang. Little Omar said he knew where the sniper was who had killed one of our soldiers—he was spending the night in a nearby mosque. Little Omar was still a new informant and any mosque is considered a sensitive site, so we pressed him to make sure his information was correct. An hour later I received another call. Little Omar was now *at the mosque* and with the sniper (a former friend), confirming the target and exact location inside the mosque. His only ask was that when we raided it, we treat him the same so we didn't blow his cover. Later that night, the Samarra Iraqi police raided the mosque under the watchful eye of our Bravo Company. As my journal reads, they "found weapons and evidence galore" but not a single shot was fired. Why? Little Omar later told us that, while the sniper was sleeping, he had placed damaged rounds in the sniper's weapon to make it inoperable. This was not the first time, nor the last, that Little Omar would put his life on the line for us.

Just like my first impressions of Little Omar—which were incomplete and superficial—the conventional wisdom on the Iraq war is ass-backward. The lesson of Little Omar is that he was not a permanent enemy; he was instead a potential ally, a conclusion we drew only after further engagement, investigation, and review of the conventional wisdom. Likewise, the invasion of Iraq was not a mistake; leaving the battlefield precipitously was the real mistake—based on surface-level perceptions and a willful blindness to facts on the ground. Just as it took time and effort to build a relationship with Little Omar, it also took time, effort—and blood—to forge a stable and governable Iraq. Even if our intelligence at the outset of the war was not fully correct, abandoning the Iraq War—not entering it—was the largest strategic blunder of the Obama administration, the ramifications of which America will be dealing with indefinitely. Our eventual strategic defeat in Iraq, which came squarely as a result of Barack Obama's policy of disengagement and retreat, came at terrible costs—in American security, in credibility, and, most important, in lost opportunity.

American retreat was the single largest ingredient in the rise of the most bloodthirsty and powerful Islamic movement in modern history, leading to an Islamic State caliphate hell-bent on striking the United States, exporting their apocalyptic ideology around the globe, and unleashing a humanitarian and refugee crisis of biblical proportions. This was Al Qaeda in Iraq's goal as well, before they were soundly defeated during and after the surge. The disintegrated security situation in Iraq following our hasty withdrawal under Obama in 2011 also served to amplify the consequences of incoherent U.S. policy in Syria and Libya during the so-called Arab Spring. The chaos in Iraq and Syria today is also directly tied to region-wide chaos, accelerating a regional power struggle between (former) Arab Sunni allies and an ambitious—and eventually nuclear—Iran. On a global scale, because America didn't follow through on a difficult war in Iraq following a successful surge strategy, we will remain heavily invested there—and less capable of checking global threats like China and Russia. We left chaos behind in Iraq and as a result are far less capable or credible there . . . or anywhere else.

But as bad as the Islamic State is today, the lost opportunity of what we gave up in Iraq (tomorrow) is worse. Understanding the full extent of this lost opportunity starts with understanding what Iraqis, enabled by American troops, had achieved in Iraq by the time Barack Obama took office. Thanks to a military and political shift of massive proportions, the environment in Iraq following the surge was nothing short of a geopolitical game changer. Iraq in 2008, 2009, and 2010 was the type of Middle Eastern country that—in the rearview mirror in 2016—America would love to have. It was allied, largely peaceful, and increasingly prosperous. In a post-surge Iraq, Al Qaeda was defeated, Iran was increasingly marginalized, Sunni-Shia political progress was developing (not perfect, but moving in the right direction), and the Iraqi economy was hitting its stride. Iraq was not, and never would be, a Western-style democracy, but it was—as Commanding General David Petraeus called it: an "Iraqracy"—Iraqi-style democracy.

And it wasn't the first time a functioning "Iraqracy" had taken shape, against all odds, inside this notoriously fractious state. Following the Persian Gulf War in 1991, Iraqi Kurds—mostly Muslim, but also including a diverse group of Christians and other minorities—were protected by an American-enforced northern no-fly zone, thereby given a de facto opening for post-authoritarian self-governance. The prospect of life without Saddam Hussein was a monumental moment for Iraqi Kurds, and elections were quickly held. But long-standing intra-Kurdish tensions simmered (also stoked by neighbors), and the political process broke down and descended into civil war. Eventually, after years of war and following American mediation, the sides brokered a settlement that eventually led to a largely united Iraqi Kurdistan. (Sounds a bit like Iraq in 2008, doesn't it?) Today the Kurdish region of Iraq stands alone as a pocket of stability, cooperation—and yes, democracy—in the Middle East. It took years and bloodshed, but the evolution of a diverse Iraqi Kurd population that included Sunni, Shia, Christian, and other sects toward pluralism, tolerance, and peace demonstrates what is possible in the Middle East. This lesson in "Iraqracy" also demonstrates what is possible if the United States uses military and diplomatic might in the right place at the right time and is willing to stick with that commitment over the long haul.

The reality of Iraq following the surge—from those who witnessed it—is that it was a massive and missed opportunity to defeat and discredit Islamists, support the development of quasi-stable, quasi-democratic, and multiethnic governance in the Middle East, and demonstrate a decent economic and societal future for average Iraqis. Before the war, Iraq had the human and historical seeds needed for modern progress: a literate populace, a history of multiethnic tolerance, the structures for central governance, a technocratic class, oil resources, modern infrastructure, and a functioning military. After years of "woulda, coulda, and shoulda" in Iraq, the sheer courage of our troops before, during, and after the 2007 surge finally unleashed this imperfect potential . . . only for the Obama administration to squander it. *Imagine*—to quote John Lennon—an allied, stable, quasi-democratic country in the heart of the Arab world today. *Imagine* that country partnering with the United States, eventually recognizing Israel's right to exist, providing a buffer to Iran, and fighting Al Qaeda (because the Islamic State doesn't exist, or is contained to Syria). *Imagine* a stable Iraq where my kids—and yours—won't have to return to fight. *Imagine.*

But don't just take my word for it. Here is Vice President Joe Biden in February 2010 on the prospects for a good outcome in Iraq:

> *I am very optimistic about Iraq. I think it's gonna be one of the great achievements of this [Obama] administration. You're gonna see 90,000 American troops come marchin' home by the end of the summer. You're gonna see a stable government in Iraq that is actually movin' toward*

a representative government. I've been there 17 times now. I go about
every two months, three months. I know every one of the major players
in all the segments of that society. It's impressed me. I've been impressed,
how they have been deciding to use the political process, rather than guns,
to settle their differences.

In 2010, even the Obama administration saw Iraq as a success. But they still didn't have a correct understanding of why Iraqis were using "the political process, rather than guns." Political progress didn't happen magically or because of meetings—it happened at the ends of M-4 and AK-47 rifles. American and Iraqi military progress, along with powerful strategic alliances with Sunni tribes and Shia leaders, had created the space for political progress, and Iraqis had taken advantage of it. (This is especially true and remarkable given that from 2005 to 2008, Iraq was a flytrap for the world's most violent Islamists.) But progress was far from perfect, requiring continued—if substantially reduced—American military and diplomatic oversight. Americans didn't have to stay in Iraq to "nation build," but instead to ensure Iraqi military and political leaders were able to cohere and mature long enough to build their own nation, an investment that would bear incalculable returns. By 2010 that could be done with far fewer troops and far less money than at any time previously in the war.

Instead, Obama's policy of unilaterally declaring victory and then unconditionally withdrawing managed to snatch defeat from the jaws of victory in Iraq—eroding a hard-won peace and undercutting the most consequential foreign policy endeavor of the post-9/11 generation. Regardless of how they spin it, the Obama administration—hell-bent on a complete withdrawal—did not want a status of forces agreement that would allow a contingent of U.S. troops to remain in Iraq. It was never a priority, and they found every excuse to abandon the agreement (contrast that with the Iranian nuclear talks, where they humped the legs of the Iranians while agreeing to extraconstitutional secret side deals in order to get a deal).

The arc of Iraqi prime minister Nouri Al Maliki's leadership also tells the story powerfully. Emboldened by the game-changing progress of the surge, in 2008 Maliki—a Shia—proactively led a multiethnic Iraqi Army against *Shia* militias in Baghdad's Sadr City and then down to Basra to confront *Shia* militias. He oversaw some of the first truly free elections, with Iraqis holding up a purple finger: one man, one woman, one vote. And yet, just a few years later, with the Obama administration contemptuously racing for the exits with no plan in place, Maliki sought greater alignment with a neighboring benefactor—Iran, and thus increasingly marginalized his potential Sunni partners.

Maliki had been willing to take a risk and choose the American tribe, until the rapid Obama military withdrawal and diplomatic disengagement drove him closer to Tehran. These military and diplomatic vacuums in Iraq both invited the rise of the Islamic State and solidified Iran's belief that they could engage in—and win—high-stakes negotiations for a path to a nuclear bomb. The Obama administration wanted *only one thing:* to get out of Iraq. Instead, we've been sucked back into, and contributed to, an even worse mess—one that the next president will be left to confront.

You still may be thinking as you read this, *Is this guy really showcasing the highly flawed, highly disputed, and highly controversial Iraq War in a chapter about American leadership in the twenty-first century?* To be clear (to quote President Obama): *Yes, I am.* The war in Iraq was no doubt flawed, disputed, and controversial, but given America's ongoing and untenable choice between strongmen and Islamists, it also represented America's best chance for a workable "third way" solution in the Middle East. Both the story of Little Omar and the story of Al Maliki are the story of Iraq. With the right leadership, the right strategy, and the will to see a tough fight through, American military forces can forge unlikely alliances and secure a beachhead of pluralism and stability for people who have never known an alternative—making America and the free world more secure in the process.

Setting aside the rationale for the war and the difficult first few

years there, Iraq—immediately before, during, and after the surge—serves as a model for what American leadership should look like in the twenty-first century: *a consequential and clear mission, the military and diplomatic might needed to accomplish that mission, the courage to act decisively and unilaterally, and a gradual, conditions-based transfer to local political and military authorities—so the outcomes of the mission are preserved and America's interests secured.*

AFGHANISTAN: "THE WRONG WAR"

Understanding local conditions and allegiances—the *on-the-ground reality*—is one of the most important aspect of any mission analysis, lest America get sucked into missions and places that drain our finite human and financial resources in pursuit of far-fetched and ultimately counterproductive endeavors. Afghanistan, cynically dubbed "the good war" by Barack Obama and other Iraq War critics, is one of those places. Not only did Barack Obama get the consequential nature of the Iraq War ass-backward, but by halfheartedly doubling down on Afghanistan, he shifted finite American resources to a place where systemic progress is simply not possible. Given that it was the incubator of the 9/11 attacks, going to war in Afghanistan in the first place was the right idea. However, starting with George W. Bush and later with Barack Obama, the scope of what is possible in Afghanistan was never grounded in reality about the Afghan people, their culture, and their history. Save for the immediate response to 9/11, Afghanistan was the real "bad war." More accurately, as military historian Bing West called it, it was simply "the wrong war."

Support for the war in Afghanistan was easy to maintain for the right reason: violent Islamists being harbored in Afghanistan attacked America on September 11, 2001. Eventually this support, thanks to criticism of the Iraq War glowing white hot, turned into reflexive support of a (creeping) Afghanistan mission that lacked critical

evaluation. Regardless of realities on the ground, and after the successful Iraq surge and Barack Obama's election, the American public and her lagging-indicator politicians stayed committed to the full fight in Afghanistan. Support slowly declined, but never plummeted. This allegiance was healthy and not wrong, but it was misplaced—as I eventually saw firsthand. Following my personal experiences in Iraq, the success of the surge there, and even after the election of Barack Obama, I was optimistic about America's chances in Afghanistan; Obama had campaigned on winning the "good war" in Afghanistan, a victory I wholeheartedly believed in.

My group, Vets for Freedom, fought like hell to try to prevent Obama from becoming commander in chief in 2008, but now that he was—I wanted him (as the American president and my commander in chief) to succeed in Afghanistan, and believed he could with more troops and the right approach. Even after Obama's halfhearted Afghanistan surge announcement included a simultaneous withdrawal timeline and fewer troops than his commanders requested, I felt compelled to do what I could to help forge a positive outcome in Afghanistan. This included publicly supporting the Afghanistan surge in print, defending it on television, and even leading a group of Afghanistan and Iraq veterans (including then citizen and Afghanistan veteran, and now Arkansas senator Tom Cotton) to Washington, D.C., to meet with Obama aides at the White House—check the trusty visitor log!—and also compel Republicans on the Hill to support Barack Obama's surge policy. As with Iraq, Afghanistan was never about partisan politics. I wanted to win in Afghanistan, and after seeing what America had accomplished in Iraq through the surge, I was willing to give our new commander in chief the benefit of the doubt.

My passion to support the cause included volunteering to deploy to Afghanistan. I arrived in Afghanistan in early 2011, and it didn't take long to realize that it is a fundamentally different place than Iraq—in all the wrong ways. If Iraq is decades behind the modern curve, Afghanistan is millennia behind. Afghanistan is biblical times with cell phones and AK-47s, completely lacking the human and historical seeds Iraq was able to leverage. The Afghan population is overwhelmingly illiterate and fiercely tribal, there is no history of effective or multiethnic governance, the country lacks an economic base necessary for revenue, the terrain is utterly unforgiving (with an impossible Pakistan border), there is almost no modern human or physical infrastructure, and the Afghan military and police are unreliable. Moreover, by the time I arrived in 2011, the Western approach to "nation building" in Afghanistan had made many things worse. The Karzai government was fundamentally corrupt and discredited throughout the country, the economy was almost entirely dependent on foreign aid, the shadow Taliban government was outgoverning the central government, and the Afghan security forces lacked the capacity to fight without overwhelming American support.

In 2011 and into 2012, my regular email dispatches from Afghanistan to friends and family back home read like a slow, reluctant descent from naïve and uninformed optimism to realistic pessimism. My 2005–06 journal from Iraq, on the other hand, reads in the opposite direction—starting out naïvely pessimistic and ending with realistic and informed optimism. Anyone who has served in both places, or just followed those conflicts closely, understands this general comparison; Afghanistan and Iraq, both Muslim countries in a similar neighborhood, are very different. A multitude of local factors—known, unknown, and unknown-unknowns—contributed to American successes and failures in each place; this certainly includes the trade-offs of effort and investment between the simultaneous theaters. Many take this tension to a hyperbolic conclusion, saying that the Iraq War caused America to "take our eye off the ball" in Afghanistan. It's a poll-tested talking point but has little basis in reality—for two key reasons. First, even if the early years of the war had been handled differently, the long-term mission would have crept into full-scale nation building either way, a result of both the Bush and Obama administration policies. Second, Afghanistan had no foundation for, or history of, centralized, democratic government. After a spectacular early success in 2001, U.S. troops on a mission of remaking Afghanistan were on a well-intentioned fool's errand.

(Afghanistan had earned the title "graveyard of empires" for a reason. Even a kill-'em-all-and-let-God-sort-'em-out scorched-earth policy has not worked in Afghanistan. The Soviet Union tried that tactic in the 1980s, only to be driven from the country in defeat and with their puppet government quickly deposed.)

The sad reality is that Barack Obama and his campaign-team-turned-JV-national-security-team never demonstrated a realistic understanding of Afghanistan or the war. As early as 2007, candidate Obama cynically used the Afghanistan war as a foil for his opposition to the Iraq War. Because he was anti–Iraq War—even during and after the surge—he had to look tough somewhere else, so he rhetorically doubled down on Afghanistan. It was his "good war." But Obama's commitment to Afghanistan was never grounded in knowledge, strategy, or reality; nor did any of his inner-circle advisers have in-depth knowledge of the country or the conflict. Obama's support for the war in Afghanistan was, is, and always has been political. His administration didn't feel the need to do something about Afghanistan. They felt the need *to be seen* as doing something about Afghanistan.

Worse than not understanding, the Obama White House was never really committed to succeeding in Afghanistan—a moral affront to everyone who served under him, and especially those who lost comrades or kin on his watch. Fearing political blowback and always with an eye toward poll numbers, Obama never sent the number of troops his commanders requested, nor did he provide rules of engagement that could have made them successful. Moreover, as a senior counterinsurgency instructor charged with studying the past, present, and future application of our military strategy, I can personally attest to the fact that the faux-counterinsurgency surge strategy Obama employed was doomed from the beginning. Rather than projecting resolve and commitment, he immediately set a deadline for withdrawal—undercutting the mission of the troops and morale of our Afghan partners, while providing the Taliban with the hope and message they needed. Because our allies and enemies knew our commitment was finite, they hedged their bets and waited us out. This reality was evident the minute I hit Afghan soil and it will persist through and beyond Barack Obama's time in office. Every Afghan I met with and served with had at least one foot out the door—prepared for an inevitable American exit. Moreover, in contrast to Bush and the Iraq surge—and Teddy Roosevelt's barnstorming in support of World War I—Obama almost never took to the podium to defend the war. The war was a pesky political necessity for Barack Obama, not a mission to be completed. The memoir of former secretary of defense Robert Gates reveals in powerful detail that President Obama's commitment to Afghanistan was never authentic. It was utterly and cynically political.

It is a dishonorable, dishonest, and disastrous way to fight a war. As a result, Afghanistan continues to slide into the hands of the Taliban (and now the Islamic State) and the Obama administration will likely keep a small number of forces in Afghanistan to keep Kabul and the central government from falling into enemy hands. In this case, the Obama administration learned the right lessons from their failures in Iraq, just in the wrong place and at the wrong time. Keeping a small number of residual forces in Afghanistan is the right thing to do but will have minimal strategic impact, whereas keeping troops in Iraq in 2011 would have had a massive strategic impact and return on investment. Iraq certainly did not fail because of efforts in Afghanistan, but the Obama administration's disingenuous political obsession with Afghanistan caused them to "take their eye off the ball" in Iraq, plunging that country into chaos and endangering the world for Americans.

LIBYA: "LEADING FROM BEHIND"

Speaking of plunging countries into Islamic chaos, the failed Libyan intervention in 2011 showcases Obama's half-baked approach to foreign affairs and the use of U.S. military force. For decades the United States maintained a consistent strategy of undermining Libyan dictator Muammar Qaddafi that included limited U.S. military operations against Libya, isolating Libya internationally, and placing sanctions on the Libyan economy. In 2003 that strategy eventually paid off, when in response to the speedy toppling of Saddam Hussein, Qaddafi gave up his nuclear weapons program and renounced his support for Islamic terrorism. While certainly not friendly in every way, Libya also normalized relations with the United States and other Western nations. Yet, while he cut most of his ties with Islamic jihadists, Qaddafi continued to oppress the people of Libya in order to reinforce his grip on power.

Then, in early 2011, the Arab Spring came to Libya, unleashing a brutal and fast-moving civil war. Eight months later, Qaddafi was captured and killed by rebel forces. With the stated goal of avoiding a massacre of Libyan civilians, NATO forces supported by U.S. airpower directly assisted Libyan rebels in overthrowing Qaddafi. The Libya conflict was emblematic of President Obama's approach to intervention: war from the air, an extremely light footprint, and "leading from behind" through maximum international cooperation. With Qaddafi toppled, Obama ran to the United Nations to declare: "Today we've set a new direction. Forty-two years of tyranny was ended in six months. From Tripoli to Misrata to Benghazi, today Libya is free. This is how the international community is supposed to work." With an election just one year away, the Obama administration was quick to hail the Libya intervention a "model" of twenty-first-century warfare.

Then, the real world happened. After Qaddafi fell, the NATO effort—helpless to fill the power vacuum on the ground—fell apart. Relying almost exclusively on hope that the Arab Spring would em power "moderate" rebels, the United States and its allies never developed a comprehensive plan. Libya soon descended into chaos, falling into the hands of violent Islamists. The attack on America's consulate in Benghazi on September 11, 2012, was a tragic symptom of the mess that was left behind after so-called American "smart power" exited the scene. Today violent Islamist militias control massive swaths of Libya—including contesting all three of the cities the president cited in his self-congratulatory UN speech. The Islamic State has also exploited the chaos, controlling more and more territory in Libya in its push to expand the so-called caliphate.

Suffice it to say, the Obama administration is no longer promoting Libya as a "model" of twenty-first-century intervention, nor—more disturbingly—are they doing anything meaningful about preventing Libya from becoming a haven for Islamic State sympathizers hell-bent on attacking America. As outlined in chapter 4, the outcome in Libya DOES. NOT. COMPUTE. for the Obama administration. In their mind, approval of the UN Security Council and "global consensus" about action in Libya was supposed to cement a good outcome, because global cooperation is the holy grail of the Left's coexist foreign policy. Instead, while it made Obama's neophyte national security team feel good about the intervention, it turns out UN resolutions have minimal bearing on how things actually develop on the ground. The guys with the guns on the ground can still get their way, regardless of what UN bureaucrats in midtown Manhattan think about them or their cause. The Obama administration professed to have learned the lessons of Iraq and Afghanistan when they intervened in Libya, but in their haste to show a new model for U.S. leadership—or followership—they violated the very same basic tenets of foreign intervention: they did not understand the local dynamics, they underestimated violent and dedicated Islamists, and they ultimately had no plan to steer the post-Qaddafi outcome in an advantageous direction.

•   •   •

Setting aside lazy and useless rhetoric about which wars were "good" or "bad" or "smart," contrasting the wars in Iraq, Afghanistan, and Libya should teach America a great deal about how and when we apply force, to what degree we apply that force, and what we should expect outcomes to look like. Every citizen is a product of their era, and every soldier inextricably linked to their wars. The entire post-9/11 wartime period is the lens of my generation—and it has undeniably shaped my worldview, just as San Juan Hill shaped Teddy Roosevelt's. We are forced to learn the lessons of war firsthand, picking up the pieces of what went wrong, fortifying the best strategic principles and tactical practices of our conflicts, and anticipating where the next threats might come from. We also experientially learn humility about the things we thought we knew, in ways merely reading history cannot teach. One year after 9/11, I was a junior in college and argued for the Iraq War on the premise that it would bring about a wave of Western-style democracy in the Middle East. Clearly, I was wrong. We've all learned that Western-style democracy won't work in Islamic countries—and where it does take hold, the results aren't always what we might want (see Egypt). Before I deployed to Afghanistan I wrote multiple pieces about how the counterinsurgency strategy used in Iraq could also be used in Afghanistan. Again, I was clearly wrong—as I outlined above. I even had high hopes for the Arab Spring when that short-lived movement first appeared, but with the Obama administration at the helm, I should have known better.

As Teddy Roosevelt's words in my black frame reinforce, our generation has learned firsthand that the arena is a messy place—full of mistakes, losses, and boatloads of critics. We have made mistakes, we have failed, and we have fallen short. But if we believe freedom, prosperity, and equality to be bedrock values of Western civilization, past failures mustn't dissuade us from advocating unapologetic American leadership in the twenty-first century. Not Wilsonian, utopian leadership, but instead Rooseveltian, steely-eyed leadership. Despite setbacks in Iraq, Afghanistan, Libya, and elsewhere, America's next generation cannot afford to be among "those cold and timid souls who know neither victory nor defeat," lest we cede the future to looming threats or others still unforeseen. Gathering threats cannot be pre-empted or defeated with isolationism, restraint, or nonintervention. Instead, with humble hearts but heroic souls, America's "good patri-ots" need to internalize the lessons of history while harnessing the attributes of victories past—forging a path for the twenty-first cen-tury to be an American century. As long as we learn the right lessons from recent experience, the arc of America's history overwhelmingly demonstrates that our values, power, and action are the true linchpin of the free world.

This doesn't mean fighting every fight, only that no other country is capable of freedom's fight. We can whine about that reality and scold other Western countries for gutting their militaries to pay for their welfare states, but unless and until another free country emerges—with a real army, instead of armies of bureaucrats—then when we have to fight, America will shoulder the leadership burden alone. Vul-nerable nations and oppressed peoples still look to America to deter aggression and affirm their aspirations for freedom—I personally saw it in the eyes of Iraqis and Afghans. America cannot accomplish everything alone, nor should we; but almost nothing of good con-sequence can be done in the modern world without American leader-ship. The world is more interconnected than ever—from commerce to information to markets—and what happens in the far corners of the world impacts America, our allies, and our interests. The question is not "Should America lead?" but instead "In what manner should America lead?"

Many Americans, especially millennials who grew up on a healthy diet of Iraq War pessimism, may not love this "America alone" reality—but they cannot ignore it. As I saw in Afghanistan, we have some great English-speaking allies willing to pull triggers with us. The Austra-lians, the British, and the Canadians immediately come to mind, and all have been longtime, faithful allies of America. But their internal politics, battlefield caveats, and tiny defense budgets prevent them from leading necessary fights. They are strong and faithful wingmen to America, but they are not capable of leading on a global or even regional scale. Only American power, reinvigorated with good citizens and economic vitality, has the realistic ability to defend a free world besieged by threats from within and without. The sooner we realize this lonely fact, the sooner we can build a realistic picture of what leading in the twenty-first century really looks like for America.

Understanding history—and then truly learning lessons from it—is the best way to establish a clear picture of what a modern American foreign policy ought to look like. So, in abbreviated fashion, what are the specific lessons of Iraq, Afghanistan, and Libya?

In Iraq, I learned: Our Islamic enemy is real and radical—but can be defeated. Local conditions are paramount and, if understood, present important opportunities. There *is* a military solution, because only military progress is a prelude to political and economic progress. Strength, numbers, and resolve work (surge), while retreat (especially arbitrary deadlines) invites chaos. U.S. troops are part of the solution, not the source of the problem. Average Iraqis want to believe the United States is there for the right reason; our job is to confirm that bias. "Iraqracy," not liberal Western democracy, is possible in the heart of the Middle East. Unilateral action is not a dirty word, and is often preferable in execution. Counterinsurgency can work, if fully executed and accompanied by overwhelming violence of action. A clear mission—understood at the lowest level—is paramount to an effective outcome. Restrictive rules of engagement (RoE) are deadly for our troops, while aggressive RoE are incredibly effective in decimating and demoralizing our enemy. Signs of *our* progress on the modern, asymmetric battlefield are often subtle (like shifting allegiances) and invisible to the naked eye—making "on the ground" truth indispensable. Maintaining support for the war on the home front is critical to maintaining momentum on the battlefield.

In Afghanistan, I learned: Our Islamic enemy is real and radical—and very adept at survival. Local conditions are paramount and, if not understood, present insurmountable challenges. There *is not* always a military solution, and investing billions in economic development without security and governmental legitimacy only makes matters worse. Strength and numbers matter, but a lack of resolve—especially when reinforced through a lack of public proclamation—infects and undermines every aspect of warfare. Arbitrary withdrawal deadlines don't work. U.S. troops are not the source of the problem, but cannot always solve the problem. Average Afghans—especially in rural areas (in other words, most of the country)—have no concept of why the United States is in Afghanistan and just want to be left alone. No form of centralized Western governance will work, only local power-sharing agreements and tribal councils. International military coalitions, while nice on paper, are more cumbersome than useful. Counterinsurgency, especially done halfway, does not work everywhere. The lack of a clear mission leads to mission creep. Restrictive RoE are deadly for our troops and ruthlessly exploited by an adaptive enemy. Signs of *enemy* progress on the modern, asymmetric battlefield are often subtle (for example, Taliban shadow government networks) and invisible to the naked eye—making "on the ground" truth indispensable.

In Libya, we learned: Our Islamic enemies are real, radical, and resourceful—exploiting advantageous power vacuums to expand their influence. Without direct U.S. military support, so-called moderate Muslim elements are rapidly defeated and co-opted by violent and vicious Islamists (see Syria as well). Local conditions are paramount and cannot be understood, let alone influenced, from a distance. Sometimes the easiest military solution—in this case an air-only effort—is not the best solution. Once you rip the lid off the country, it's impossible to put the cover back on. Absent a better solution, an allied despot who disavows support for Islamists is better than *hoping* U.S.-induced instability will sort itself out. Strength and numbers matter, but only if you use them. The U.S. military is not the problem, but can make the problem worse. International military coalitions, while worthwhile to solidify "global consensus" for action, do not preordain a positive outcome; if anything, they allow for the shirking and shifting of responsibility. "Leading from behind" equates to U.S. followership and allowing the outcome to define itself. The Libya intervention is a model of what *not* to do in the twenty-first century—all of the action, with none of the follow-through plan. The mission in Libya was clear, but it was incomplete; the war may have ended for us, but it has not ended for the people of Libya and the Islamists preying on and exploiting them.

Three different conflicts, with three very different sets of lessons. No conflict is the same, no engagement is the same, and the threats facing America are very different. Yet the default setting of both left-wing "coexist" types and right-wing "restraint" types is to lump them together, blurring the lessons into a broad case for military inaction, blaming America first, and retreating from the world. Those are, of course, the wrong lessons. Instead, with humility and realism about the limits of American foresight and capabilities, we need to build a muscular framework for defending the free world in the dangerous twenty-first century. Firmly grounded in the rightness of American values, establishing core principles (as opposed to hard-and-fast rules) for U.S. foreign policy leadership helps answer the question, "In what manner should America lead?" From there we apply those principles to the immediate threats in today's world and, in the spirit of Teddy Roosevelt, the principled approach is revealed regardless of political party or popular passions. Successful operations apply these *eight principles;* operations that fail usually violate one—or many—of them:

1. Name, know, and gauge the enemy. My initial education on the differences between Islamist groups came over many nights in the guard tower at Guantanamo Bay, speaking with a member of my

platoon who grew up a Coptic Christian in Egypt and spoke flu-
ent Arabic. He would translate the conversations and explain the
dynamics between the more fair-skinned Afghan detainees and the
darker-skinned Arabs, who, as descendants of the prophet Muhammad, considered themselves spiritually and historically superior. The
Islamist enemies we face in Iraq, Afghanistan, and Libya are different versions of the same enemy: violent and political Islamists committed to establishing—and expanding—a caliphate and forcing
non-Muslims to submit. The Taliban and the Muslim Brotherhood,
which compared to the Islamic State look tame, are committed to the
same end game. The worst thing we can do is assume—as many in
the foreign policy intelligentsia did—that an extremely radical and
violent group like the Islamic State will "collapse under the weight of
its own evil." Such a statement—just like claiming that Muslims will
stop joining the Islamic State if they have jobs or that climate change
causes Islamic terrorism—reflects a dangerous lack of understanding
about these groups, as well as the grievances (legitimate or otherwise)
they are exploiting. Just as Russian and Chinese communism took different forms, Islamism is not a monolith. Iran has similar ambitions,
but it is obviously important to recognize that their Shia version of
Islam has been, and remains, at war with Sunni Islam. Properly gaug-
ing the threat allows us to apply the appropriate level of response, at
the appropriate time. Whereas the Islamic State must be violently, in-
discriminately, and immediately eradicated from this earth—with the
support of U.S. advisers, aviators, and trigger pullers—combating an
Iranian proxy like Hezbollah (especially under an Iranian nuclear umbrella) requires a different approach.

**2. Understand, and account for, local conditions, cultures, and
power dynamics.** Ultimately, uncontrollable local and cultural factors
can serve as the most significant constraint on the factors we do control. Personally witnessing the huge difference between what is possible in Iraq versus what is possible in Afghanistan instilled in me a

healthy and abiding dose of realism that I believe should permeate America's foreign policy. Add to that reality the cultural chasms between the United States and places like China, Russia, and Iran, and we would be foolish to believe a one-size-fits-all approach will ever work. Before we intervene on a large or small scale, America's political and military leadership must both understand and take into account local complexities and power dynamics. They must also think through how changing those dynamics will impact our security and the long-term mission we aim to accomplish—including the size, scope, and possible unintended consequences. Properly implementing this principle requires substantially increasing and empowering America's intelligence services.

3. Outline a clear, honest, and feasible *long-term* mission. No modern American war has been started without an articulation of what was declared, at the time, to be a clear and limited mission. In Afghanistan we were going to crush Al Qaeda and topple the Taliban—but it quickly expanded into full-blown nation building. In Iraq the original mission was to remove Saddam from power and preempt Iraqi deployment of weapons of mass destruction—but we quickly shifted to a more ambitious endeavor of democracy promotion. In Libya the mission was narrowly focused on protecting Libyan civilians from massacre, not on deposing a dictator—but eventually American planes helped hunt down and kill Qaddafi. In each case, either infeasible mission creep or an unstated secondary mission obscured the clarity of the cause. Only in the case of Iraq—and it took until 2007—was a clear, honest, and feasible mission ever outlined that was grounded in hard-earned experience and local realities. We need to realize that, in conflicts of consequence, easy and short-term outcomes are rarely possible—and the attempt to do wars on the cheap (Iraq pre-surge) or only from the air (deposing Qaddafi in Libya) can have massive unintended consequences. None of our adversaries are going anywhere soon, making long-term military, diplomatic, and economic planning and execution critically important. It also means deterring conflict is *highly preferable* to engaging in conflict.

4. The American military is a force for good. As outlined throughout this book, I believe America has always been an exceptional nation that is a force for good in the world. Acting under this premise doesn't mean being arrogant or belligerent; it only means having confidence in the value of our commitment to political freedom, economic freedom, and religious freedom. Of course, just like any other nation, we are a flawed nation, full of fallen people. America has made many mistakes, we have unnecessarily killed innocent people, and we have fallen short of our values. But, on the whole, America has been a force for good in the world—freeing people from tyranny, lifting people from poverty, saving people from disasters, and keeping the world's shipping lanes open for free trade and global commerce.

My experience also shows, quite clearly, that in contested areas military progress is *the* essential precursor to political and economic progress. The use of American force is, on balance, a good thing. These facts, which are abstract for many, were validated during both of my tours to combat zones. Our actions are not perfect, but those who dwell on our imperfections either miss the forest for the trees or simply have an ideological ax to grind. Or they live in a fantasy world where democracy, free markets, and allies emerge in a vacuum—even when history shows us that force of arms is the necessary precursor. Enemies don't defeat themselves, and shipping lanes don't protect themselves. When Democrats and Republicans embrace this principle, the old adage "partisan politics stops at the water's edge" really is possible. Teddy Roosevelt did it and our generation did it—it's not hard. America's failures abroad are failures for all of us.

5. America *is* the world's sheriff. In order to secure America and her interests, we must be robustly engaged in the world. America must be unafraid to act unilaterally when necessary because, as discussed later in chapter 8, today's international institutions are impotent,

obstructionist, and outright hostile to American interests. This reality does not mean we act rashly or belligerently, but instead requires
that America act muscularly and proactively—as a means to *deter* our
enemies, *reassure* our allies, and *maintain* global trade markets. In the
past this role was called, including by Teddy Roosevelt, the "proper
policing of the world." My experience shows how difficult this really
is. The world is so disparate, chaotic, and complex that American
boots cannot be everywhere, nor should they be. Instead, like a good
sheriff's department, American boots, ships, and airpower should be
in the neighborhood, either embedded or just over the horizon, and
proactively prepared to shape outcomes, deter violence, and support
our friends. When we intervene, sometimes we can leave quickly; but
other times, mission success will dictate that we must stay.

This means staying in regions where we are engaged, and finding new locations from which to project American power. The real
and constant threat of immediate American intervention—the willingness to "pay any price, bear any burden"—actually *lessens* the likelihood of conflict, as bad actors think twice about causing trouble.
This approach does not mean searching for fights or starting wars; on
the contrary, peace is possible only by reintroducing the real threat of
American intervention and thereby restoring respect for, and fear of,
America around the world. Otherwise we end up containing, managing, and refereeing bloody and consequential conflicts from the
sidelines, hoping they end in our favor rather than influencing the
outcome (a situation very similar to what America's inner-city police
departments face right now). By strongly and proactively addressing
international flash points—a concept Ronald Reagan dubbed "peace
through strength" and *Wall Street Journal* columnist and author Bret
Stephens calls "broken windows foreign policy"—America can deter
weaker foes and prevent large-scale conflict. We should enlist local
friends and international allies as sheriff's deputies whenever possible;
but without America confidently in the lead—with a shiny golden
badge seen by all—the twenty-first century will be neither free, prosperous, nor peaceful.

6. American strength and resolve are fundamental. Being in the neighborhood does little good if America is unwilling to act decisively or, more important, overwhelmingly to defeat a threat. Present or not, indecisiveness and equivocation undercut our allies and embolden adversaries. Worse, America cannot afford to quit fights when they become difficult. Osama bin Laden called America a "paper tiger" for a reason: he believed America did not have the resolve to finish a fight with Islamism. While he was correct about American public opinion, he was proved wrong by the Iraq surge—only to be validated by Barack Obama's unilateral withdrawal. American resolve, should we muster it, is the ingredient our enemies most fear. Ronald Reagan's "peace through strength" adage is correct, as is the inverse—weakness is dangerous and invites challenge. Strength also requires untying the hands of our warfighters by altering battlefield rules of engagement (RoE) that are currently slanted against them. Our enemies hide among civilians, limiting our options and endangering our troops—and that must change. Our troops should always get the benefit of the doubt, and should be empowered to punish the enemy no matter their cowardly tactics.

Resolve also requires hard truths. When confronting Iran and the Islamic State, what is our Hiroshima and Nagasaki moment? If we believe the threat to be no less severe than Nazism, what will bring our enemies to their knees? And how will America muster the resolve? The unwillingness to do whatever is necessary to defeat our enemies means wars drag out longer, at unnecessary cost in American lives and treasure. Following the Obama administration, delivering decisive destruction to our enemies will require a renewed focus on fostering citizens and patriots, as well as a defense restoration similar to the Reagan buildup of the 1980s.

7. The freedom agenda is not dead, but must be more realistic. Many of the most persuasive critics of America's post-9/11 foreign policy make the case that any form of democracy is incompatible with any form of Islam. As skeptical as I am about Islamic reformation, my

experience and interactions in the Middle East—especially in Iraq—showed me that certain Muslim populations, in certain places and at certain times, can actually buck this trend with the help of America. Iraqracy, or quasi-democracy, is eventually possible where societal ingredients exist that can either supersede or suppress hard-core Islamic law. It was eventually forged—after decades—in the Kurdish region of Iraq after the Gulf War, and could have happened throughout Iraq after the surge, with a long-term commitment from the United States. There's also no reason why it could not have secured a beachhead in Iran—a highly educated country. We could have exploited popular protests in 2009 far better, either helping to topple the regime entirely or at least forcing the issue toward a far better nuclear deal. Instead, we sat back passively and feebly.

That said, attempting to impose democracy militarily across the *entire* Middle East is a bad idea, a waste of resources, and chock-full of unintended consequences. Often America pours mountains of humanitarian aid into vulnerable countries, without the necessary military component, hoping democracy will take root; instead the situation only gets more violent, more chaotic, and full of corruption. Ultimately, sustainable "Iraqracies"—no matter where in the world—require the *capability for* some level of sustainable shift in underlying societal preferences and opportunities combined with the will of America to shepherd that shift. Teddy believed others should "receive liberty," and so do I; in addition to ruthlessly hunting and killing our enemies, the challenge of the twenty-first century is finding the realistic opportunities for freedom promotion without blindly charging (or tepidly applying) American power in the service of unwinnable quagmires. This also means publicly and actively supporting freedom dissidents in all corners of the world. Doing this requires also remembering another Teddy Roosevelt maxim, delivered in March 1910 before the General Assembly of Cairo University in Egypt: "The training of a nation to fit itself successfully to fulfill the duties of self-government is a matter, not of a decade or two, but of generations." The balance between see-

ing the possible and knowing the limitations is the gray area freedom's statesmen must navigate in the twenty-first century.

8. Strategic victory matters, and is attainable. After bad outcomes in Iraq, Afghanistan, Libya, and elsewhere, some on the left and the right have taken soft solace in the argument that "winning" wars is an outdated adage. Modern, asymmetric wars have followed a familiar pattern: an overwhelming tactical battlefield victory, followed by a drawn-out insurgency and eventual strategic defeat. Iraq—as a result of the surge—is the only place where strategic victory was truly in our grasp. Strategic victories—especially if they take many years in an aggressive counterinsurgency fight, as in Iraq—really matter and have lasting consequences. Likewise, stepping back and realizing that a war is strategically unwinnable, as in a place like Afghanistan, helps guide how much additional American investment should be made. Calling for strategic victory does not mean clinging to failing efforts, but instead identifying which efforts—and when—merit the long-term American effort needed to win. Obtaining strategic victory requires applying the level of resources needed to match the threat—at home and abroad. It also means committing to conditions-based withdrawal instead of timeline-based withdrawal, not an easy task for a country wedded to a four-year political cycle. Finally, retreating—rather than winning—almost always creates more collateral damage (that is, civilian casualties) than if America had stuck around, stuck with the fight, and aggressively killed the enemy in pursuit of tactical and strategic victory. Civilians are unfortunately going to die in war, but in the face of cowardly enemies and in the pursuit of American security, those deaths often bring about a future where far more lives are saved and many more people prosper.

Applying these principles will require a level of commitment America cannot currently muster, let alone stomach. Some of the specific poli-

cies I recommend later in the book may make people uneasy, mostly because most Americans have no idea how dangerous the world really has become, and how alone America really is. I also have no illusions about how wide the gap is between what I assert in these pages and where the appetite of the American people, especially young people, currently lies. An aggressive, assertive, and confident American foreign policy is not possible without the allegiance of good—and unapologetically patriotic—citizens. The extent to which the twenty-first century is an American century has as much to do with the education of American middle school students as it does with the number of American aircraft carriers; both are ultimately necessary, but the latter will not be sustainable without the former.

The other potential impetus for an assertive and muscular U.S. foreign policy would be something nobody wants: a large-scale direct attack on American citizens in our homeland. I believe a strong and aggressive American posture—fighting them "over there"—is best served to prevent such an attack; this fact is what makes the past seven years of American retreat and disengagement from the world so dangerous. Even though our FBI has done yeoman's work countering the homegrown terrorism threat, America's "coexist" posture has only *increased* the likelihood of more attacks—either directly or through the use of so-called lone wolves. (I hate the term *lone wolf*—since jihadists who decide to attack us internally are neither alone, nor wolves. They are motivated by fellow Islamists abroad who actively recruit them, and they are cowardly sheep—not brave wolves.)

Under President Obama we have "unclenched our fist" and instead of reaching out in good faith, our enemies have taken full advantage of our weakened posture. While the Islamic State circulates images of horrific torture on social media, our State Department creates hokey "Think Again, Turn Away" social media accounts (yes, they *actually* named it that) that—I guarantee—are not reaching impressionable young Muslims. While the Iranian regime chants "Death to America," our president botches negotiations that actually ensure their path to a

nuclear bomb, while freeing up billions of frozen assets for use as terror funds. And while the world gets more dangerous, our military has
been hollowed out—physically and psychologically.

But I still have hope. The idea of America is what stirred in the
hearts of thousands of Americans who volunteered to serve after 9/11,
just like it stirred in my soul when, in 2005, I volunteered to leave my
job on Wall Street to lead an infantry platoon in Iraq. And, once there,
the idea traveled with me. In addition to my black frame with Teddy
Roosevelt's quote, I had a sheet of paper stapled above my dusty work-
station in Iraq that simply read, "They want to believe . . ." My experience on the ground during hundreds of interactions with Iraqis of all
backgrounds, locations, and religious affiliations demonstrated that the
idea of America—as distant as it may be to some—lingers in the hopes
of those we interact with. People who encounter Americans across the
globe have seen the movies and the television shows and heard the
apocryphal stories. They want to believe that America is a beacon of
opportunity, lined with golden streets and perpetual peace. They want
to believe we can offer them a better life, right where they live. They
want to believe that the reason we send our men to foreign lands is to
liberate, not to subjugate. The problem comes when, eventually, we fail
to meet the expectations of local populations—either not quickly or
not holistically enough. But, even when we do fall short, the hope still
lingers, and creates opportunities for partnerships that no other country in the world could facilitate.

Little Omar wanted to believe. When we eventually asked him why
he flipped so enthusiastically to our side, he simply said, "How could
I not work with people who came across the ocean to help save and
rebuild my city?" While most of the leadership of the insurgency in
Samarra, Iraq, was composed of dedicated jihadists, many of their foot
soldiers were impressionable youth—swept up by Islamist rhetoric and
lacking an alternative belief system. When confronted by the possibility of America—up close and personal, in Little Omar's case—they
will consider, and fight for, an alternative. (Drones can't do this, by the

way; and neither can diplomats in guarded compounds.) Little Omar did not want a job; he wanted a future. He wanted to believe. As I wrote in my journal at the time,

> *This fact gives me hope. It's not like he [Little Omar] quit being a Muslim, quite to the contrary. He is still enrolled in an Islamic school and had finals last week. But he has seen the human side, that killing innocents is wrong. If Omar can turn—and not forsake his beliefs—then there is hope. Islam has its problems, but it is not necessarily destined to violence. It may be prone to violence, but it is not destined. And if we engage each other, meet each other, learn from each other, hope and understanding can occur. In fact, we can fight together to defeat extremism and violence.*

The last sentence is most important, and the precursor to the rest. We must fight together—something Little Omar dedicated his life to, and is remembered in death for. On June 15, 2006, Little Omar sent me the following poem in a text message: "Salam Allah [God greets you], to people who my heart likes their mention, when they are far from me, they are in my heart, may the Most Merciful [Allah] guard them." A prayer asking Allah to guard *us*—the outsiders, the supposed infidels. The next morning, he was found shot in the head, just outside the city. An Al Qaeda cell murdered Little Omar—driving him out to the desert and shooting him in the back of the head. Delivering the $2,500 condolence payment to his humble and timid father was excruciating, especially while Little Omar's father talked about all the good things his son had said about the Americans and the courage of Mr. Assad. Little Omar is gone, but his life and death perpetually remind me of three powerful realities: people all around the world want to believe in America, good people of different backgrounds fighting together can accomplish big things, *and* our enemy is utterly ruthless and unrelenting.

As Teddy Roosevelt said, "there is little place in active life for the timid good man. . . . The good citizen in a republic must first of all be able to hold his own. He is no good citizen unless he has the ability which will make him work hard and which at need will make him fight hard."The world today requires America to fight hard, both abroad and at home, to shore up our values and ultimately maintain and project our power. Recent wars have given Americans pause; but recent stumbles cannot cause Americans to lose sight of the fact that in the long run "others receiving liberty" is ultimately a good thing, one that will increase the cause of peace around the world. Either America will lead the free world—with her good citizens and good patriots getting in the arena—or we will watch from the sidelines as the world slowly (or quickly!) falls into the hands of theocrats, authoritarians, and bureaucrats. And then freedom slips away. Making the twenty-first century an American century will require the continued defense—and carefully waged promotion—of freedom, free markets, and free peoples. History suggests there is simply no viable alternative.

PART III

★ ★ ★

The Power of Looking Ahead | The Future of Our Republic

SEVEN

★ ★ ★

Equal of Opportunity: Revitalizing the American Dream

We are bound in honor to strive to bring ever nearer the day when, as far is humanly possible, we shall be able to realize the ideal that each man shall have an equal opportunity to show the stuff that is in him by the way in which he renders service. There should, so far as possible, be equal of opportunity to render service; but just so long as there is inequality of service there should and must be inequality of reward.

—TEDDY ROOSEVELT, 1910

The erosion of equal opportunity is among the greatest threats to our exceptionalism as a nation. But it also provides us with an exciting and historic opportunity: to help more people than ever achieve the American Dream . . . upward mobility and equal opportunity is not a partisan issue, it is our unifying American principle.

—SENATOR MARCO RUBIO, ADDRESS ON FIFTIETH ANNIVERSARY OF THE WAR ON POVERTY, JANUARY 8, 2014

On a beautiful fall afternoon in October, a citizen of rural Illinois took to a modest speaker's platform in the small farming town of Alton, Illinois. It was October 15, 1858, and citizen Abraham Lincoln was running for the U.S. Senate against incumbent senator Stephen Douglas. The spirited campaign featured a series of seven lengthy debates across the state. Known famously as the Lincoln-Douglas Debates—or "the Great Debates of 1858"—they centered on the most contentious topic of the day: slavery and its future in America, especially in new territories. The debates also served as a preview of the 1860 presidential election, a contest that would also feature Lincoln and Douglas in large part because, like Roosevelt's speech in France, newspaper coverage of their debates was ubiquitous—with major newspapers across the United States reprinting the debates in full. Over the course of two months, the two men eloquently defended their positions—wrestling over central questions of personhood, citizenship, state sovereignty, fundamental rights, democracy, and equality.

In Alton that day, before an assembled crowd of more than six thousand voters, citizen Lincoln made his closing argument on equality:

> *I think the authors of the Declaration of Independence intended to include all men, but they did not mean to declare all men equal in all respects. They did not mean to say all men were equal in color, size, intellect, moral development or social capacity. They defined with tolerable distinctness in what they did consider all men created equal—equal in certain inalienable rights, among which are life, liberty and pursuit of happiness. This they said, and this they meant. They did not mean to assert the obvious untruth that all were actually enjoying that equality, or yet that they were about to confer it immediately upon them. They meant to set up a standard maxim for free society which should be familiar to all—constantly looked to, constantly labored for, and, even though never perfectly attained, constantly approximated, and thereby constantly spreading and deepening its influence, and augmenting the happiness and value of life to all people, everywhere.*

Fifty-two years later, citizen Teddy Roosevelt spoke the very same words standing on an ornate stage in front of a much different audience. Repeating the words of Lincoln to his French audience at the Sorbonne, it was the *only* quotation Roosevelt used during his ninety-minute "Citizenship in a Republic" speech. This is certainly no coincidence.

Roosevelt revered Lincoln, in much the same way conservatives today hold up Ronald Reagan and seek to continue his legacy. Roosevelt sought to continue the Lincolnian legacy, believing they shared a similar vigor for truth, courage, and action. At his inauguration Roosevelt wore a ring that contained a lock of Lincoln's hair. Roosevelt invoked Lincoln often as president and later wrote a biography of the sixteenth president in 1909—just one year before his speech at the Sorbonne (this could have been why he used this quote in his speech). By historical happenstance, a six-year-old Teddy Roosevelt was even present for President Lincoln's funeral, with a rare photograph showing him peering out of his family's Broadway Avenue home in New York City as Lincoln's casket passed below. Side by side on Mount Rushmore, history remembers them together alongside two of America's greatest founders. They were, in many ways, kindred spirits.

Having hammered home the centrality of "good citizens" to a great republic in the core of his speech, Roosevelt used Lincoln's historic words to pivot to the most important "public good" he believed those good citizens should advance: *the continuous pursuit of* "equality of opportunity" for everyone. In making this point, Roosevelt points to Lincoln, who, as he always did, pointed to the Declaration of Independence, which powerfully states:

> *We hold these truths to be self-evident, that all men are created equal,*
> *that they are endowed by their Creator with certain unalienable Rights,*
> *that among these are Life, Liberty and the pursuit of Happiness. That*
> *to secure these rights, Governments are instituted among Men, deriving*
> *their just powers from the consent of the governed.*

Even if it was unequally applied at the time, the word *equal* is arguably the most important word in the Declaration's preamble. Lincoln clarifies: "[The founders] did not mean to assert ... that all were actually enjoying that equality, or ... that they were about to confer it immediately upon them." Lincoln's point, echoed by Roosevelt throughout the speech, is that equality is never truly equal and never truly attainable; but must always be held up for pursuit—"looked to ... [and] labored for" in every way. Many basic elements of the Declaration's endowed equality took far too long to take hold, but the pursuit has been constant ever since—from the Emancipation Proclamation in 1863, to the Nineteenth Amendment in 1920, to Martin Luther King Jr.'s "Dream" in 1963. Equal freedom, equal treatment, and equal justice are founding promises of America—even if, at times, they have been a long time coming.

From Lincoln to Roosevelt and beyond, this elevation of "equality" is a defining characteristic of both the *republican* and *Republican* tradition. Republican Abraham Lincoln led a war to emancipate enslaved black Americans; Republicans in Congress led the charge for women's suffrage and Republican legislatures across the country ratified it (eight of nine Democratic legislatures voted *against* ratification); a Republican president and Republican-controlled Congress granted citizenship to Native Americans; and it was Republicans in Congress who overcame a Democratic filibuster to pass the Civil Rights Act of 1964. In each case, the *republican* activists who championed these social movements—and the *Republicans* who advanced and voted for their codification—appealed directly to the Declaration of Independence's basic and unalienable rights endowed *equally* by a Creator, not a government. Each case was a fulfillment of America's founding premise, not a rejection or transformation of it. America's founders understood that republican government exists to secure these rights, not bestow them.

By modern standards, these beliefs—among others related to liberty, role of government, and free enterprise—could only place America's founding republicans in league with modern conservative Republicans. The founders had plenty of disagreements among themselves—some violently so!—but it's hard to dispute that even those disagreements fall within the conservative end of today's political spectrum. This is not intended to be a partisan statement—I'm not writing a Republican book for Republicans, nor am I looking to parse out the differences between 1776-era Federalists, Anti-Federalists, or Democratic-Republicans (the prescient name of the party formed by Thomas Jefferson and James Madison in 1792). Instead, comparing the principles of our founders to the principles of modern-day conservative Republicans is meant to clarify where, more or less, the small-*r* republican ideals of our founding in 1776 still live more than two hundred years later: ideas of individual liberty, limited government, religious faith, free enterprise, and equal opportunity. These founding ideals—later codified by the Constitution and Bill of Rights—are what make America, by definition, *exceptional*. America is not exceptional because we are proud, powerful, or rich. America is exceptional because of the principles upon which she was founded—principles that, at the time of our founding, were considered unfeasible by the rest of the known political world.

America's first *republican*, George Washington, along with his founding compatriots, fully understood this reality. From the balcony of Federal Hall on Wall Street at his first inaugural address, Washington said, "the destiny of the republican model of government [is] justly considered, perhaps, as deeply, as finally, staked on the *experiment* entrusted to the hands of the American people." America was, from the first shot heard 'round the world to John Hancock's bold signature on the Declaration of Independence, an experiment: an experiment in self-government and an experiment in human freedom. In Europe and around the world, government "of the people" was seen as dangerous and peaceful transfers of power deemed a naïve prospect. Surely a constitution—just a scrap of paper—could not command such authority and allegiance? Such an experiment was doomed to fail! So said the cynics and the critics. Yet thanks to the courage of generations, thanks to men and women in the arena, an exception was achieved and an experiment validated. America has seen exceptional results since—pride, power, and wealth experienced by many—but only the perpetuation of the equal and exceptional ingredients instilled at the founding keeps America truly special. All republicans—Republicans or Democrats—can agree on that; the only question is who in America will truly fight for it today, and how.

Lincoln's statement is an expression of America's tradition of equality, but Roosevelt refines it further. When discussing equality, neither Lincoln nor Roosevelt is talking about *absolute* equality or equality of *outcome*—as stated earlier, both knew such a goal is impossible and counterproductive. Instead, "we are bound in honor to refuse to listen to those men who would make us desist from the effort to do away with the inequality which means injustice," said Roosevelt. "The inequality of right, opportunity, of privilege." Full equality is never possible, and is not just. People will never be, in practice, equal—nor is it possible for people or governments to forge equal outcomes. Attempting that quickly turns equality into an injustice, redistribution, socialism, or worse. But on the point of *equal opportunity*, Roosevelt is unequivocal:

> *We are bound in honor to strive to bring ever nearer the day when, as far is humanly possible, we shall be able to realize the ideal that each man shall have an equal opportunity to show the stuff that is in him by the way in which he renders service. There should, so far as possible, be equal of opportunity to render service; but just so long as there is inequality of service there should and must be inequality of reward.*

Equal opportunity is also known as the American Dream, the ability for anyone—man, woman, black, white, young, old, rich, or poor—

to "show the stuff that is in him." This dream has fueled the American psyche for more than 240 years and has produced a country of strivers, innovators, pioneers, workers, and high achievers. The preservation of that dream in each generation has produced citizens who are afforded equal opportunity to leverage their talents and skills to pursue happiness and leave a better life for the next generation. Nothing more, but nothing less. Just as the greatness of a country is determined by the goodness of its average citizens, *equal opportunity* for those good citizens to succeed is fundamental to a great republic's success. Good citizens use their equal opportunity to achieve the American Dream, all of which keeps the American experiment exceptional. Put even more simply, *Good citizens plus equal opportunity equals an American Dream for individuals and an exceptional America for all.*

The inverse is also true. Without "good citizens," the equation fails—hence Roosevelt's emphasis on citizenship in the speech. The ability to work, willingness to fight, necessity of strong families, and baseline of character remain fundamental. However, even with good citizens, the American Dream and American exceptionalism are lost without both the perception and the reality that an equal opportunity to "pursue happiness" is available to all Americans, regardless of station in life. This is where good citizens are required to go beyond "efficiency" as individuals and "also must have those qualities which direct the efficiency into channels for the public good." The phrase "public good" can mean many things, to many people; Roosevelt mentions different attributes in the speech but always comes back to the core theme of being "equal of opportunity."

At a basic level, today's formulation of equal opportunity is commonly understood to mean that all Americans are treated similarly—that is, equal justice—and are unimpeded by societal barriers, inherent prejudices, or societal preferences that inhibit social mobility. The good news is that, from slaves to women to Native Americans to blacks to the gay community, the concept of equal justice has proliferated powerfully, if imperfectly, in America. Likewise prejudices and societal preferences against individuals live largely at the ideological margins of society, having been addressed by a commitment to assimilation and America's embrace of pluralism and real tolerance. America is not perfect, but the arc of equality—to channel Martin Luther King Jr.—has bent continually in the right direction. Today the real impediment to equal opportunity exists from societal, political, or economic limitations to *social mobility*. Differences of mental ability, physical capability, and family ties will always exist and will always keep the playing field uneven to some degree, but systemic barriers to advancement, seen or unseen, are intolerable and ought be the focus of "good citizens"—as they were for Roosevelt. The ability for anyone to rise, anyone to succeed, or anyone to pursue happiness—my children or yours—remains the preeminent "public good." Unfortunately, social mobility is heading in the wrong direction in America today.

For much of America's history, the "man who does his work well," in Roosevelt's words, was able to get ahead. Work hard enough, get an education, save money, be responsible—and doors will open. A 2014 Pew Research Center poll showed that 60 percent of Americans still believe most people who want to get ahead can do so if they work hard enough. Unfortunately, this perception—which reflects healthy optimism about the American Dream—is increasingly disconnected from the lives of many Americans, especially those lacking financial and familial means. Many studies have been done, and lots of statistics compiled, that demonstrate a plain, simple, and difficult reality today: even if you play by the rules, it is getting harder to get ahead in America. Pew called 2000–10 "the lost decade" with a middle class that "has shrunk in size, fallen backwards in income and wealth, and shed some . . . of its characteristic faith in the future." Eighty-five percent of Americans in the survey say it's more difficult than ever to maintain their standard of living. These numbers, and this sentiment, have only worsened since 2010. Income, wealth, and net worth all continue to trend downward for the poor and middle class; debt, on the other hand, continues to rise. Overall, too often the poor are staying poor and the middle class are either stuck where they are, or sliding slowly backward. Working hard and playing by the rules doesn't pay off the way it used to.

The causes for this are many. Many of our country's poor are trapped in a self-fulfilling dependency cycle that meets their basic needs but provides few avenues up and out. A soft bigotry of low or, worse, *no* expectations keeps the poor, poor. The jobs that are accessible for the poor and middle class don't pay off the way they used to—with increases in living costs outpacing basic wages, technological advances replacing low-skilled jobs with high-skilled jobs, and global competition and regulations sending companies, and their opportunities, overseas. Moreover, today's good-paying jobs require education and skills that many of America's students don't have. Instead they get a high school diploma from a public school that fails to prepare them adequately for the modern job market, or come out of college saddled with mountains of debt and four years of intellectual coddling that didn't prepare them for the real world. America's twentieth-century education model, already saddled with a postmodern curriculum, is not serving twenty-first-century students well at all. Most important, the advantages traditionally instilled by a family in the home—the ingredients for good citizenship—are undercut by high divorce rates, out-of-wedlock children, and broken families. The family unit is the first and indispensable step toward equal opportunity, and it remains in crisis. Not having a healthy family life makes getting an education more difficult, and not having a good education makes getting a good job more difficult; lack of good opportunity in all three areas—family, education, and employment—is an unholy mix that has led to a "social mobility gap" America must address.

The Left claims to carry this mantle, making "income inequality" their signature issue—and they're not entirely wrong to do so. While in absolute terms, more than 80 percent of Americans have higher incomes than their parents did, in relative terms the wealth gap has grown considerably. Most of America's wealth has collected at the top, with America's highest earners today accumulating significantly more wealth than ever, while income accumulation at the bottom of the economic ladder is stagnant, and falling. In absolute terms the tide might be rising overall, but that overall rise does not solve for the fact that the discrepancy in boat size is rising much faster—the rich are building bigger yachts and the poor are sticking with their fishing boats or, sadly, life rafts. Launching off from this reality is where the Left continually misses the mark. Rather than address the *root cause* of social immobility (the ability for small boats to become big boats) they publicly denounce the symptom of "income inequality" (how dare you have such a big boat!).

Teddy Roosevelt warns of this impulse in his speech, saying, "The gravest wrong upon his country is inflicted by [the] man . . . who seeks to make his countrymen divide primarily in the line that separates class from class, occupation from occupation, men of more wealth from men of less wealth." The Left's argument devolves into divisive class warfare, pitting economically insecure voters against rich bogeymen. Likewise, their policy prescriptions, no matter how well intentioned, are tried, tired, and have proven counterproductive. For more than a half century, the Left's universal and undeterred so-called solution to poverty has been more government intervention, more government programs, and more wealth redistribution. Always more spending; always just a few more billion dollars away from a "New Deal" or "Great Society." Take from the rich and give to the poor—"from each according to his ability, to each according to his needs"—say Barack Obama, Hillary Clinton, and Bernie Sanders, echoing Karl Marx. It may work at the ballot box, but more than fifty years after LBJ's "War on Poverty" was declared, it's quite clear that government control of economic distribution doesn't work in implementation.

The Left still operates as though the government stands at the center of all things, owning and controlling all the resources and choosing which to dole out to whom, either by picking winners and losers through the tax code or redistribution of taxpayer dollars. However, government-centric redistribution is not the approach America was founded on, and not what built the most prosperous nation—from top to bottom—that the world has ever seen. America was founded on economic freedom, not economic predestination; our founders believed in equal opportunity and individual choices, not equal outcome via government mandates. A proper understanding of these principles has lifted more men, women, and children out of poverty than any system in human history. America's free-market, capitalist system is the reason that, for all our problems, America is the first country in the world where our poorest people struggle with *obesity* and have more technology in their pockets today than NASA had when it sent a man to the moon. We may struggle with social mobility today, but it's still great to be an American.

The ongoing fight to preserve the American Dream is why I introduced the word big-*R Republican* earlier in this chapter—not to make a partisan statement or laud Republicans for past achievements, but instead to remind them—and in fact chide them (and *me*)—to continue the *republican* and *Republican* tradition for the equal opportunity that enables the social mobility that enables the American Dream. Republicans, especially conservatives, are ceaselessly accused of not caring about the little guy and instead advancing policies that ensure the rich only get richer, at the expense of the little guy. That is not why I'm a conservative, and I've never met a conservative who seeks that. But complaining about this characterization won't fix it, either. It is not enough for those of us who vehemently oppose the scourge of social immobility to simply rail against the left-wing, centrally planned, big-government policy failures that suppress upward mobility for the least among us. Income inequality is perfectly acceptable—in fact healthy—as long as social mobility, both up and down the ladder, is possible. Poorer Americans shouldn't look at the rich and say, "Shame on you." Instead we should look at wealthy Americans and say, "Someday I could be rich like you. And if I'm never rich, my son or daughter could be!" As long as this American Dream is strong and social mobility possible, Americans understand inevitable income inequality.

The problem comes when the evidence suggests not only that America is less equal, but that Americans are also less economically and socially mobile—that the deck is stacked against the little guy in favor of the rich, elite, and well connected. We are at one of those moments and therefore have a decision to make. We can allow the Left to continue their rhetorical attack on income inequality and advance larger and more intrusive government as a response, or instead start building the case for both the freedom *and* opportunity that enable, and can renew, social mobility—and the American Dream. At those moments, Roosevelt says, "[r]uin looks us in the face if we judge a man by his position instead of judging him by his conduct in that position." Republicans, conservatives, and all republicans need to muster the courage, led by good citizens who understand the need to fight for the public good, to both identify and confront the societal barriers to social mobility and propose proactive solutions that restore equal opportunity in America (some of which are highlighted in the policy chapter). It's our job to keep the focus on "conduct," not "the position." The Left is not going to do it; only the right side of the political spectrum has the ability to restore America's founding premise.

America can be a very polarized place, with each side fervently invested in its view of the world and special interests on all sides ensuring that nothing changes. The same could be said of Roosevelt's time and he provides yet another powerful reminder to citizens engaged in domestic ideological battle, especially one full of powerful, competing, and entrenched interests. He proposed a two-part retort to ideological gridlock. First, "perhaps the most important thing the ordinary citizen, and, above all, the leader of ordinary citizens, has to remember in political life is that he must not be a sheer doctrinaire," said Roosevelt. "The closet philosopher . . . who from his library tells how men ought to be governed under ideal conditions is of no use in actual governmental work."

Conservatives—myself included—understand this error is inherent to progressivism, but conservatives fall prey to the same folly. Modern conservatives must look at problems as they *are,* not as they *used to be* or as we *think they are.* The challenges of 2014 are not the challenges of 1980, and conservative solutions must adjust accordingly. Of course the core principles of conservatism remain the same, but their efficacy may require different applications. Simply proposing more marginal tax cuts and eliminating federal agencies—while principled—may not be the policy prescriptions that improve opportunity in America. This is not an issue of messaging (making sure people know conservatives *care*) but is instead the sincere pursuit of opportunity-based solutions that will improve the lives of citizens. The endowed and equal pursuit of the Declaration never changes, but how we get to that end can and does change.

Roosevelt continues with his second retort, equally valid for both the Left and Right. "The citizen must have high ideals, and yet he must be able to achieve them in practical fashion. No permanent good comes from aspirations *so lofty* that they have grown fantastic and have become impossible and indeed undesirable to realize." Whether we choose to internalize it or not, this country is split roughly evenly between Republicans and Democrats. Both sides often prefer to pretend they can wave a magic wand and make their view of America happen. Not only does that not work, but as Roosevelt points out in his speech, such a position often means "the man of fantastic vision who makes the impossible better [is] forever the enemy of the possible good." Arguments become stale, entrenched, and impassable—not just between the Left and the Right, but also within the Right. Moreover—as I've learned at almost every turn of my conservative life—the hypothetical island of conservative ideological purity is never pure enough for a self-appointed few. One slip of the tongue, one word of cooperation, one picture with the wrong person, or one suggestion of a deal can bring the full wrath of the self-appointed purity police (enter, Facebook and Twitter!). The same happens on the left but is at least equally prominent on the right.

Being in the arena does not mean fighting zealously *only* for lost

causes; in fact, perpetually and intentionally pursuing extreme or controversial positions can, for some, be a convenient way to never actually
enter the arena. Relishing positions that offend or inflame is another
way to avoid actual debate or political relevance, further making impossible positions the enemy of the good. Roosevelt had this position
pegged as well, calling out the "one-sided fanatic, and still more the
mob-leader, and the insincere man who to achieve power promises
what by no possibility can be performed, are not merely useless but
noxious." Today, noxious often lives behind 140 characters or in the
comments section of an online news story or blog post, basking in a
self-fulfilling glow of vitriol.

Speaking of purity, the man most conservatives hold up as our
standard-bearer—former president Ronald Reagan—was very Rooseveltian in his approach to leadership and public policy. Reagan was
a transformative conservative leader, but he was also a pragmatist—
a believer in the 85 percent solution who knew how to avoid gridlock and make things happen even with Democratic majorities in
Congress. Reagan was a rock-ribbed conservative who, for goodness' sake, launched a primary against a sitting *Republican* president
in 1976; he was a conservative crusader but he ultimately went to
Washington to govern, not die on the hill of principle. He was the
"real reformer" Roosevelt spoke of, who never compromised on core
principles or for the sake of compromise itself, but he was also not
an "empty phrase-maker" with an impractical vision. By projecting a
hopeful and optimistic spirit and forging a genuine, personal friendship with liberal Speaker of the House Tip O'Neill, Reagan was able
to substantially cut taxes for everyone, shrink government where he
could, and restore America's military—all things conservatives laud
him for. However, lest we forget, President Reagan also raised some
taxes and granted amnesty to three million illegal immigrants. Those
instances—which can be fully understood only in the context of their
time—do not disqualify Reagan for greatness; instead they demonstrate a man "with stumblings and shortcoming, yet [who] does in

some shape, in practical fashion, give effect to the hopes and desires of those who strive for better things." Reagan was *in* the arena but did not pretend he was in there alone. As a result, Reagan knew the "triumph of high achievement" and America is better for it.

But, as some conservatives need to finally realize, it's no longer the 1980s—and the challenges facing America today may require new variations of what Reagan proposed. Conservatism, just like progressivism, is not a fixed end in and of itself, but instead is a means to a more important end: an equal shot at the American Dream for as many as possible. As a conservative, I believe fervently that lower taxes, fewer regulations, and more individual freedom give people more opportunity to succeed. But what if those policies *alone* are not sufficient to ensure equal opportunity and social mobility in America today? What if more liberty for the individual isn't always enough, because a complex tax code and maze of regulations are rigged to benefit the wealthy and well connected at the top? What if cutting taxes (say, reducing the top rate from 39 percent to 35) is less consequential because businesses aren't expanding, wages are lower, or companies have offshored both? What if a good, middle-class job no longer pays enough to support a family and raise multiple children? What if America's public institutions— even with school choice—no longer reinforce character and values, let alone prepare our kids for twenty-first-century employment?

Modern conservatism not only needs to have answers to these pressing questions that meet people where they are at in their lives; we also must accept the fact that not every solution to modern problems fits neatly into an ideological box. Roosevelt also speaks to this point, saying, "We ought to go with *any man* in the effort to bring about justice and the equality of opportunity, to turn the tool-user more and more into the tool-owner." There is no reason to work together with ideological opponents to seek equal *outcomes,* but in pursuit of "justice and the equality of opportunity" conservatives must be willing to work in good faith with partners across the spectrum to advance the American Dream.

. . .

In setting up Lincoln's quote in his speech, Roosevelt lauded the former president for espousing a view of equality "with his usual mixture of idealism and sound common sense." I can think of no better formulation—principled idealism grounded in common sense. As someone who grew up in and still lives in "middle America," "flyover country," and/or "bitter-clinger land"—pick your descriptor—it's painfully obvious how much common sense is lacking in elite circles and the policies they propose. It all goes back to that fact that so few students—who then become professors, lawyers, activists, and policy makers in America's government and institutions—have a sound grasp of what truly makes America exceptional. I saw a great deal of this during my two years as a graduate student at Harvard University's John F. Kennedy School of Government. Most of the students and faculty were wonderful people with the best of intentions—especially if we left the pesky Declaration of Independence, Constitution, and free market out of the discussion. In a business-related policy class in my first week on campus, one of my classmates openly declared, "I don't understand the private sector. It seems like just one, big, ambiguous mess to me. How can you control it?" Think about that quote! I could catalog dozens more like it—all of which reveal a preference for centrally planned policies, often in pursuit of solving what they deem to be the "greatest threat" of our time—global climate change. Lots of big-government "idealism," just not much common sense or humility. And lots of climate change policy, *always* climate change policy.

Although I do include a limited list of policy prescriptions later in the book, this is not a policy book. Unlike many of my classmates at Harvard, I don't believe there is a silver-bullet policy solution to every challenge we face. Instead, wherever possible, I prefer to look at the problem of social immobility through Roosevelt's commonsense formulation. In order to ensure social mobility and unleash the American Dream, we need less complicated regression analysis from the Harvard Kennedy School and a lot more common sense from Main Street America. Like the folks I go to church with, buy groceries with, and send my kids to school with, most Americans are idealists with common sense—they seek a higher standard of living but don't expect anyone to give it to them or a government program to solve it for them. They make trade-offs, balance their checkbooks, and put in overtime at work. They ask only that the basic rules of the free-market playing field be the same for everyone, not just a few. The words of Lincoln and Roosevelt both reveal the very same sentiment.

Today, average Americans—especially aspiring entrepreneurs and small business owners—see and sense impediments to social mobility and the American Dream that can't simply be solved by a good job and an honest day's work. With people squeezed at the bottom and boxed out from the top, social immobility in America today must be attacked at both the macro-mobility and micro-mobility levels, leveraging solutions that create more wealth and growth opportunities for all (grow the economic pie!), as well as tailored policies (or removal of policies!) to ensure the playing field of opportunity is simple and fair for everyone.

Even if he could not have foreseen the depth of our modern challenge, Roosevelt anticipated the unique and particular challenges to social mobility—starting at the bottom. The first perpetuates a system of dependence that can "make men feel that the same reward will come to those who shirk their work and those who do it." When government programs—welfare or otherwise—cease to provide a "helping hand now and then" and instead create a systemic culture of dependency, they trap those at the bottom rung of society in a cycle of poverty. The problem is not that the programs make people poor, it's that they often *keep* them poor. Obviously a good many Americans—for reasons of disability, age, health, or family situation—are in need of some government assistance, and it should be there for them. But when, for instance, the Social Security Disability Insurance program is structured in a way that severely punishes those who attempt to overcome a disability or an accident to rejoin the workforce and earn their own income, government is doing a great job of providing the wrong incentives.

Roosevelt isn't referring to the disabled worker trying to get by. He is referring to "the thriftless, the lazy, the vicious, the incapable" who— "if [they] lie down, it is a waste of time to try and carry [them]; and it is a very bad thing for every one if we make men feel that the same reward will come to those who shirk their work and those who do it." This is common sense, but it applies to a relatively small portion of the population. Most Americans, regardless of their station in life, would like a path to a better and independent life. For those people there still exists today a baked-in, chronic, and institutional social immobility that prevents real equity of opportunity. Oftentimes their family structure is strained—leading to instability for children and short-term thinking for adults. Oftentimes only one parent is in the home, or only one parent working—making employment and child care difficult, let alone saving for the future. Oftentimes the public schools are lacking in both academic excellence and character development, with a lack of options for parents. A small few have real school choices, even fewer a parent or teacher to mentor them individually. If kids do make it to college, they are often saddled with substantial debt and few distinguishable skills. Oftentimes, especially in inner-city communities, children grow up mistrusting authorities and lacking strong role models—turning instead to gangs or crime to fill familial, economic, and moral holes in their lives. Even if family and education are there, citizens looking to improve their lives often lack the technological infrastructure, training, and connections needed to become entrepreneurs or small business owners.

The American Enterprise Institute (AEI) has done a great job in recent years pointing out that local and state governments actually block the path to upward mobility. One bad law can snuff out the dreams of aspiring entrepreneurs—particularly low-income ones—with burdensome red tape. As an example, so-called occupational licensing laws at the state and local level do little to protect the public's health and safety, but they are very good at creating barriers to join these middle-class occupations, fostering the very income inequality that so frustrates the Left. In fact, across many occupations, these laws do little but protect the incomes of the entrenched, licensed few, while freezing out others. AEI cites a 2012 study by the Institute of Justice that found that emergency medical technicians—a career where people come into contact with life-or-death situations—get trained, on average, for about thirty-three days. Yet that same study found that licensing requirements were far lengthier for professions like interior decorators, barbers, hairdressers, and nail salon staff. How does that make sense? This isn't a "red state versus blue state" phenomenon, either; some states, like Louisiana, that lean conservative have terrible occupational licensing regimes that create a drag on economic growth and opportunity. These types of laws, which only satisfy government's appetite for more control, squash Roosevelt's dream of equal opportunity—especially for those at the bottom of the income ladder.

This phenomenon has also been powerfully demonstrated by the rise of Uber—the smartphone app that allows you to instantly and conveniently order a private car service. Besides making travel much easier for users of the service, Uber has made it very simple for individuals to become Uber drivers, allowing them to choose their schedule and level of service. Sick of dealing with the cab company cartels? Leave, join Uber, and make money. Out of work and need income? Join Uber and make money. Need a second job or want *more* income on your own schedule? Join Uber and make money. It's more than an application; it's an empowerment tool—for users and drivers. But, as you might imagine, the old-line cab companies don't like Uber because it's undercutting their bottom line. Cab companies have become stale, unresponsive, and entrenched—meaning *ripe* for competition like Uber. But rather than innovate to compete, they reach out to political patrons to create new regulations to block Uber under the guise of "safety" and/or "liability." It's a classic example of statist stasis that prevents people from taking control of their own social mobility. Ropublicans and republicans should run these types of regulations over with a truck!

As Roosevelt also points out, the problem is just as bad—if not worse—at the top of the economic ladder; which brings me to the second impediment to social mobility: a "special privilege" that Roosevelt believes undermines equal opportunity. He calls it an "inequality of reward" in society, saying,

> *The individualism which finds its expression in the abuse of physical force is checked very early in the growth of civilization, and we of to-day should in our turn strive to shackle or destroy that individualism which triumphs by greed and cunning, which exploits the weak by craft instead of ruling them by brutality.*

There will always be unequal amounts of social connection, political connections, and famous last names—I learned this the *first* time I met a Rockefeller family member at Princeton. Rich, famous, and powerful people are not the problem—and the vast majority add substantial value to America: building businesses that provide job opportunities, running institutions that address problems, and making laws to improve governance. John D. Rockefeller himself, in fact, was an incredibly generous American! The problem comes when there is a sense—and a reality—that many of the rich, famous, and powerful people (the "elite") in America today play by a different set of political and economic rules than the rest of us. I'm not simply referring to the Enrons and the Solyndras of this world—this is not just a problem of crooks and criminal cronies.

Today, the inequality that overwhelmingly benefits America's elites happens mostly at the confluence of big government and big business. Government is so big, so complex, and so intrusive that only elite individuals and large businesses with armies of accountants and lawyers are able to navigate the maze of domestic and international rules, regulations, and mandates. Not only can these elites circumvent the maze of government largesse, but their accountants and lawyers are also able to exploit loopholes, exceptions, and subsidies to ensure they succeed—and prevent others from doing so in the process. Political advantages for elites can also create insurmountable barriers to entry for regular Americans. The elite can do it all legally because their accountants and lawyers work with powerful and well-connected lobbyists who work behind closed doors to craft legislation that benefits—you guessed it—the corporations and powerful individuals. This symbiotic relationship—big government helping big business, and vice versa—is not a new concept; it happened just as much in Roosevelt's time and even before then. However, the problem today is far worse because government is so much more complex, powerful, and unchecked than it has ever been.

As Mark Levin points out in *The Liberty Amendments*, the federal government is "the nation's largest creditor, debtor, lender, employer, consumer, contractor, grantor, property owner, tenant, insurer, health-care provider and pension guarantor." There is almost no aspect of society today that government does not touch in some way. As a result, the "big ambiguous mess" of the Harvard student's free market has been replaced by the even bigger and even more ambiguous mess of the federal government—and therein lies the problem. In a free market, individuals with the best ideas, best products, and best services make the most money, but in a world controlled more and more by government, the individuals with the best lobbyists, best accountants, and best lawyers can make the most money. Sure, the market still matters, but it matters less—especially for those on the lower end of the economic ladder. From their view, every new law, mandate, regulation, or tax loophole represents yet another rung they must climb just to start a business or expand an existing business. Moreover, while they are merely surviving the tax code, the elites are manipulating it to their advantage. Even incentives like minority-hiring preferences are best exploited by big businesses more interested in the tax break and the public relations boost than so-called social justice.

This is not a Democrat problem or a Republican problem—this is an American problem, and a serious threat to our republic. The Left leverages the problem to attack the wealthy and instigate class warfare—a practice Roosevelt called "the prime factor" in the fall of great republics. Unfortunately, the Right has not done a good job providing a nondivisive, non-class-warfare, and pro-market alternative. The Left talks about pulling down the rich while the Right talks mostly about "pulling up the bootstraps." Conservatives must also demand this Roosevelt mantra, from top to bottom: "the only safe standard is that which judges each man on his worth as a man, whether he be rich or whether he be poor, without regard to his profession or to his station in life."

We should do everything we can to level the opportunity playing field by making it easier for the folks at the top to fail and easier for the those at the bottom to succeed. At the top, no individual, no business, and no institution is *too big to fail* in America. America was built as much by failure as it was by success. Conservatives should fight big-government, big-business cronyism that amounts to nothing more than riskless corporate welfare for the rich in return for bottomless campaign cash for politicians. We should slash corporate loopholes, end rigged tax incentives, and stop picking corporate winners and losers. For those at the bottom, we must fight for a system that reduces barriers to opportunity and empowers people to help themselves. We should make accountants irrelevant by dramatically simplifying the tax code, we should put lawyers out of business by drastically reducing regulations, we should invest in technology and infrastructure for those who need it the most, and we should give every student a real opportunity at success by fundamentally overhauling America's education system.

In order to attack opportunity inequality from the top and bottom, conservatives must also come to grips with the fact that, with the deck so stacked in favor of elites, simply "increasing liberty" for individuals is not sufficient to ensure access to social mobility up the economic ladder. Giving a few more citizens more freedom will not necessarily result in better outcomes, especially if those citizens are not pursuing good citizenship. Opportunity is an application of freedom, not the definition of it. Therefore, if average Americans have a few more individual freedoms but the elites are still able to manipulate the system to their advantage, then additional freedom is utterly insufficient. More individual freedom in the hands of those still facing a stacked deck does not necessarily improve social mobility. In order for real equality of opportunity to proliferate, conservatives must be just as aggressive and unabashed in fighting *against* forms of corporate cronyism and political collusion as they are about fighting *for* individual liberty. Finally, at the end of the day, we also must fight to advance policies—left or right—that facilitate and forge the making of more of Roosevelt's "good citizens."

The wealthy can, and must, do their part. Roosevelt said, "I decline to recognize the mere multimillionaire, the man of mere wealth, as an asset of value to any country.... If he has earned or uses his wealth in a way that makes him a real benefit ... then he does become an asset of real worth." A great modern example of this is Charles and David Koch, CEO and executive vice president, respectively, of Koch Industries. Not only do their businesses choose to stay in the United States and employ more than sixty thousand Americans (sixty thousand livelihoods), but they produce thousands of retail products that Americans want, need, and use in their daily lives. This is good in and of itself; but in addition to creating jobs and wealth for many, the Koch brothers use their wealth to a "real benefit" for America, not just themselves. While I disagree with many of their views on foreign policy and national security, they are true champions of individual freedom and free enterprise, and have spent millions fighting *for* policies they believe will create economic growth for all and *against* corporate cronyism and political patronage that benefit an elite few. They have fought against the very subsidies, tax credits, and protective tariffs that stack the economic deck in favor of most major businesses, including their own. Nonetheless, their critics are ferocious—and disingenuous. The mainstream media assumes that like so many others in big business, their political giving must be in pursuit of special privilege. But if you look at their principles and, more important, their giving—the Koch brothers have put their money where their mouths are. Despite what the Left might say, an argument for equal opportunity is not about the rich or the poor; it is about "good citizens" who come in all sizes, shapes, and pocketbooks.

Advancing these arguments in the real world is not easy. I have learned that firsthand through my work to deliver timely and quality health care to America's veterans—another "little guy" currently being crushed under the weight of big government. The fact is, what veterans want and need most is what Roosevelt points to in the speech: *equal opportunity* to get decent health care. Unfortunately, despite having a $160 billion budget and an army of 340,000 employees, the Department of Veterans Affairs still cannot manage to provide timely and quality health care to veterans who have earned that care. From secret lists of appointment requests that were hidden from inspectors, to veterans dying while waiting for care, the system is dysfunctional, the bureaucratic culture toxic, and the health-care delivery model outdated. Veterans and their families are forced to live with this fact. It is so bad, in fact, that most members of Congress dedicate a number of full-time caseworkers to helping veterans in their states and districts try to navigate the VA. Think about that for a second—getting care from the VA can depend on the power and effectiveness of a politician and his team. If your senator cares about the VA, you *might* have a chance. If he doesn't? Good luck. That's not equal opportunity. That's big-government incompetence and a travesty of justice.

Nothing changes, because the VA bureaucracy—outdated and bloated—is almost entirely unaccountable and has lots of friends inside and outside government looking to protect its failed model. The VA's public employee unions and old-line veterans' organizations are more interested in protecting the VA than in giving veterans what they want by reforming the system to fit their needs. The only solution for defenders of the VA is to convince reelection-seeking members of Congress that the department is always in need of more money. The *next* $5 billion is always going to fix the system. Just the *next* $5 billion.

If you ask veterans what they actually want, 90 percent simply want the *choice*—the simple choice—to either see a VA doctor or go to a private doctor if they cannot be seen in a timely or convenient manner. But that simple choice—and real accountability for workers who deserve to be fired for gross incompetence—is extremely difficult to get. The VA bureaucracy only wants to grow and will never reform itself, traditional veterans' groups have long ceased to be watchdogs and are instead VA lapdogs, and members of Congress want feel-good bills and photo ops, but not the tough reforms needed to truly deliver for veterans. As a result, special interests maintain a stranglehold on important policy matters related to veterans, making reforming the VA an extremely difficult proposition. It takes sustained outside advocacy—straddling the line of policy and politics—in order to even create the conditions where folks in Washington, D.C., *might* do the right thing by veterans. Without the pressure of outside organizations and efforts, the individual veteran is unlikely to ever be afforded a real VA health-care choice that empowers them and incentivizes the VA to treat them like customers. Armies of advocates—of "good citizens"—must fight back. Efforts to change the status quo may fall short or may succeed, but our faces will be "marred by dust and sweat and blood." We must be in the arena for veterans, and all Americans crushed under the weight of failed government.

This is just one example, at one department, in the federal government. Across our federal behemoth, the deck is stacked in favor of government growth and government control, just as it is on the big business side of the ledger. Only good citizens, bonding together and supported by those who use their wealth for "real benefit," can create the conditions for real opportunity to flourish.

• • •

As you know by now, Roosevelt spends the vast majority of his speech talking about citizens, but he also makes an important point about the type of leaders republics need in order to maintain equal opportunity. Speaking to his elite audience of French academics and dignitaries at the Sorbonne, Roosevelt says,

> *It is well if a large proportion of the leaders in any republic, in any democracy, are, as a matter of course, drawn from the classes represented in this audience to-day; but only provided that those classes possess the gifts of sympathy with plain people and of devotion to great ideals.*

The Left gushes with the "sympathy with plain people" Roosevelt describes, but for decades the big-government policies they've advanced have only exacerbated entrenched poverty for "plain people" while building a maze of government regulation and bureaucracy that America's elite happily exploit. Politically, the Left benefits from this unfortunate reality by decrying the resulting "income inequality" and then proposing even more government intervention as the solution. After years of class warfare, postmodernism, and investments in government growth, the Left has truly forgotten the "great ideals" upon which this country was built and that make this country exceptional.

As outlined in previous chapters, the rise of Barack Obama is the powerful example of a cultural seduction that fundamentally misunderstands America's exceptionalism. Following his inauguration, Obama went on a worldwide American apology tour, during which he made the following statement: "I believe in American exceptionalism, just as I suspect the Brits believe in British exceptionalism and the Greeks believe in Greek exceptionalism." He is wrong about America yesterday and today, but I fear he could eventually be proven correct. If America's good citizens do not do what is necessary to preserve what makes America truly special, then our exceptionalism can and will be lost. Just like everything else in this world, American exceptionalism is not inevitable. It does not perpetuate itself. It must be fought for, and defended, by every single generation.

Unlike big-government advocates and big business cronies, the good citizens of America—such citizens being the most important ingredient to a great republic—must be unabashed about their special interest: the dogged pursuit of a vibrant American Dream that keeps America exceptional. We must be so grateful for the equal opportunity our founders gave us that we are willing to leap into the arena to fight for it. We are either "free people" in name only, dependent on a government, or we are truly free people fighting—day in and day out, in our own lives and in the lives of others—to ensure the vitality of our experiment in self-governance and equal opportunity. Our founders dedicated their "lives, their fortunes, and their sacred honor" to gifting us freedom, defeating the most powerful empire in the world to do it. The least we can do, as good citizens of a great republic, is enter the arena in our neighborhoods, schools, communities, councils, and churches to grant the same gift of freedom to the next generation. Then, as "good patriots," we must boldly face the world—and the threats it contains.

EIGHT

★ ★ ★

The Wise Statesman:
Threats to a New
American Century

It is the duty of wise statesman, gifted with the power of looking ahead, to try to encourage and build up every movement which will substitute or tend to substitute some other agency for force in the settlement of international disputes. It is the duty of every honest statesman to try to guide the nation so that it shall not wrong any other nation. But as yet the great civilized peoples, if they are to be true to themselves and to the cause of humanity and civilization, must keep in mind that in the last resort they must possess both the will and the power to resent wrong-doings from others. The men who sanely believe in a lofty morality preach righteousness; but they do not preach weakness, whether among private citizens or among nations. We believe that our ideals should be so high, but not so high as to make it impossible measurably to realize them. We sincerely and earnestly believe in peace; but if peace and justice conflict, we scorn the man who would not stand for justice though the whole world came in arms against him.

—TEDDY ROOSEVELT, 1910

The clash of civilizations will dominate global politics.
                              —SAMUEL HUNTINGTON, 1993

F our years after Teddy Roosevelt spoke at the Sorbonne, his
   French audience was engulfed in a world war. A web of alliances
had maintained a precarious balance of power in Europe for four decades, but a frantic arms race in the early twentieth century, especially
between the British and German empires, exposed the tenuous nature of the resulting peace. War was triggered—or at least justified—
following the political assassination of Archduke Franz Ferdinand,
heir to the throne of Austria-Hungary. Kaiser Wilhelm's Germany
stood by Austria-Hungary, declared war, and quickly turned its gaze
west to France. Britain and France mobilized to defend Western Europe, and a pitched battle of bloody trench warfare ensued for years.
The Great War took 16 million lives, roughly half of those on that
Western Front.

As president, Teddy Roosevelt had witnessed both the ambition
and instability of Kaiser Wilhelm, and recognized the powerful and
possibly nefarious potential of Germany's emerging industrial and
military stature. Roosevelt had a great deal of respect for the German
people and did not consider imperial Germany an outright foe, but he
also understood how the emergence of Germany as the strongest military power in Europe could upset that teetering continent. Germany
was powerful, but it was not free and was not content to simply coexist.
He had no idea Germany would instigate a world war in his lifetime,
but he understood that the balance of power is never fixed, and that
peace—while always desirable—was not the normal international condition (a point utterly lost on the Coexist Left today). This recognition,
along with the need to enforce his Roosevelt Corollary to the Monroe
Doctrine, contributed to a substantial defense buildup—most substantially to the U.S. Navy—during Roosevelt's presidency.

Years before war broke out across Europe and the world, Roosevelt's vision for American engagement in the world provided useful

context to his historic Sorbonne speech. Roosevelt was not just a man who studied history, but also someone whose understanding of historical context allowed him to shape history. As such, Roosevelt ended his 1910 speech with a pointed, and eventually prophetic, reminder to his French audience: "We sincerely and earnestly believe in peace; but if peace and justice conflict, we scorn the man who would not stand for justice though the whole world came in arms against him. . . . You and I belong to the only two republics among the great powers of the world. . . . For [France] to sink would be a loss to all the world." Four years later France was fighting for its very existence, and Teddy Roosevelt had the opportunity to show exactly what kind of friend he was to the free world. The advent of war provided yet another opportunity for him to shape history.

When world war broke out in Europe in 1914, isolationism was the firm preference of the American public. Most Americans felt, justifiably, that two vast oceans and a history of nonintervention would shield the United States from the ambitions of European empires. President Woodrow Wilson reflected that sentiment by quickly proclaiming the United States "officially neutral," taking neither side and refusing to place blame with Germany. This stance was initially popular with the American public but was made increasingly untenable by the aggressive actions of Germany—most especially the tragic sinking of numerous American civilian ships by a new weapon of war, the submarine. The unrestricted use of submarine warfare against neutral ships eventually forced Wilson's hand and America reluctantly entered World War I.

On April 2, 1917—nearly three years after the war began in Europe—Woodrow Wilson asked a joint session of Congress for a declaration of war against Germany, famously pronouncing, "The world must be made safe for democracy." Less well known are the litanies of long-forgotten justifications for U.S. nonintervention given by Woodrow Wilson over the preceding three years. Following the infamous torpedoing of the American civilian ship *Lusitania* by a German submarine in 1915, Wilson said, "There is such a thing as a man being *too proud to fight*." Overwhelming domestic criticism of that remark later forced him to retract the statement, for fear of looking weak abroad. As late as January 1917, with both sides locked in deadly trench warfare, Wilson was still calling for "peace without victory." And just weeks before being forced into war, Wilson mused about the possibility of "armed neutrality."

Wilson may be credited with the phrase "making the world safe for democracy," but it was former president Teddy Roosevelt who poked, prodded, and pushed him into the defense of France, and by extension, the shaping of the free world in the war's aftermath. For the final four years of his life, with his health steadily deteriorating (he passed away on January 6, 1919), Teddy Roosevelt crisscrossed America urging preparation for war against Germany, making the case for intervention on the side of the Allies, and ultimately the need for "total" victory—as a means to *prevent* future wars. At times Teddy was publicly deferential to the current commander in chief; other times he could not contain his anger, declaring Wilson "cowardly" and "weak" and ceaselessly mocking Wilson's "too proud to fight" statement. Roosevelt even wrote a hasty and fascinating book in 1917—titled *The Foes of Our Own Household*—that eviscerated Wilson's naïveté and equivocation in real time. Wrote Roosevelt, "We are in the war. But we are not yet awake."

Once President Wilson gave his famous speech and war was declared, Roosevelt both publicly and privately supported Wilson's execution of the war. In fact, in a personal meeting with Wilson shortly after war was declared, the fifty-six-year-old former colonel asked for only one thing: the opportunity to assemble a volunteer division of former soldiers, led by Roosevelt, that could be dispatched immediately to Western Europe. Dubbed the "Roosevelt Division" by historians, the concept was eventually rejected by Wilson on the grounds that it would interfere with the new draft process. But the French wanted Roosevelt and the morale boost he would bring, with the prime minister of France saying, "The name of Roosevelt has legendary force in this country." He urged Wilson to send Roosevelt. Ultimately, Teddy never made it to World War I, but all three of his sons did—with his youngest giving his life over the skies of Germany.

During World War I, a friend dubbed Roosevelt "the Bugle That Woke America" for his unrelenting commitment to American involvement. But Roosevelt woke America to much more than a war; he woke America to leadership on the world stage. Roosevelt understood, long before World War I and Woodrow Wilson, that the United States was no longer just a regional power, but instead a global power with an emerging responsibility to engage an increasingly interconnected world. The defense of a fragile free world required a powerful and assertive American republic. America in the early twentieth century may not have wanted to be engaged with the world, but the world was engaging—and challenging—America. Rapid advances in communications and transportation, alongside the ability for deadly tools of war to be projected farther and with more lethality, meant that America could no longer just police her shores, or even the Western Hemisphere. The affairs of both the Pacific and Atlantic would increasingly impact America—and America could either shape them, or be shaped by them.

Roosevelt knew all of this at the time of his 1910 speech, and also understood the mood of the American public. He knew that average Americans had little interest in foreign affairs and that aggressive foreign interventions were generally greeted with protest from isolationists (called "anti-imperialists" in his time). As such, Roosevelt was careful to articulate that his extension of the Monroe Doctrine, which justified U.S. intervention in the Western Hemisphere, had nothing to do with American territorial interest or colonies. Instead he framed it as a responsibility to prevent further European meddling in America's backyard—a reality that came true in World War I. While noisy anti-imperialists still howled about this extension, known as the Roosevelt Corollary, the move was popular with most Americans and Roosevelt recognized that fact. Americans were skeptical of the world but proud of America's strength and values, and would support policies that successfully projected American strength and defense.

The same dynamic exists in America today. Following fifteen years of difficult war with violent Islamists—and sloppy outcomes on the battlefield—the American people are increasingly skeptical of American engagement abroad. A malaise of so-called war-weariness hangs over the American consciousness like a wet blanket, exploited not just by the Coexist Left, but also by modern-day "anti-imperialists" on the right. Right-wing isolationists—led first by Congressman Ron Paul and more subtly by his son, Senator Rand Paul—have seized on the complexity, cost, and many mistakes of our fight against Islamists to reenergize a noisy minority of isolationists (or self-styled "non-interventionists") inside the conservative spectrum. These isolationists argue that the principle of limited government should automatically translate into a smaller defense capability and a dangerously high threshold for intervention. They argue, like the Coexist Left, that America is largely to blame for many of the threats that face her. And they argue that America can retreat to her shores and restrain her involvement in the world. Oftentimes and unfortunately, their perspective descends into various black-helicopter conspiracy theories, like questioning the origins of the 9/11 attacks, lionizing traitors like Edward Snowden, and accusing defense contractors of instigating war.

More dangerously, they have few serious answers for developments like a surging Islamic State and a rising and increasingly assertive China. They argue against fighting the Islamic State, declaring it cannot be America's problem, while ignoring the global reach and expansionist abilities of emboldened Islamists. In the case of China, modern isolationists cling to the belief that open markets alone will inevitably induce good outcomes, when history and evidence have shown that collectivist political ideologues have grown adept at leveraging open markets. The attraction of this isolationist "let someone else fight" philosophy is undeniable, but it runs headlong into an increasingly interconnected world where commerce, politics, and yes—military actions, kinetic or cyber—happen on a global scale. Understanding this new modern reality, isolationists have taken to renaming their position "restraint" rather than "isolationism." It may be a clever phraseology and rebranding—just like liberals renaming themselves "progressives"—but the same old ineffectual ideas underwrite this new label.

Nonetheless, average American citizens and many conservatives remain understandably skeptical of foreign intervention abroad because of how recent wars have turned out. From Iraq to Afghanistan to Libya, it's admittedly difficult to find the immediate upside from fifteen years of war. But, like support for Teddy Roosevelt's aggressive policy of policing the Western Hemisphere, this is where both the Coexist Left and isolationist right misread the American public for the long haul. It's not that average Americans are anti-action, antiwar, or anti-intervention; they are just against *ineffectual* and *half-assed* American action. Americans still believe we are a force for good, and that we should win decisively and quickly, even if most Americans have a limited sense of what this notion truly means. To the contrary, most American battlefield victories have been long, complicated, and difficult, and during these messy fights—like today's fight against Islamism or yesterday's against the Soviet Union—the public must be reminded of America's indispensable role as the guarantor of free peoples and be continually rallied to that cause. Instead from both the Coexist Left and isolationist Right today, they are rallied in the opposite direction. "War-weary" Americans have been put in the mood for isolationism by many of their political leaders, from both the Left and the Right, and are pumped full of one of Barack Obama's favorite lines: "it's time for nation building at home."

Unfortunately neither history nor her unknowable next chapter is in the same mood. No amount of American retreat, restraint, or "nation building at home" will prevent foreign threats from gathering on the horizon. In this sense, the overarching geopolitical context of 2016 feels a lot like Teddy Roosevelt's 1910, with America unsure of her role in the world at the same time the world simmers with the potential for chaos and conflict—as the geopolitical tectonic plates shift. If you had told Teddy Roosevelt or any American in 1910 that in just eight years both the German and Ottoman empires would cease to exist, the Middle East would be carved up and remade, and both France and the United Kingdom would exhaust themselves in self-defense, they would hardly have believed it. Less than a decade after Roosevelt spoke at the Sorbonne, the entire global chessboard was reshuffled— and America emerged as the free world's leader.

Separated by more than a century, the years 2016 and 1910 are of course worlds apart domestically, internationally, geopolitically, militarily, societally, and economically. But the hearts of men remain the same. My experience as a soldier, advocate, and student of history is that human nature has not changed, and will not change; dangerous ideologies still lurk today—overtly and covertly—inside the hearts of men, ambitions of civilizations, and halls of elite institutions. This is of course one of the oldest ideological dividing lines, with liberals seeing man as inherently good and perfectible and conservatives asserting that man is perpetually fallible and therefore not perfectible. Conservatives are unfortunately correct. We may live in a post-colonial and post-imperial age, but we don't live in a post-ideological or post-authoritarian age. The threats the free world faces may not currently come in the form of standing armies or fascist dictators, but they still exist—not because of new tactics or forms of terror, but because of dangerous ideologies, ambitious civilizations, and powerful international impulses that are making a strong bid for supremacy in the twenty-first century and beyond.

From the opening chapter of this book, I've emphasized the idea that history is not over, that we must remember it and live in it— with clear eyes, conviction, and courage. Every generation grapples with history: its past impacts, current manifestations, and lessons for the future. History can also be tempting, either retrospectively oversimplifying contested outcomes or lulling current practitioners into self-deceptive certainty. We happen to live in one of those self-deceptive periods in history. Many American elites, leftists, libertarians, and complacent conservatives believe that with big threats like Nazism and communism in the dustbin of history, America at the height of its power, and international institutions growing in size and scope, the big questions have mostly been answered. They believe that with wars between major powers seemingly a thing of the past, religious affiliation waning in most corners of the world (except Islamists, of course), and the Internet connecting people in real time, the existential questions of war, peace, and freedom are largely twentieth-century relics—or even nineteenth-century relics, as Secretary of State John Kerry said of military actions by Russian president Vladimir Putin. To this influential cadre of American elites, the twenty-first century will be dominated by topics like climate change, global governance, reparations, and social justice. Except, what if history has other plans?

The fall of the Berlin Wall in 1989, the dissolution of the Soviet Union in 1991, and the subsequent end (or, in retrospect, long pause) of the Cold War reshaped the world's balance of power. Following a redemptive victory in the 1991 Gulf War, America found itself the undisputed global hegemon, leading a free world—with no discernible global threats—into a new century of limitless potential. The 1990s saw a substantial "peace dividend," not just in America, but especially throughout Europe, where governments slashed their military capabilities to finance exploding welfare states and outsourced their existential defense to America. With the march of freedom seemingly in perpetual motion, Western elites started to look past the building blocks of the nation-state system; instead cutting defense spending and eroding state sovereignty in favor of an amorphous, but surely benevolent, international order. Entities like the European Union and United Nations seemed the wave of the future;

individual countries, large armies, and competing ideologies a thing of the past. For a brief moment, the West took a pause to sing "Imagine" with John Lennon.

That brief moment produced two competing—and compelling—views of the future, each with very different and renewed implications for the world in 2016. In 1989, political scientist Francis Fukuyama wrote an essay—and later a book—asking if we're witnessing "The End of History?" His theory was that "the triumph of the West . . . is evident . . . in the total exhaustion of viable systemic alternatives to Western liberalism . . . marking the *end point* of mankind's ideological evolution and the universalization of Western liberal democracy as the final form of human government." At the same time, he bemoaned the rise of postmodernism (the idea that all truth is relative and all viewpoints equally valid), believing it threatened to undermine the intellectual underpinnings of the West. Fukuyama caveated his theory, recognizing that other potential ideologies (naming Islam in his original essay) could alter this trajectory—hence the question mark: *The End of History?*

In response, political scientist Samuel Huntington wrote a 1993 essay—and later a book as well—asking if the world would soon, or eventually, see "A Clash of Civilizations?" His theory was that "nation states will remain the most powerful actors in world affairs, but the principal conflicts of global politics will occur between nations and groups of *different* civilizations. The clash of civilizations will dominate global politics." He agreed with Fukuyama that wars between Western nations were over but argued that civilizational conflict would happen at two levels: the micro-level for physical territory along contested borders and civilizations, as well as at the macro-level as "states from different civilizations compete for relative military and economic power, struggle for control of international institutions," and promote their cultural values. As a result, he saw no such end to history and made a prediction that the next world war would be between civilizations, mostly likely between the West and Islam. Still almost a full decade from 9/11, Huntington also recognized the unknowable—hence the question mark: *The Clash of Civilizations?*

Two huge questions—*End of History?* or *Clash of Civilizations?*—each with multiple corollaries and many shades of gray. They are not new, but cannot be ignored today because when boiled down to their essence, only one can be correct—with huge implications for the future of the free world. At the turn of the twenty-first century, American elites and Western intelligentsia largely internalized Fukuyama's "End of History" view, planning for a century of increased peace, prosperity, and international cooperation while slashing individual defense budgets. At the same time, they dismissed his warnings about the rise of postmodernism, simultaneously embracing a "coexist" mind-set toward the world. But then history happened. The 9/11 attack revealed a simmering civilizational chasm, and the world—most especially the United States—awoke and was compelled to respond. That response, alongside the simultaneous economic and military rise of China in the new century, proved Huntington's "Clash of Civilizations" view increasingly viable. Even Fukuyama walked back his thesis, recognizing that the world's power balance was ever shifting.

Not only has Western democracy not ushered in the end of history, but the free world is increasingly under siege. The notion that freedom, capitalism, and equality will inevitably prevail has run headlong into the reality that in just the past decade the condition of freedom and civil liberties globally has actually declined. According to a 2015 report from Freedom House, a watchdog organization dedicated to global freedom, "acceptance of democracy as the world's dominant form of government, and of an international system built on democratic ideals, is under greater threat than at any point in the last 25 years." Or, put another way, freedom is under greater threat today than at any point since the Cold War ended. From overt examples like Russia's invasion of Ukraine and the Islamic State's rise, to more subtle dictatorial developments in places like China and Turkey, world events are sliding in the wrong direction. We got the worst of both worlds from

Fukuyama's thesis—Western leadership that views the march toward freedom as inevitable, but at the same time disputes many of the values that built the West. It's an unholy mix of unilateral disarmament and postmodernism, the combination of which creates a Western vulnerability that leaves emerging civilizations licking their chops to challenge us.

Huntington, like Fukuyama, saw America and the West in a dominant position—but with a key difference in the outcome. With the West "at an extraordinary peak of power in relation to other civilizations" and able to assert our will militarily, economically, and through international institutions, Huntington posited that the non-Western world would fight back, whereas Fukuyama argued non-Western countries would largely and eventually fall in line. The former—an escalating tug-of-war with proud civilizations—has ensued, a prediction made increasingly true since 9/11, as the United States was forced to assert its military and diplomatic power in the Middle East while attempting to maintain an edge in the Pacific.

The result is a growing "the West versus the Rest" reality that, as Huntington predicted, is being actively stoked in places where Western values like individualism, equality, the rule of law, democracy, free markets, and the separation of church and state *are not* the cultural norm. Moreover, with many Western societies culturally undermining themselves from within, it has really become "America versus the Rest." Non-Western civilizations, and the old and new ideologies they advance, pose a very real threat to the free world. The West did not produce these threats and may not even fully recognize them yet, but eventually, the United States—the only leader of the West—will be compelled to confront, or will simply collide with, civilizations with an inherent desire, and growing means, to challenge and supplant freedom.

Whether we like it or not, Fukuyama was wrong about history, and Huntington's thesis has held true—manifest today in three civilizational threats to America, any of which has the possibility of strangling the free world either slowly or quickly if they are not addressed both strategically and forcefully. Huntington correctly predicted two of today's threats in his work—the Islamic civilization and Chinese (or Confucian) civilization. From the Islamic State to Iran's pursuit of nuclear weapons, the rise of Islamism—both Sunni and Shia versions—is a clear and present danger to America, Europe, and free people everywhere. At the same time, while the United States has been engaged in the Middle East, an increasingly nationalist China has taken full advantage—utilizing long-term economic growth to expand its military power and sphere of influence. In recent years the Chinese have become only bolder, more assertive, and more authoritarian in their advances and are looking for opportunities to test America's mettle.

The third threat is a civilization that Huntington overlooked, largely because its manifestation had yet to fully cohere in the 1990s. It's the emerging global civilization. While not a civilization by any conventional definition, it fits all the criteria of one. Forsaking clan, village, region, ethnic group, religion, or nationality, modern globalists—Teddy Roosevelt's "citizens of the world"—share a cultural identity in that they have *no* national identity. Globalists share a common language ("internationalese"), history (anti-Western), religion (none), customs ("diversity"), and institutions (UN, nongovernmental organizations, etc.). As Huntington points out, civilizations can be large or small, and while the global civilization is not currently large in size, its influence— through elite media and institutions—is vast. Today, with America's military disarmament and global disengagement on full display—and with a fellow global citizen in the White House—globalists are aggressively driving their postmodern, post-Western, and post-American worldview. Between violent Islamists, ambitious Chinese autocrats, and dystopian globalists, history is definitely not over for the American civilization.

THE SCOURGE OF ISLAMISM

The Treaty of Westphalia in 1648, which effectively created the foundations of the modern nation-state, ended the Thirty Years' War—a bloody war of religion, pitting Catholics against Protestants across Europe. From that moment forward, in fits and starts, the world's civilizations entered—in one form or another, voluntarily or violently—a modern international system that recognized the "state" as the fundamental ingredient. One civilization proudly resisted this development successfully for nearly three hundred years, hewing instead to religious tradition and teachings that see no separation between mosque and state (there is no "give unto Caesar that which is Caesar's" in the Quran). The Islamic civilization, in the form of the Ottoman Empire and its declared form of purist government (the "caliphate"), had a long tradition of self-rule and rejection of the Westphalian system. That is, until the Ottoman Empire sided with Kaiser Wilhelm's German Empire in World War I, and following its defeat, it was carved up (purposely, if problematically) into nation-states by the European victors. The modern nation-states of Iraq, Syria, Lebanon, Jordan, and Israel were a result of this agreement, generally referred to as the Sykes-Picot Agreement.

Islamism and Islamists—defined as those who believe in the complete supremacy and imposition of Islam both violently and nonviolently—view the official end of the Ottoman Empire in 1924 as a catastrophic loss of their divinely ordained form of governance, a *unified Islamic caliphate*. And they point the finger of blame squarely at Western civilization and Sykes-Picot. Modern Islamist movements, in all of their mostly Sunni manifestations—Saudi Arabian Wahhabi Salafism, the Egyptian Muslim Brotherhood, Afghan mujahideen, Palestinian Hamas, global Al Qaeda, the Islamic State, and others— seek an end to both the Westphalian international state system *and* the West. (As does the Shia version, Iran.) The Islamic State, being the most recent and most powerful manifestation of this Islamist thread, has made this point clearly in its justifications and propaganda. They have declared a new caliphate, which is the reason why they attract so many Islamists from across the globe. The Islamic State's declared leader and caliph, Abu Bakr Al Baghdadi, said in a rare 2014 speech that, in addition to the religious underpinnings for their self-declared caliphate, the Islamic State's "blessed advance will not stop until we hit the last nail in the coffin of the Sykes-Picot conspiracy." Moreover, an Islamic State strategy document obtained by U.S. intelligence officials in 2015 outlines their goal of uniting all Islamist groups into a unified terror army, especially in Afghanistan and Pakistan, and then triggering nuclear Armageddon by attacking India. The Islamic State not only wants to destroy the modern world; they are hell-bent on inducing their apocalyptic and prophetic "end of the world."

Iran, the Shia Muslim standard-bearer of Islamism, has also made opposing the West a lodestar since its Islamic Revolution in 1979. Unlike any other nation on earth, the revolutionary Islamic Republic of Iran was literally founded on the premise of opposition to the West and America—with their bold seizure of the American embassy in 1979 serving as a literal and symbolic rejection of the Western system. Not only do both Sunni and Shia Islamists seek their own pure Islamic governance structures, but they also dream about the destruction of Israel, America, and the entire construct of Western civilization—and actively pursue the weapons, and the leverage that comes with them, to make that dream a reality.

Even the terrorist attacks on September 11, 2001, have a centuries-old connection. On September 11, 1683—more than three centuries ago—an alliance of Christian armies led by the king of Poland came to the defense of the Gates of Vienna in Austria, turning back the farthest advance of the Ottoman Empire's Muslim army. For the next three hundred years, and throughout the twentieth century, Islam was in cultural, technological, and geographic retreat from the West. Osama bin Laden, while also galvanized by immediate circumstances, believed that—first in Afghanistan against the Soviet Union, and then on 9/11 against America—he was putting Islam back on the offensive. He saw the attacks on the date of September 11 as both a metaphoric and literal continuation of the unsuccessful 1683 siege of Christendom. In the mind of Osama bin Laden, the wars he unleashed in the twenty-first century are part of drawing the far enemy (America) into his neighborhood, where he could bleed us dry physically and financially. The larger point is that whether the West does or not, modern Islamists still live in history and believe they will come out on top—eventually. We barely remember 2001, whereas they are motivated by 1683 and 1924. We're sedated by postmodern multiculturalism; they're motivated by end-times theology.

The threat Islamism poses goes even deeper. While the Islamic State, Al Qaeda, and Iran—through Hezbollah and other proxy forces—lead the military fight, there is a stealth enemy afoot as well. Saudi Arabian oil money funds radical, anti-Western Islamic schools (madrassas) and mosques across the Muslim world, in Europe, and even here in the United States. This is not to say that rank-and-file Muslims are seeking out radical madrassas or mosques, but rather that many Muslim leaders who build, finance, and lead those institutions use them to radicalize the larger population. Groups like the Muslim Brotherhood and the Council on American-Islamic Relations (CAIR) have quietly advanced this mission for decades. Likewise, on the demographic front, average Muslims aren't necessarily having ten kids because they hope to form Muslim majorities in European countries; but many radical Muslim leaders exploit these developments as opportunities to spread their radical and violent ideology, and eventually—in twenty-five, fifty, seventy-five years—will attempt to insert Islamic law into these societies. The same goes for how radicals will exploit the ongoing refugee crisis to seed Europe with radicalized young Muslim men. Like bin Laden, Islamists take a very long, aggressive, and subversive view of the future. Islamists will not conquer Europe militarily; they will do so demographically first, and then politically.

At this point, I can already hear the Coexist Left, and the "perpetual pragmatists" of today, demanding—yelling—"*The Islamic State is not Islamic! . . . and, for that matter, Islam is a religion of peace!*" Of course I reply with the obligatory, obvious, and quite personal response that there are millions of peaceful Muslims in this world. As I discuss in other portions of this book, I've met, worked with, fought with, and personally helped many Sunni and Shia Muslims. They can be kind, courageous, and fiercely loyal; but, alas, the problems of Islam do not lie with the sensibilities of rank-and-file Muslims or how most of them practice their faith, but instead with the Quran they read, the various religious interpretations that emanate from it, and the (millions!) of Islamists who embrace jihad as a tactic to advance it.

It doesn't take a Quranic scholar to identify the core reasons why Islamism has taken root and isn't going anywhere soon. Islam is neither a religion of peace nor a religion of violence; it is a religion of submission. The word *Islam* itself translates to English as "submission" (not "peace," as revisionists attempt to argue)—submission to God (Allah), submission to God's word (the Quran), and submission to the life and teachings of God's prophet Muhammad (the Hadith). To adherents, the text of the Quran and teachings of Muhammad are infallible, inflexible, and unquestionable—making the text of Islam the real challenge. Moreover, if the Quran and Hadith are reordered and read chronologically, the text starts with harmonious and peaceful passages and evolves toward more dominant and violent passages—mirroring the life of Muhammad. As he accumulated devotees, power, and a conquering army, Muhammad changed his approach to spreading his new faith; he captured Mecca through persuasion, but took Medina by the sword. In both scenarios—peaceful and violent—the outcome was the same. Non-Muslims paid a second-class-citizen tax (*Jizya*), converted to Islam, or were killed. Either way, they submitted. The aims of Islamists today—all around the globe—are the same.

Prior to the life and teachings of Jesus and the New Testament, many of these same attributes could be said of the Bible and Christianity. The Bible's Old Testament also contains violent passages; but a key distinction makes these two Abrahamic religions very different. The Quran has no "New Testament," which means a painful reformation like the one Christianity eventually emerged from—peace over violence, equality over slavery, and separation of religion and state—could be a long way off for Islam, if possible at all. Islam simply has no theological "new testament" positioned to supersede its "old testament" Quran. Making matters even more complicated, Islam is not just a religion, but also a system of governance (sharia law, in various forms), a judicial and penal system, and a cultural way of life for devout Muslims; meaning Islamism, and some argue more mainstream political Islam, cannot peacefully coexist with representative government and the modern nation-state system. Again, millions of Muslims have joined modernity and choose to live peacefully, liberally, and inclusively; but those Muslims do so by disregarding intolerant and violent Quranic passages that are no less authoritative today than they were a thousand years ago. They also must openly and courageously confront fervent Islamists who choose to interpret the Quran as it is written, not as modernity views it. This confrontation, on a large scale, is what made Iraq's budding post-surge "Iraqracy" so important.

These facts do not mean that America is at war with Islam, but it does mean we are, and will be, at war with Islamism—because they are at war with us, and have been, in modern form, for almost one hundred years. Al Qaeda and the Islamic State, and Iran and its proxies, are the latest manifestations of an Islamist movement that has no plans of receding and certainly no plans of "coexisting." They seek land, they seek power, they seek demographic and political advantages, and they actively seek the military means, especially nuclear weapons, to bring the West to its knees—and in the case of the Islamic State, hasten end-times. They seek our subjugation and destruction. The longer the West lives with the comfortable delusion that Islam is a religion of peace—especially as the demographic tables are dramatically turned on us in Europe and across the globe—the more difficult we make our task of dealing with future, and even more contentious, confrontations with both violent and political Islamism. In doing so America cannot bow to leftist elites who, in agreement with Islamists, point smugly to the land divisions in the Sykes-Picot Agreement as the cause of Middle Eastern violence and assert that there is only a choice between dictators and Islamists. Drawing lines on a map a century ago did not make the Islamist bloodshed inevitable. Moreover, failing to defeat Islamism *and provide a viable alternative* only ensures that more blood will be shed in the Middle East and around the world in defense of freedom and pluralism for Christians, Jews, moderate Muslims, and other "infidels."

THE CHINA MODEL AND CHINESE DREAM

The three thousand years of Chinese civilization make Islam's 1,300 years look like a warm-up. Like Islam, the Chinese boast many ancient and important achievements, like the invention of paper, printing, gunpowder, and the compass. They are proud of their long and consequential cultural history, and rightfully so. However, China's modern history lacks that luster, starting with a republican revolution in 1912 that ended more than two thousand years of dynastic rule but quickly descended into a century of internal strife. Coups, civil war, and revolution ultimately led to the creation of the People's Republic of China in 1949, the Chinese nation-state that exists today. The infamous insurgent and communist revolutionary Mao Zedong was modern China's first leader, and implemented the "Great Leap Forward" in 1958, a period of sheer state coercion intended to catch China's economy up with the Western world that ultimately led to the direct death of more than 45 million Chinese. While most in the West see Mao as a ruthless dictator and mass murderer, official Chinese history—and current Chinese leadership—lauds him as the revered father of modern China's rising power.

The Chinese, like Islam, look back on the past two centuries and wonder how such a storied and massive civilization finds itself playing second fiddle to the United States, and beholden to a Westernized international system stacked against them. China does not oppose the nation-state system outright like Islamists do; instead they have been involved begrudgingly while actively seeking rival structures, especially in the last decade. China was a founding member of the United Nations and the UN Security Council but quickly found itself in a contested status for twenty years over a dispute centered on Taiwan that remains relevant to this day. China was a late addition to global economic organizations like the World Trade Organization (WTO) because of both global skepticism about China's record and Chinese skepticism toward great powers and the global stage. For the latter half of the twentieth century, legitimate concerns over global communism and the balance of power between the United States and the Soviet Union kept China on the fringes of international affairs, a period during which China ultimately undertook economic reforms that led to its current mixed model, the "China Model."

The China Model combines a closed authoritative political system with a quasi-open economy, allowing the Chinese economy to grow quickly (if precariously) while the Chinese Communist Party retains absolute power. Communist China learned the lessons that the former Soviet Union learned too late, that some amount of economic liberalization is needed in order to maintain an economic base capable of sustaining military power and consolidating political control. But according to American foreign policy intelligentsia since the end of the Cold War, it wasn't supposed to happen this way. Led by "elite" *Mc*-ademics like Thomas Friedman and his "Golden Arches" theory—an economic adaptation of the Democratic Peace theory—economic liberalization in China would lead to gradual political liberalization, and largely peaceful intentions. Instead, by underestimating the level of state control and the depth of cultural supremacy in China, the opposite occurred and China has exploited international markets to expand its economic prowess, extend its military influence, crack down on internal political dissent, and stoke communist nationalism. Worse, China is gleefully if quietly proliferating its "Model," breathing new life into international communism and encouraging other budding authoritarian regimes to follow suit. Empowered by ideologically agnostic international institutions and a current U.S. administration that also ignore the nature of regimes, look for countries like Cuba—which the United States recently normalized relations with in return for no political reforms—to adopt the China Model, along with the nefarious influence it enables.

For the ruling Communist Party and its benefactors, the China Model has been a success. Despite market variations, inside Chinese government–controlled "think tanks," academic institutions, and military circles, there is an increasingly bold belief that China is on the cusp of becoming the world's most consequential nation— first economically and militarily, then regionally (a Chinese Monroe Doctrine), and finally globally. Beijing sees a weakened U.S. economy (as they challenge the dollar's supremacy and watch America's swelling debt), eroding American leadership and political will globally, and the literal shrinking of the U.S. military as signs that American hegemony is ending and a new era of the proud—or some might say, arrogant—Chinese civilization is beginning. Even though it is better shrouded, many Chinese leaders (not all, but many) possess a belief in Chinese cultural supremacy with the same ideological and evangelical fervor as Islamists. In this way, and especially with Xi Jinping's nationalist rise to the presidency in 2012, the China Model has given rise to a new class of Chinese political and military leaders who believe in a "Chinese Dream" of military power and communist collectivism.

The Chinese Dream—first the title of a book by a hawkish Chinese general and now the central theme of Xi Jinping's tenure—is not the dream of empowering free individuals to achieve, like the American Dream, but instead a collectivist dream of a great and powerful nation. Said Xi Jinping in December 2012, "This dream can be said to be the dream of a strong nation. And for the military, it is a dream of a strong military ... *to achieve the great revival of the Chinese nation.*" The Chinese Dream, as articulated repeatedly by Xi Jinping and Party leadership, has nothing to do with Western constructs of freedom and everything to do with leveraging Chinese economic and military power to first establish regional dominance, and then eventually shape a China-dominated world that, to quote a top Chinese government–controlled "think tank," establishes "a global hierarchy where *order is valued over freedom, ethics over law,* and *elite governance over democracy and human rights* [italics added]." Reads a bit too much like a directive from the First Order from *Star Wars: The Force Awakens.* Peaceful rise, violent rise, or something in between, if the twenty-first century is a Chinese century then it will not be a free century, a prosperous century, or a peaceful century. Plain and simple, a rising China—armed with a "model" and a "dream"—represents an eventual existential challenge to America and the free world.

And the Chinese are putting their muscle where both their money and their mouth are. Leaked internal documents repeatedly reveal that China's most important foreign policy priority is "how to manage the decline of the United States," and they are building a military capable of—eventually—challenging American power in the Pacific and around the world. Over the past decade, China has embarked on an ambitious military modernization program, aggressively increasing the size, sophistication, and lethality of its armed forces with an obsessive focus on capabilities that *specifically* neutralize American advantages. China is not only building its own aircraft carriers; it is building sophisticated missiles specifically designed to destroy American aircraft carriers. Furthermore, a nuclear-armed China is right now building man-made islands in the South China Sea from which to project its growing military power. The Chinese military is chasing next-generation capabilities in the air, land, and sea—far beyond what experts believe would be needed for self-defense, or even regional hegemony. The Chinese are also spending massive amounts of money on "soft power" domestic and international propaganda machines. But don't just take my word for it. In one of his first moves after taking power, Xi Jinping issued orders to his military to focus on "real combat" and "fighting and winning" wars—a stark departure from China's previously benign "nothing to see here" rhetoric. While China says it is rising peacefully, a growing body of public and private evidence suggests the opposite.

Yet, while China has huge potential and nefarious intentions, it also faces serious obstacles to becoming a modern power. They are the world's most populous nation but are confronted by major demographic problems. A long-standing "one-child" policy (recently updated to two) that favors boys has created a gender gap with unknowable consequences, and China's massive population will get old before the country gets rich—creating entitlement liabilities that are unsustainable (much like America's). China may have an economy that rivals America's in sheer size, but much of its growth has been fueled by forced population relocation from rural areas, economic exploitation abroad (which continues to undermine China's global popularity), and massive state-directed investment, especially in manufacturing. Their economy is limited by a lack of middle-class consumers and entrepreneurial talent, each of which they're currently outsourcing and insourcing, respectively. Attempts to open up their stock market have invited substantial volatility—and unchartered risk. Their aggressive military actions have driven regional countries into the American orbit, stunting their regional options for strategic alliances in the near term. But domestic politics could ultimately be their downfall. As Chinese leaders double down on authoritative policies, China's youth—with access to wealth, information, and world travel—will continue to demand more say in their nation's political system, leading to more domestic instability. China's challenges are real, but they are not insurmountable.

America's governing and economic "model" is superior to China's and our "dream" is real, not manufactured. American free enterprise—properly oriented, unleashed, and positioned—carries the day against central planning and failed political philosophies every time. But because the superiority of America and American power is not inevitable, the prospect of the twenty-first century being a Chinese one is not inconceivable. In fact, if America continues to decline in power and posture, Chinese predominance is more likely than most care to admit; especially since China, like Islamism, is playing a long game—with Xi Jinping projecting 2049 as the high-water mark of his aforementioned Chinese Dream of national greatness and regional and global power. Even with this rise, violent conflict with China is not inevitable or even likely on a large scale; but, like with Islamism, American weakness and equivocation only invites more challenge and violence, and if America does not maintain its economic and military edge, then China could eventually usher in a new era of collectivism.

AN EMERGING GLOBAL CIVILIZATION

Teddy Roosevelt was an unapologetic advocate of American values and leadership, but he was also an internationalist—acknowledging in his Sorbonne speech that "[i]nternational law will, I believe, as the generations pass, grow stronger and stronger until in some way or other there develops the power to make it respected." A few weeks later, while accepting the Nobel Peace Prize in Oslo, Norway, Roosevelt even called for a "League of Peace" managed by great powers and dedicated to keeping peace . . . by force of arms if necessary. A student of history, Roosevelt knew that the arc of Western history—from the humanist Renaissance to the Protestant Reformation to the Treaty of Westphalia—had slowly evolved toward a managed international order biased in favor of Western ideas of representative governance, individual freedom, and free markets. He had no illusions about the fact that an increasingly interconnected world would include some global structures, but the nature, scope, and mandate of those structures were critically important to Teddy Roosevelt, and they are even more so to us today. The original concept of Roosevelt's "League" was to protect national sovereignty, not attempt to supersede it.

Nine months after America's entry into World War I, and ten months *before* the war's conclusion, President Woodrow Wilson laid out America's terms for an enduring postwar peace in "Fourteen Points." Wilson's Fourteen Points for world peace, while never ratified by the U.S. Senate nor codified internationally, nonetheless served as the (failed) framework for postwar negotiations with Germany. The most prominent point was the fourteenth—an international League of Nations that would "[afford] mutual guarantees of political independence and territorial integrity to great and small states alike." Wilson sought an equal international body where disputes could be aired, debated, and hopefully resolved before bullets started flying. Roosevelt, acknowledging the laudable goal of a lasting peace (which he had proposed *before* Wilson), nonetheless forcefully opposed the League of Nations and the Fourteen Points, believing they would "simply add one more scrap to the diplomatic wastepaper basket [because] most of the fourteen points could be interpreted to mean anything or nothing." As we say in the military, *they briefed well—but had little connection to reality*.

Worse, Roosevelt believed a universal League of Nations—as envisioned by Wilson—would subjugate great powers, like the United States, France, and Great Britain, to equal footing with lesser, and less free, powers. Unchecked, loose interpretations of ambiguous mandates combined with a forum for lesser powers—and dictatorial regimes—could eventually become a powerful bludgeon against the free world. Roosevelt preferred a "compact by the allies and well behaved neutrals" that would "admit other nations only as their conduct . . . warrants it."

Such an arrangement—a loose compact of like-minded countries as opposed to an international mandate of any country—would ensure, as Roosevelt wrote, that "our territorial possessions, to our control of immigration and citizenship, to our fiscal policy, and to our handling of our domestic problems generally [would] not be brought before any international tribunal." (I recommend such an arrangement in the next chapter.)

Fast-forward one hundred years and we see that global institutions—like the United Nations and International Criminal Court (ICC)—have affirmed Roosevelt's suspicions. These institutions, and a sprawling web of others like them, were started under the admirable auspices of peace, conflict resolution, and equal justice. And for most of the twentieth century, these institutions largely served Western interests, with the UN Security Council advancing democracy expansion and the ICC prosecuting tin-pot dictators and bloodthirsty war criminals. But this is not likely to be the case in the twenty-first century. These international institutions, conceived to protect and advance the Western order, are being gradually captured—and wielded—by a powerful new civilization that would like to hold the West, and especially America, to account for so-called sins of the past. Increasingly enabled, and thereby emboldened, by America's current "coexist" foreign policy, a powerful *global civilization* is actively working to use international organizations to undermine the West's dominant position, inadvertently opening the door to Islamists and Communist China to fully arrive on the scene.

The emerging global civilization is a combination of two forces, one complacent and the other militaristic. Previous chapters highlighted a new generation of "citizens of the world" that manifests in a soft anti-Americanism and deference to all things international, diverse, and multicultural. "International feeling swamps . . . national feeling" for this group of postmodern do-gooders; they are not *the* problem, but they are a big part of the problem. Their naïveté (much like average Muslims who tolerate extreme views) unwittingly advances the *real* "foe of mankind" inside the global civilization—the globalists. Globalists are militant, anti-Western internationalist elites, largely from postmodern Europe, who are hell-bent on "coexisting." Globalists believe, like Islamists, that Western-controlled international institutions simply advance new forms of Western economic, cultural, and political imperialism and colonialism. With the levers of international institutions at their fingertips, self-loathing globalists are gathering together lesser powers (regardless of regime type), cataloging Western "injustices," and arming themselves with international "regulations" by which they can level the international playing field. Various international global climate change agreements (schemes) demonstrate this dynamic powerfully.

While more benign in nature, the globalist pursuit of utopia—regardless of flag, freedom, or creed—ultimately seeks a similar end to that of Islamists and Chinese communists: the end of the modern nation-state system as the fundamental construct of global affairs, replaced with a top-down form of global governance. Islamists want a caliphate, communists want a Chinese Dream, and globalists want One World government. These three threats cannot "coexist" together forever, but currently constitute an alliance against their shared enemy: America. Globalists would like to eventually do away with state sovereignty, unilateral action, and any form of warfare (just or unjust), believing their perfected state of humanity will create a coerced condition of global consensus, mutual understanding, and economic fairness. In doing so, they can box in America—and everything that comes with it. They ignore the fallen nature of man, instead putting their faith—and fate—in the hands of postmodern, perfected men. Skinny jeans, neutral genders, and blue helmets are their uniform.

Globalists don't just believe that history is over; instead, like Islamists but with atheistic fervor, they believe they can usher in a perfected end to human governance and thereby history. They demand fellow adherents forsake clan, village, region, ethnic group, religion, and nationality. The European Union (EU) is an excellent example of the globalist worldview. As part of the post–Cold War I peace dividend—and partly in an attempt to check American hegemony—Europe voluntarily transformed itself into an anti-nation-state system, stripping economic, political, and geographic sovereignty away from individual countries and giving them an ill-defined and ambiguous form of governance with power concentrated in the hands of unaccountable EU bureaucrats. Just a few years removed, member states now have neither sovereignty nor a powerful civilization capable of projecting military might, preventing harmful Muslim mass immigration, or preserving cultural influence—and are thus relegating themselves to second-class international status. The outcome of the EU was not power, influence, or the perfection of human governance, but instead the massive transfer of power away from nation-states (the people) into the hands of unelected and unaccountable technocrats. For globalists, the instructions say to lather, rinse, and repeat across the twenty-first century.

As Samuel Huntington points out, civilizations can be large or small, and while the global civilization is not currently large in number, their influence is vast. Opposing their agenda does not mean opposing all international institutions, but instead approaching international cooperation through a pro-freedom lens: encouraging voluntary association and voluntary exchange with freedom-defending societies while opposing the globalist push for collective consensus and coercion. Good-faith, principled international engagement is a must of American foreign policy in the twenty-first century, but submitting the future and interests of the United States to unelected, unaccountable, and unaligned international bodies undermines our security and dilutes the special nature of our country. Principles we take for granted today—open markets, freedom of speech, equality under the law, religious liberty, and government by consent of the governed—are not the principles of globalists, so help us God (wait, they don't believe in God).

The balance Roosevelt tried to strike in his critique of Wilson's Fourteen Points in 1918 was correct, and we need to find a way to reestablish a similar balance today—lest we cede the future to globalists, and by extension, Islamists and Chinese communists.

Other threats to freedom, of course, exist, like Vladimir Putin and his desire to reestablish Russian greatness (Cold War II). But understanding threats to freedom does not mean seeing a civilizational bogeyman behind every corner. America has never had permanent enemies, and we seek a just peace wherever possible. Two of today's most powerful economies and former violent enemies—Germany and Japan—are living examples of America's willingness to not only see past historical transgressions, but instead actively promote a prosperous future for former enemies. America seeks freedom, not perpetual enemies—another reason why America is a truly exceptional nation in human history.

Iraq—and the war my generation fought on her soil—represents another such example. As it turns out, Francis Fukuyama—the aforementioned author of *The End of History*—also wrote extensively about the outcome in Iraq. After supporting the war initially as a means of freedom promotion, Fukuyama withdrew his support in 2006 and declared the war an inevitable disaster, saying, "Before the Iraq war, it was clear that if we were going to do Iraq properly, we would need a minimum commitment of five to ten years." On these points, he was both wrong and right. He was right that Iraq would require a long-term commitment, but he was wrong that the war—as bad as it was in 2006—was bound to fail.

The Iraq War in 2006—which I waged and witnessed at that time—was not going well. Violence was rising, Iraqi power-sharing failing, and domestic public support waning. The choice and potential outcomes for George W. Bush could not be starker: American retreat followed by violent Islamist chaos *or* resolute American commitment that would produce a long-term and contested outcome. If we left Iraq, we could cut our losses and violence would ensue; if we stayed, browbeating globalists. Only American power—unapologetically and shrewdly applied—has the ability to ensure the free world gets stronger and more secure in these moments. We must learn the lessons of the past, but we also cannot shrink from the world just because our past isn't perfect. We cannot do it alone, but without America leading the way—serving as the free world's sheriff with a shiny golden badge seen by all—the twenty-first century will be neither free, prosperous, nor peaceful.

we might just muddle along. Or, if things really went our way, may victory was still possible. Nobody knew for certain, and the future the Middle East hung in the balance. After invading the country, li erating oppressed minorities, and investing in a quasi-representativ government, would America leave behind an Islamist hotbed in Ira or stand resolute? The answer to this question ultimately determined whether Iraq would be a foe-turned-friend like Germany or Japan, or would contribute to the civilizational march of Islamists. The stakes of the Iraq War in 2006 (just like in 2011) were that high.

The history books of World War I always remember President Woodrow Wilson "making the world safe for democracy," but they fail to mention his shortsighted insistence just three months earlier that "peace without victory" was still possible—an utterance Teddy Roosevelt knew was nonsense. In the face of even the most forceful and evident threats, men will always hesitate, equivocate, and look for the exits—look at President Obama today as a tragic example. Fights like World War I, World War II, and the first Cold War look clear in retrospect but were highly contested in their times. A certain subset of Americans, like Wilson, have always been—and will always be—"too proud to fight," either outright opposing necessary fights from the outset, or quickly jumping ship at the first sign of resistance. Like Teddy Roosevelt's vigorous defense of France and the free world during World War I, my experience in the Iraq War—both on the battlefield and at home—forged an experiential belief in the powerful, principled, and resolute application of American power. We could have finished our victory in Iraq, but instead we chose to leave early and lose—to horrific consequence.

Like the trajectory of the Iraq War, the fragile moments in history where Wilson's "peace without victory" clash with Roosevelt's "total victory" are where wars are won or lost—and dangerous ideologies either defeated or emboldened. Like the Iraq War in 2006 and 2011—two defining decision points—the future will see many more of these moments, with ruthless Islamists, Chinese nationalists, and

A PRESCRIPTION

★ ★ ★

Advancing Citizenship
in a Republic

As a conservative who subscribes to the founding premise of our country, there are many policies I believe America needs today—many of which have been mentioned in these pages. I believe our government needs to be drastically smaller, our tax code simpler, our spending constrained and debt slashed, our border secured, our legal immigration protected from manipulation, our health care privatized, our VA overhauled, our energy resources maximized, our students afforded real school choice, our unborn babies protected, and our Second Amendment rights ardently protected. I also love the idea of fighting for an Article 5 "Convention of States," a constitutional path whereby state legislatures—The People—can rein in our federal government to its original and limited purpose.

But this book is not a catchall for every conservative prescription, and is not meant to spell out a comprehensive governing philosophy. Instead, my aim is to heed the words of Teddy Roosevelt and reinvigorate good citizenship, ensure equal opportunity, and reinforce American leadership. Doing those things—the basic blocking and tackling of our republic—will help ensure America remains the freest, strongest, and most prosperous country in the world. In that spirit, below are fifteen brief policy suggestions (five per section) that I believe would place America on the path to leading yet another century.

GOOD CITIZENSHIP

1. Teach Citizenship and the Constitution. In order to graduate, high school students—public school, private school, or home school—should have to pass the same basic civics test that immigrants are required to pass in order to become new U.S. citizens. Moreover, America's founding documents—Declaration, Constitution, Bill of Rights, Federalist Papers, etc.—should form the basis for national civics educational parameters that prepare students for the mandatory test. Such a curriculum would have to be closely guarded and based on original texts, lest it be captured by revisionist agendas. Other efforts—like celebrating and promoting Freedom Day (April 13) and Constitution Day (September 17)—should be accelerated as a means to further educate students and Americans about the constitutional source of our exceptional nation . . . and the simple and powerful importance of patriotism.

2. A Common Language. Assimilation to American life is a fundamental tenet of perpetuating good citizenship; moreover, assimilation ensures that no matter race, creed, or country of origin, new immigrants are set up to succeed in America. In addition to immersion in U.S. history and civics, new immigrants should be encouraged, incentivized, and ultimately pressured to learn and use the English language. Not only is English the language of America; it is the language of our commerce, our politics, and our media. It is the language of equal opportunity, just as it is the language of our common civic discourse. Citizens who don't learn English will always be at a disadvantage, which puts America at a disadvantage. Our country must remain a melting pot, not a tossed salad of multiculturalism.

3. Select(ive) Service. Today, male U.S. citizens from ages eighteen to twenty-five are required to register with the Selective Service for possible conscription into the military. Most don't think twice about the box-checking exercise and therefore remain detached from the concept of service to our country. I don't believe in universal national service because it would be used to massively grow government and pursue all kinds of social agendas. But what if, instead, we made the Selective Service process substantive and meaningful? Why not create an alternate list of able-bodied Americans, male and female, who are willing to serve, especially in times of need? After high school, and before they turn twenty-five, these youth would sign up for a one-time basic military training and then maintain annual fitness standards. This "Minutemen Corps" would not only be prepared to support national emergencies, but, more important, would put "skin in the game" for a large swath of able-bodied, young Americans. In times of war or urgent need, these Americans could be mobilized for active military service. Signing up for this Minutemen Corps would be voluntary but membership would come with substantial educational and employment preferences, student loan forgiveness, and tax benefits.

4. More Family, Less Government (Schools). School choice in public schools has expanded educational options for some in America, and that choice should be greatly expanded. Same with school vouchers. But if government schools (public schools) continue to fail to reinforce American principles, then citizens ought be further empowered to educate their kids—their future "good citizens"—at home. George Washington, Abraham Lincoln, and Teddy Roosevelt were all homeschooled—why not make it much easier for kids today? Legislation should be pursued that protects the fundamental right to homeschool, streamlines and simplifies the process to homeschool, channels some tax dollars to follow the kids rather than default to local school districts, financially empowers parents to educate their kids, and ensures that school districts are not able to erect barriers to homeschooling.

5. Make Elections Competitive Again. The Left seeks to level the election playing field by limiting money in politics, to no avail. Money is speech, and should not be restricted. However, money in politics is concentrated in too few geographic locations due to the proliferation of noncompetitive congressional districts. Using various means, states should be shoehorned away from gerrymandered congressional districts and instead be pushed to establish political boundaries based on geographical reality, not political or racial prejudice. I have no idea whether conservatives or liberals would benefit from this development; but I do know that dozens—if not hundreds—of congressional seats would instantly become competitive, diluting the influence of a limited set of seats and forcing a much wider debate among the electorate. Moreover, in order to foster a shared civic experience, Election Day should be made a national holiday and early and mail-in voting should be minimized.

EQUAL OPPORTUNITY

1. Dramatically Simplify the Tax Code. The tax code should be radically simplified and consolidated. A flat and fair tax rate should be set, with any deductions and incentives benefiting only the attributes of good citizenship—honest work, service to country (see No. 3 above), and industrious families. Loopholes, especially for those of financial means, should be slammed shut—ensuring that those at the top of the economic ladder actually pay their rate, making lawyers, accountants, and lobbyists less powerful, and making the tax code more accessible for all. Moreover, corporate tax rates should be substantially reduced and regulations significantly simplified, incentivizing businesses to stay in (or return to) America and clearing barriers to entry for new smaller businesses. The federal government and states should aggressively seek out, reduce, and eliminate burdensome licensure requirements and exclusionary licensure fees. Save for jobs that legitimately impact immediate physical or public safety, the government should get out of the business of dictating the background, training, and experience of many common occupations and instead allow the market to dictate who succeeds and who fails.

2. Invest in Twenty-First-Century Infrastructure. Good roads, bridges, and freeways will always be critical to the success of commerce in America, and spending to maintain this conventional infrastructure should remain a priority. But even more important to commerce today is the virtual superhighway—accessible, cheap, and high-speed Internet access. Few businesses today can thrive without an Internet presence; moreover, the Internet empowers anyone with access to pursue his or her interests, passions, and happiness. When it comes to high-speed Internet access, fiscal hawks should spare no expense because the Internet is the infrastructure of the twenty-first century. America should be the most wired, connected, and high-speed country in the world—especially in inner cities and rural areas, where those on the lower end of the economic ladder often congregate. In the 1950s, President Eisenhower created the Interstate Highway System; we need an Interstate Internet System in America—free from regulation and taxation.

3. Equip Women to Choose. Women should be equipped and empowered either to feel comfortable staying at home with children—the most important job in the world—or to stay in the workforce and also be great mothers. If mothers choose to stay at home with children, the tax code should support that choice by providing deductions or credits for the rearing of children as well as homeschooling (if they so choose). If mothers choose to stay in the workforce, accommodations should be made to ensure that that decision is honored. Options like the ability to work from home and/or part-time, more paid maternity and family leave allocations, more robust worker protections for pregnant employees, and child-care support for those gainfully employed should be advanced. These options can mostly apply to men as well.

4. Higher Education Empowerment. Many of the best jobs in the twenty-first century have everything to do with technical skills and nothing to do with a liberal arts education, yet we have a system weighted heavily toward a four-year undergraduate education. While four-year degrees remain a factor in more opportunity and higher wages, many students are defaulting to a four-year degree when a more focused—and far less expensive—technical or community college degree would better prepare them in specialized skills badly needed in the modern economy. Policies should be pursued to ensure students have a better sense of what their education will prepare them for, and the type of career it will afford them. Rather than defaulting to the undergraduate degree, we should do a better job of making sure students understand the technical and technological options available.

5. Civil Service Overhaul. America needs civil service reform across the federal government. Bad employees should be able to be expeditiously fired and good employees empowered. The closest thing to immutable job security is a job in the federal government, which creates a corrosive and unaccountable culture. The concept of "public employee unions" is an affront to good governance, as they no longer exist to protect worker protections but instead to ensure it is nearly impossible to remove poor-performing employees. The crony and corrosive influence of public employee unions should be fought at every turn. My former organization's efforts to reform extremely burdensome employee protections at the Department of Veterans Affairs is an example of how government can be made more accountable and more responsive.

AMERICAN LEADERSHIP

1. Substantially Increase Defense Spending. The world is getting more complex, more uncertain, and more dangerous. The threats and countermeasures of the future will be asymmetric and digital, but also nuclear and kinetic—think aggressively weaponizing space, fielding more underwater drones, and guarding against a devastating electromagnetic pulse attack. America must be nimble enough to prepare for all potential threats, but also robust enough to ensure we have every capability—the sheer weight—necessary to confront our adversaries. This means investing heavily in future weapons systems, modernization of existing systems, hardening our electric grid, and substantially enhancing both digital and human intelligence. It also means maintaining—and expanding—the personnel baseline (the number of troops!) needed to support expansive national security efforts. In order to ensure that increases in spending are channeled effectively, serious reforms must be pursued in how the Defense Department procures future weapons systems and how the Pentagon personnel system is structured. We need to spend more on defense, but need to be smart about it.

2. A Tougher (Not Kinder) Military. While many of these trends are long-standing, Obama's military has accelerated a safety-obsessed Pentagon, a politically correct and socially engineered military culture, and a litany of rules of engagement (RoE) that endanger our trigger pullers. Risk mitigation and soldier safety have become the military's holy grail, rather than fostering a warrior ethos; politically correct social promotion—especially through obsessively advancing women in combat and "gender neutral" roles—has replaced the focus on warfighting capability; and White House and Pentagon lawyers have obsessively imposed RoE that tie the hands of our commanders and warriors, and empower our enemies to exploit our delicacy. Radicals who exploit women, children, and civilians to shield themselves should be unapologetically killed—full stop. The next commander in chief needs to ruthlessly reinstill a warrior culture in our military that is prepared to kill bad guys, not check politically correct boxes.

3. Authorize the Long War with Violent Islamism. America today may not want to be at war with Islamism, but Islamism is at war with us. We should declare war on Violent Islamism in a manner that recognizes the current manifestation of the threat (Islamic State, Al Qaeda, etc.) and sees no time frame, borders, or limitations. This is not to make a case for endless war, but instead the realization that this generational threat is not going away, and our Congress would be well served to pass an Authorization for the Use of Military Force that comprehends this reality. Only a sustained American commitment will put the scourge of Islamism on the retreat, and the weight of congressional authorization would help ensure more institutional legitimacy in this generational cause. (And, for the record, a larger Guantanamo Bay detention facility is a perfect place to hold and interrogate the Islamists we capture on the battlefield.)

4. Establish a League of Democracies. As laid out in the previous chapter, international institutions like the United Nations and International Criminal Court (ICC) no longer serve the interests of the United States and the West. Instead, as Roosevelt predicted, smaller and hostile states now use these institutions to box in, castigate, and shame America on the world stage. Rather than submit to this self-inflicted persecution, America should end our financial support of the UN and ICC and instead use our geopolitical weight to establish an alternative "League of Democracies" (or similar name). Admission to the League would be voluntary, but also contingent on a real commitment to both freedom principles and defense spending. The League would be empowered to act unilaterally or collectively in defense of individual or shared values and interests. Collectivist states like China and Russia would no longer have veto power over American action, ensuring our diplomatic and military sovereignty is preserved.

5. An Active Beacon of Freedom. The American story—from world wars to Iraq to Guantanamo Bay—is one of Americans giving their lives, and doing difficult things, so *others* can live free and peacefully. We have not been perfect, but we have been ruggedly principled. We should not be afraid to propagandize—unapologetically—the role America has played in ensuring the world is a freer place. Moreover, America must continue to support freedom and democracy promotion around the world. Political dissidents—fighting theocratic, collectivist, and authoritarian regimes—still have only one real champion in the world: the United States of America. We must continue to seek formal and informal avenues to support freedom fighters and empower their cause, wherever the cause exists, including demands for political liberalization of regimes that benefit from economic liberalization and global markets (for example, the China Model).

AN EXHORTATION

★ ★ ★

The Great Devotions

It is not the critic who counts; not the man who points out how the strong man stumbles, or where the doer of deeds could have done them better. The credit belongs to the man who is actually in the arena, whose face is marred by dust and sweat and blood; who strives valiantly; who errs, who comes short again and again, because there is no effort without error and shortcoming; but who does actually strive to do the deeds; who knows great enthusiasms, the great devotions; who spends himself in a worthy cause; who at the best knows in the end the triumph of high achievement, and who at the worst, if he fails, at least fails while daring greatly, so that his place shall never be with those cold and timid souls who neither know victory nor defeat.

—TEDDY ROOSEVELT, 1910

Come on now all you young men, all over the world. You are needed more than ever now to fill the gap of a generation shorn by the war. You have not an hour to lose. You must take your places in Life's fighting line. Twenty to twenty-five! These are the years! Don't be content with things as they are. "The earth is yours and the fullness thereof."

Enter upon your inheritance, accept your responsibilities. Raise the glorious flags again, advance them upon the new enemies, who constantly gather upon the front of the human army, and have only to be assaulted to be overthrown. Don't take No for an answer. Never submit to failure. Do not be fobbed off with mere personal success or acceptance. You will make all kinds of mistakes; but as long as you are generous and true, and also fierce, you cannot hurt the world or even seriously distress her. She was made to be wooed and won by youth. She has lived and thrived only by repeated subjugations.

—WINSTON CHURCHILL, 1930

This book humbly seeks to project, onto our era, the timeless truths and insights of Teddy Roosevelt's 1910 "Citizenship in a Republic" speech. But both his speech and this book mean very little if they don't compel people to enter the arena. Ultimately conviction—just like Facebook ranting—is worthless without action. It's one thing to remember a speech or read a book, and an entirely different thing to put down that book and step boldly into the real-world arena; to step forward and selflessly advance the American experiment in human freedom and flourishing. Not the latest fad, or your interpretation of social justice; but to advance the core of what makes America special—constitutionally protected freedom, citizenship, equal opportunity, and the duty to preserve all three. As Roosevelt powerfully exhorted, the exceptional principles of America's founding were entrusted to us—the "good citizens" of our generation—to preserve and perpetuate.

If you're not going to enter the arena now, then when will you? If not in 2016—with America's cultural and civic decay in plain sight at home and American leadership falling apart across the world—then when? Whether you're Winston Churchill's twenty-five-year-old or a seventy-five-year-old retiree, America needs you—and those questions should ring in your ears *today*, not tomorrow. There is a job you can do, a family you can lead, a cause you can champion, a group you can join, a team you can coach, a candidate you can support, a business you can start, a child you can raise, a tough assignment you can volunteer for. *Something!*

But many of us won't take that next step, because the arena is a tough place. It is a contested space, full of problems, possibilities, and—ultimately—people. The arena is an intensely personal place—full of nice people and nasty people alike. Working with people for larger principles—rather than manipulating people for self-interest—is not an easy thing to do. There will be disagreements and confrontations, winners and losers; I can guarantee there will be friction. And while we might be civil about it, others—especially the militant Left, but also some supposed friends—will not be. You will be falsely attacked, shamelessly and personally. Nothing worth doing in life is easy, and critics will be everywhere, friends fleeting, and failure likely. Resistance will meet you at every turn—in your job, your community, on the Internet, and with your friends and family; but most powerfully, resistance will come from within. Inner resistance comes in different forms. It comes in the form of piled-up excuses, complications that never resolve themselves, and creeping cowardice that lives within all of us. It's never the right time to step up and there is always a reason *not* to fight; too often our inner "no" wins out over the difficult "yes." Doing nothing is easy; taking a stand is tough.

This inner resistance is what has made the "Man in the Arena" quote such a powerful reminder in my brief life. It's why I printed out the quote, put it in that frame, and stuffed it in my green duffle bag of life, and it's why I hope you'll do the same. My life has seen many twists and turns, up and downs—I've succeeded and I've failed. I get attacked, in one form or another, nearly every day. Nothing is perfect, and nobody is remotely perfect; I would be utterly lost without the grace and redemption of Jesus Christ. I suspect you've experienced much of the same. Each twist, each scar, and each unexpected complication in life can lead to a callous inner resistance, a reason not to stick your neck out again; not to pick yourself up, dust yourself off, and continue to fight. Incredible people—friends and family—make all the difference at those times, no doubt; but without principles, without believing in something greater than yourself, life gets very shallow, sedentary, and sad. Mustering the courage to enter the arena—critics, complications, and cowardice all—is the only way to both live a life of meaning and ensure you pass the same possibility to the next generation of Americans.

That is what makes the arena, despite the critics and setbacks, the most rewarding place you can be. You will face criticism, but you will also meet the most amazing, purposeful, and passionate people in your life. You will be challenged, you will be inspired, and you will find resolve you didn't know you had. The "great enthusiasms, the great devotions" spent for "a worthy cause" will infuse your life with a purpose that self-centered, small, and silly pursuits will never fulfill. In 1895, Winston Churchill found himself amid a firefight in Cuba and remarked, "Nothing in life is so exhilarating as to be shot at without result." I concur, both on the battlefield—and in the arena of life. The more you fight in the civic arena, the more you realize—unlike the battlefield—that most of the time you are shot at "without result." Your opposition will bluster, they will bluff, they will flat-out lie, and they will beat their chest—but if you stand your ground, standing in the right, you can prevail.

Our society loves to say "all things in moderation," which is a nice sentiment, but not conducive to the arena. I'm certain both Teddy Roosevelt and Winston Churchill would soundly reject it—which is partly why we see them as great men. Moderation—the mushy middle of the comfort zone—is what keeps so many people from doing what is necessary to make real change, or make their dreams really come true. What if America's founders had said, let's take the moderate path and strike a deal with our British masters. What if Lincoln had said, the moderate choice is to compromise on a fifty-fifty split on slavery. Or what if Reagan had said, "Tear down a portion of that wall!" Going big for worthy causes, both nationally and in your local community, is the lifeblood of humanity. Moderation makes cowards—and bores—of even the best man. Dust, sweat, blood, valiance, daring . . . these are not words of moderation, these are words of action. America needs men and women of fortitude, toughness, and purpose. We need good citizens and good patriots. So, permit me to ask again:

> *Are you striving valiantly?*
> *Is your face marred by dust and sweat and blood?*
> *Are you spending yourself in a worthy cause?*
> *Are you daring greatly?*
> *Are you in the arena?*

If you're in the arena, you'll know. If you think you might be, you probably aren't—which makes seizing this day, this moment, the most important thing you can do for the country we both love.

Much of what has transpired in my own life, including the arguments made in this book, would likely never have happened without four simple words I'll share in closing. In the summer of 1999, a stoic Vietnam War veteran, a man whose name I cannot recall, looked me in the eye and said, "Pete, whatever you do, *don't miss your war.*" I was nineteen years old, and the stark statement ricocheted around my brain like a stray bullet. I knew nothing of the military—let alone war. I was not from a military family, and couldn't tell you the difference between the Army and the Marine Corps. While I was captivated by our lunch conversation, it was not what I expected to hear from the war buddy of a family friend. Most veterans speak of reluctant service, shades of gray, haunting memories, and impossible choices. Many don't speak of war at all. But his unique statement was intentional, serious, and anything but cold or flippant. He said it with certainty that I had yet to hear in my short life, except from a pulpit. (And they didn't teach *that* in church.) To my virgin ears, he sounded cavalier. Was he a warmon-

ACKNOWLEDGMENTS

★ ★ ★

First and foremost, thank you—and *I love you*—to my wife and best friend, Samantha, the toughest, kindest, and coolest girl I've ever met. She supported me in this project, even when the finish line seemed so distant. Our boys—Gunner, Boone, and Rex—motivate our shared love of country, loathing of terrorists, and commitment to a free and secure future. Speaking of those three boys: this book is for you guys. I love you so much.

Thank you to my father, Brian, and mother, Penny, who love and support me through thick and thin. More than any two people, they built the foundation on which I—and my brothers, Nate and Phil—stand. They love Jesus and our country, and live it each day—serving as a steady source of support, wisdom, and encouragement. I also thank my brothers, two patriots in the arena in their own right.

Two other people were central and indispensable to this project. The first is Nat Hoopes, my college roommate and best of friends. I'm quite certain he's edited—excuse me, rewritten—most everything I've ever written. We wrote the *Daily Princetonian* 9/11 response op-ed together, he edited my Iraq after-action report, and he made my 2006 *Wall Street Journal* op-ed fit to print. He's been the "content editor" of my life and was with me at each step of this project—for which I am grateful.

The second person is David Bellavia, a true hero of the Iraq War—

and a friend for life. He was, and is, a fellow Vets for Freedom devotee and is the author of the bestselling war memoir *House to House* (as well as the future, hypothetical bestseller, *The Politics of Valor*). He has encouraged me to write this book for many years, and it never would have happened without him. I would go to war with David, in any capacity and at any time. Unending thanks to everyone involved with Vets for Freedom as well—especially its other founders, Wade Zirkle, Knox Nunnally, and Mark Seavey. We fought the good fight, and made a difference.

Thank you to Jim Hornfischer, my literary agent, for believing in this project and making it happen. Thank you to Mitchell Ivers, Natasha Simons, and everyone at Threshold Editions and Simon & Schuster for believing in me and this book. And thank you to Matthew Baum, professor at Harvard's Kennedy School, for working through this book's initial proposal during my graduate work. While the final version looks nothing like my original proposal, it was sharpened by your challenge.

Each step of my life has made this possible as well. Thank you to the community of Forest Lake, Minnesota—most especially my lifelong friend and spit brother, Jimmy Knutson. Thank you to my church community of Eagle Brook Church and pastor Bob Merritt, a man who charts the course each Sunday and has supported me through bright and dark days. Likewise to all the members of my brief, spirited, and ultimately failed 2012 Senate campaign—we'll get 'em next time! Thank you, Nate Swanson, for taking time to review multiple chapters.

Thank you to the Princeton basketball program, especially Coach John Thompson Jr., for teaching me to persevere . . . and reinforcing that I wasn't meant to be a basketball player! Thank you to Princeton ROTC, especially LTC Matthew McCarville and MAJ Randall Newton, for patiently forging an Army officer. Thank you to my fellow staff and trustees of the *Princeton Tory*, for having the courage of your convictions—amazing Princetonians and patriots all. Thank you to my other Princeton roommates and incredible friends: Kyle Wente, Ryan

Feeney, Andy Kane, and Brian O'Toole (who smoked me in my first debate, freshman year). And thank you to Professor Robby George and former professor Patrick Deneen for being lone voices of conservative reason during my time at Old Nassau.

Thank you to my former colleagues at Concerned Veterans for America—fellow patriots dedicated to mobilizing veterans to fight for a free and prosperous America. It was an honor to work with you all, each and every day. A special shout-out to Joe Gecan, my Partner-in-Scrappiness from the beginning, Marine Dan (Caldwell) for feedback on multiple chapters, and Kate Pomeroy for encouraging this project from the beginning. I also benefited greatly from the insight and encouragement of my good friend and bestselling author Sean Parnell. Same to my dear friend Karen Vaughn.

A huge thank-you to the *Weekly Standard*'s Bill Kristol, a personal friend and mentor who has supported me—and so many of America's youngest warfighters—in active and earnest ways for over a decade. Bill, you are truly one of the good guys. Likewise to the amazing staff at *National Review* for affording me so many opportunities over the years—including twice sending me to Iraq to report on the surge in 2008. Thank you to all the great conservatives at the Manhattan Institute, who do yeoman's work on the island of Manhattan. And thank you to the guys at Power Line Blog in Minnesota who regularly reprinted my missives from the battlefield, including my first deployment in Guantanamo Bay in 2004—giving me a start and platform.

Thank you to my new colleagues at Fox News Channel—especially everyone at *FOX & Friends*, *The Kelly File*, and *Outnumbered* who have afforded me so many wonderful opportunities. Likewise to so many other great shows on Fox News and Fox Business. From the top executives to the hosts to the producers and bookers, I'm grateful to work with such smart, hardworking, and talented people.

Finally, thank you—most personally and passionately—to everyone I've ever worn the uniform with. You are the best "men in the arena" I have ever known. To start, this includes the faithful interpreters and allies—Muslims all—who supported and fought with us, especially my great friend Ali, "John Kerry," "Steve-O," Mr. Assad, Bakr, Omar, and Little Omar (RIP) in Iraq, and Esmatullah and Abdul in Afghanistan. To the "Peacemakers" platoon and Charlie Company from the New Jersey Army National Guard in Guantanamo Bay, Cuba, and the year we endured together, especially CPT Jurandir Ajaujo, SFC Robert Merz, SPC Kenneth Froehner, and the late—KIA in Afghanistan—SPC Jorge Oliveira. To the "Little Bastards" platoon, Charlie Company, and all "Iron Rakkasans" in Iraq and the combat mission we forged together, especially MAJ Steven Delvaux, CPT Chris Brawley, CPT Pete Carey, CPT Dan Hart, 1SG Eric Geressy, 1LT Mike Horne, SFC Ismael Godoy, SPC Jason George, PFC Kris Sapp, and our leader, COL Michael Steele. To our hodgepodge training unit in Afghanistan and the problem set we tackled, most especially MAJ Michael Murray and MAJ Chip Rankin. A grateful nation, and this soldier, will especially and always remember the warfighters who never made it back from the battlefield—365 days a year.

The legacy of those soldiers, the country they served, the love and forgiveness of Jesus Christ, and the blessings of a wonderful family are the heart and soul of this book. I pray each is honored through this humble submission.

THE SPEECH

★ ★ ★

You've read my interpretation of Teddy Roosevelt's historic speech, through the portions cited throughout this book. Now I encourage you to engage with Roosevelt's entire speech—drawing your own conclusions about its implications for America today. Trigger warning: it might compel you to heed his words, and enter the arena.

TEDDY ROOSEVELT
The Sorbonne, Paris, France
April 23, 1910

Strange and impressive associations rise in the mind of a man from the New World who speaks before this august body in this ancient institution of learning. Before his eyes pass the shadows of mighty kings and war-like nobles, of great masters of law and theology; through the shining dust of the dead centuries he sees crowded figures that tell of the power and learning and splendor of times gone by; and he sees also the innumerable host of humble students to whom clerkship meant emancipation, to whom it was well-nigh the only outlet from the dark thralldom of the Middle Ages.

This was the most famous university of mediaeval Europe

at a time when no one dreamed that there was a New World to discover. Its services to the cause of human knowledge already stretched far back into the remote past at a time when my forefathers, three centuries ago, were among the sparse bands of traders, ploughmen, wood-choppers, and fisherfolk who, in hard struggle with the iron unfriendliness of the Indian-haunted land, were laying the foundations of what has now become the giant republic of the West. To conquer a continent, to tame the shaggy roughness of wild nature, means grim warfare; and the generations engaged in it cannot keep, still less add to, the stores of garnered wisdom which were once theirs, and which are still in the hands of their brethren who dwell in the old land. To conquer the wilderness means to wrest victory from the same hostile forces with which mankind struggled on the immemorial infancy of our race. The primeval conditions must be met by the primeval qualities which are incompatible with the retention of much that has been painfully acquired by humanity as through the ages it has striven upward toward civilization. In conditions so primitive there can be but a primitive culture. At first only the rudest school can be established, for no others would meet the needs of the hard-driven, sinewy folk who thrust forward the frontier in the teeth of savage men and savage nature; and many years elapse before any of these schools can develop into seats of higher learning and broader culture.

The pioneer days pass; the stump-dotted clearings expand into vast stretches of fertile farm land; the stockaded clusters of log cabins change into towns; the hunters of game, the fellers of trees, the rude frontier traders and tillers of the soil, the men who wander all their lives long through the wilderness as the heralds and harbingers of an oncoming civilization, themselves vanish before the civilization for which they have prepared the way. The children of their successors and supplanters, and then their children and their children and children's children, change and develop with extraordinary rapidity. The conditions accentuate vices and virtues, energy and ruthlessness, all the good qualities and all the defects of an intense individualism, self-reliant, self-centered, far more conscious of its rights than of its duties, and blind to its own shortcomings. To the hard materialism of the frontier days succeeds the hard materialism of an industrialism even more intense and absorbing than that of the older nations; although these themselves have likewise already entered on the age of a complex and predominantly industrial civilization.

As the country grows, its people, who have won success in so many lines, turn back to try to recover the possessions of the mind and the spirit, which perforce their fathers threw aside in order better to wage the first rough battles for the continent their children inherit. The leaders of thought and of action grope their way forward to a new life, realizing, sometimes dimly, sometimes clear-sightedly, that the life of material gain, whether for a nation or an individual, is of value only as a foundation, only as there is added to it the uplift that comes from devotion to loftier ideals. The new life thus sought can in part be developed afresh from what is roundabout in the New World; but it can developed in full only by freely drawing upon the treasure-houses of the Old World, upon the treasures stored in the ancient abodes of wisdom and learning, such as this is where I speak to-day. It is a mistake for any nation to merely copy another; but it is even a greater mistake, it is a proof of weakness in any nation, not to be anxious to learn from one another and willing and able to adapt that learning to the new national conditions and make it fruitful and productive therein. It is for us of the New World to sit at the feet of Gamaliel of the Old; then, if we have the right stuff in us, we can show that Paul in his turn can become a teacher as well as a scholar.

Today I shall speak to you on the subject of individual citizenship, the one subject of vital importance to you, my hearers, and to me and my countrymen, because you and we are great citizens of great democratic republics. A democratic republic such as ours—an effort to realize in its full sense government by, of, and for the people—represents the most gigantic of all possible social experiments, the one fraught with great responsibilities alike for good and evil. The success of republics like yours and like ours means the glory, and our failure of despair, of mankind; and for you and for us the question of the quality of the individual citizen is supreme. Under other forms of government, under the rule of one man or very few men, the quality of the leaders is all-important. If, under such governments, the quality of the rulers is high enough, then the nations for generations lead a brilliant career, and add substantially to the sum of world achievement, no matter how low the quality of average citizen; because the average citizen is an almost negligible quantity in working out the final results of that type of national greatness.

But with you and us the case is different. With you here, and with us in my own home, in the long run, success or failure will be conditioned upon the way in which the average man, the average women, does his or her duty, first in the ordinary, every-day affairs of life, and next in those great occasional crises which call for heroic virtues. The average citizen must be a good citizen if our republics are to succeed. The stream will not permanently rise higher than the main source; and the main source of national power and national greatness is found in the average citizenship of the nation. Therefore it behooves us to do our best to see that the standard of the average citizen is kept high; and the average cannot be kept high unless the standard of the leaders is very much higher.

It is well if a large proportion of the leaders in any republic, in any democracy, are, as a matter of course, drawn from the classes represented in this audience to-day; but only provided that those classes possess the gifts of sympathy with plain people and of devotion to great ideals. You and those like you have received special advantages; you have all of you had the opportunity for mental training; many of you have had leisure; most of you have had a chance for enjoyment of life far greater than comes to the majority of your fellows. To you and your kind much has been given, and from you much should be expected. Yet there are certain failings against which it is especially incumbent that both men of trained and cultivated intellect, and men of inherited wealth and position should especially guard themselves, because to these failings they are especially liable; and if yielded to, their—your—chances of useful service are at an end.

Let the man of learning, the man of lettered leisure, beware of that queer and cheap temptation to pose to himself and to others as a cynic, as the man who has outgrown emotions and beliefs, the man to whom good and evil are as one. The poorest way to face life is to face it with a sneer. There are many men who feel a kind of twisted pride in cynicism; there are many who confine themselves to criticism of the way others do what they themselves dare not even attempt. There is no more unhealthy being, no man less worthy of respect, than he who either really holds, or feigns to hold, an attitude of sneering disbelief toward all that is great and lofty, whether in achievement or in that noble effort which, even if it fails, comes to second achievement. A cynical habit of thought and speech, a readiness to criticize work which the critic himself never tries to perform, an intellectual aloofness which will not accept contact with life's realities—all these are marks, not as the possessor would fain to think, of superiority but of weakness. They mark the men unfit to bear their part painfully in the stern strife of living, who seek, in the affection of contempt for the achievements of others, to hide from others and from themselves their own weakness. The role is easy; there is none easier, save only the role of the man who sneers alike at both criticism and performance.

It is not the critic who counts; not the man who points out how the strong man stumbles, or where the doer of deeds could have done them better. The credit belongs to the man who is actually in the arena, whose face is marred by dust and sweat and blood; who strives valiantly; who errs, who comes short again and again, because there is no effort without error and shortcoming; but who does actually strive to do the deeds; who knows great enthusiasms, the great devotions; who spends himself in a worthy cause; who at the best knows in the end the triumph of high achievement, and who at the worst, if he fails, at least fails while daring greatly, so that his place shall never be with those cold and timid souls who neither know victory nor defeat.

Shame on the man of cultivated taste who permits refinement to develop into fastidiousness that unfits him for doing the rough work of a workaday world. Among the free peoples who govern themselves there is but a small field of usefulness open for the men of cloistered life who shrink from contact with their fellows. Still less room is there for those who deride or slight what is done by those who actually bear the brunt of the day; nor yet for those others who always profess that they would like to take action, if only the conditions of life were not exactly what they actually are. The man who does nothing cuts the same sordid figure in the pages of history, whether he be a cynic, or fop, or voluptuary. There is little use for the being whose tepid soul knows nothing of great and generous emotion, of the high pride, the stern belief, the lofty enthusiasm, of the men who quell the storm and ride the thunder. Well for these men if they succeed; well also, though not so well, if they fail, given only that they have nobly ventured, and have put forth all their heart and strength. It is war-worn Hotspur, spent with hard fighting, he of the many errors and valiant end, over whose memory we love to linger, not over the memory of the young lord who "but for the vile guns would have been a valiant soldier."

France has taught many lessons to other nations: surely one of the most important lessons is the lesson her whole history teaches, that a high artistic and literary development is compatible with notable leadership in arms and statecraft. The brilliant gallantry of the French soldier has for many centuries been proverbial; and during these same centuries at every court in Europe the freemasons of fashion have treated the French tongue as their common speech; while every artist and man of letters, and every man of science able to appreciate that marvelous instrument of precision, French prose, had turned toward France for aid and inspiration. How long the leadership in arms and letters has lasted is curiously illustrated by the fact that the earliest masterpiece in a modern tongue is the splendid French epic which tells of Roland's doom and the vengeance of Charlemagne when the lords of the Frankish hosts were stricken at Roncesvalles.

Let those who have, keep, let those who have not, strive to attain, a high standard of cultivation and scholarship. Yet let us remember that these stand second to certain other things. There is need of a sound body, and even more of a sound mind. But above mind and above body stands character—the sum of those qualities which we mean when we speak of a man's force and courage, of his good faith and sense of honor. I believe in exercise for the body, always provided that we keep in mind that physical development is a means and not an end. I believe, of course, in giving to all the people a good education. But the education must contain much besides book learning in order to be really good. We must ever remember that no keenness and subtleness of intellect, no polish, no cleverness, in any way make up for the lack of the great solid qualities. Self-restraint, self-mastery, common sense, the power of accepting individual responsibility and yet of acting in conjunction with others, courage and resolution—these are the qualities which mark a masterful people. Without them no people can control itself, or save itself from being controlled from the outside. I speak to a brilliant assemblage; I speak in a great university which represents the flower of the highest intellectual development; I pay all homage to intellect and to elaborate and specialized training of the intellect; and yet I know I shall have the assent of all of you present when I add that more important still are the commonplace, every-day qualities and virtues.

Such ordinary, every-day qualities include the will and the power to work, to fight at need, and to have plenty of healthy children. The need that the average man shall work is so obvious as hardly to warrant insistence. There are a few people in every country so born that they can lead lives of leisure. These fill a useful function if they make it evident that leisure does not mean idleness; for some of the most valuable work needed by civilization is essentially non-remunerative in its character, and of course the people who do this work should in large part be drawn from those to whom remuneration is an object of indifference. But the average man must earn his own livelihood. He should be trained to do so, and he should be trained to feel that he occupies a contemptible position if he does not do so; that he is not an object of envy if he is idle, at whichever end of the social scale he stands, but an object of contempt, an object of derision.

In the next place, the good man should be both a strong and a brave man; that is, he should be able to fight, he should be able to serve his country as a soldier, if the need arises. There are well-meaning philosophers who declaim against the unrighteousness of war. They are right only if they lay all their emphasis upon the unrighteousness. War is a dreadful thing, and unjust war is a crime against humanity. But it is such a crime because it is unjust, not because it is a war. The choice must ever be in favor of righteousness, and this is whether the alternative be peace or whether the alternative be war. The question must not be merely, Is there to be peace or war? The question must be, Is it right to prevail? Are the great laws of righteousness once more to be fulfilled? And the answer from a strong and virile people must be "Yes," whatever the cost. Every honorable effort should always be made to avoid war, just as every honorable effort should always be made by the individual in private life to keep out of a brawl, to keep out of trouble; but no self-respecting individual, no self-respecting nation, can or ought to submit to wrong.

Finally, even more important than ability to work, even more important than ability to fight at need, is it to remember that chief of blessings for any nations is that it shall leave its seed to inherit the land. It was the crown of blessings in Biblical times and it is the crown of blessings now. The greatest of all curses is the curse of sterility, and the severest of all condemnations should be that visited upon willful sterility. The first essential in any civilization is that the man and the woman shall be father and mother of healthy children, so that the race shall increase and not decrease. If that is not so, if through no fault of the society there is failure to increase, it is a great misfortune. If the failure is due to the deliberate and willful fault, then it is not merely a misfortune, it is one of those crimes of ease and self-indulgence, of shrinking from pain and effort and risk, which in the long run Nature punishes more heavily than any other. If we of the great republics, if we, the free people who claim to have emancipated ourselves from the thralldom of wrong and error, bring down on our heads the curse that comes upon the willfully barren, then it will be an idle waste of breath to prattle of our achievements, to boast of all that we have done. No refinement of life, no delicacy of taste, no material progress, no

sordid heaping up riches, no sensuous development of art and
literature, can in any way compensate for the loss of the great
fundamental virtues; and of these great fundamental virtues the
greatest is the race's power to perpetuate the race.

Character must show itself in the man's performance both
of the duty he owes himself and of the duty he owes the state.
The man's foremost duty is owed to himself and his family; and
he can do this duty only by earning money, by providing what
is essential to material well-being; it is only after this has been
done that he can hope to build a higher superstructure on the
solid material foundation; it is only after this has been done that
he can help in his movements for the general well-being. He
must pull his own weight first, and only after this can his sur-
plus strength be of use to the general public. It is not good to
excite that bitter laughter which expresses contempt; and contempt is what we feel for the being whose enthusiasm to benefit
mankind is such that he is a burden to those nearest him; who
wishes to do great things for humanity in the abstract, but who
cannot keep his wife in comfort or educate his children.

Nevertheless, while laying all stress on this point, while not
merely acknowledging but insisting upon the fact that there
must be a basis of material well-being for the individual as for
the nation, let us with equal emphasis insist that this material
well-being represents nothing but the foundation, and that the
foundation, though indispensable, is worthless unless upon it is
raised the superstructure of a higher life.

That is why I decline to recognize the mere multimillionaire,
the man of mere wealth, as an asset of value to any country; and
especially as not an asset to my own country. If he has earned
or uses his wealth in a way that makes him a real benefit, of real
use—and such is often the case—why, then he does become an
asset of real worth. But it is the way in which it has been earned
or used, and not the mere fact of wealth, that entitles him to

the credit. There is need in business, as in most other forms of human activity, of the great guiding intelligences. Their places cannot be supplied by any number of lesser intelligences. It is a good thing that they should have ample recognition, ample reward. But we must not transfer our admiration to the reward instead of to the deed rewarded; and if what should be the reward exists without the service having been rendered, then admiration will only come from those who are mean of soul. The truth is that, after a certain measure of tangible material success or reward has been achieved, the question of increasing it becomes of constantly less importance compared to the other things that can be done in life. It is a bad thing for a nation to raise and to admire a false standard of success; and there can be no falser standard than that set by the deification of material well-being in and for itself. But the man who, having far surpassed the limits of providing for the wants, both of the body and mind, of himself and of those depending upon him, then piles up a great fortune, for the acquisition or retention of which he returns no corresponding benefit to the nation as a whole, should himself be made to feel that, so far from being desirable, he is an unworthy, citizen of the community; that he is to be neither admired nor envied; that his right-thinking fellow countrymen put him low in the scale of citizenship, and leave him to be consoled by the admiration of those whose level of purpose is even lower than his own.

My position as regards the moneyed interests can be put in a few words. In every civilized society property rights must be carefully safeguarded; ordinarily, and in the great majority of cases, human rights and property rights are fundamentally and in the long run identical; but when it clearly appears that there is a real conflict between them, human rights must have the upper hand, for property belongs to man and not man to property.

In fact, it is essential to good citizenship clearly to understand that there are certain qualities which we in a democracy are prone to admire in and of themselves, which ought by rights to be judged admirable or the reverse solely from the standpoint of the use made of them. Foremost among these I should include two very distinct gifts—the gift of money-making and the gift of oratory. Money-making, the money touch, I have spoken of above. It is a quality which in a moderate degree is essential. It may be useful when developed to a very great degree, but only if accompanied and controlled by other qualities; and without such control the possessor tends to develop into one of the least attractive types produced by a modern industrial democracy. So it is with the orator. It is highly desirable that a leader of opinion in democracy should be able to state his views clearly and convincingly. But all that the oratory can do of value to the community is enable the man thus to explain himself; if it enables the orator to put false values on things, it merely makes him a power for mischief. Some excellent public servants have not that gift at all, and must merely rely on their deeds to speak for them; and unless oratory does represent genuine conviction based on good common sense and [is] able to be translated into efficient performance, then the better the oratory the greater the damage to the public it deceives. Indeed, it is a sign of marked political weakness in any commonwealth if the people tend to be carried away by mere oratory, if they tend to value words in and for themselves, as divorced from the deeds for which they are supposed to stand. The phrase-maker, the phrase-monger, the ready talker, however great his power, whose speech does not make for courage, sobriety, and right understanding, is simply a noxious element in the body politic, and it speaks ill for the public if he has influence over them. To admire the gift of oratory without regard to the moral quality behind the gift is to do wrong to the republic.

Of course all that I say of the orator applies with even greater force to the orator's latter-day and more influential brother, the journalist. The power of the journalist is great, but he is entitled neither to respect nor admiration because of that power unless it is used aright. He can do, and often does, great good. He can do, and he often does, infinite mischief. All journalists, all writers, for the very reason that they appreciate the vast possibilities of their profession, should bear testimony against those who deeply discredit it. Offenses against taste and morals, which are bad enough in a private citizen, are infinitely worse if made into instruments for debauching the community through a newspaper. Mendacity, slander, sensationalism, inanity, vapid triviality, all are potent factors for the debauchery of the public mind and conscience. The excuse advanced for vicious writing, that the public demands it and that demand must be supplied, can no more be admitted than if it were advanced by purveyors of food who sell poisonous adulterations.

In short, the good citizen in a republic must realize that he ought to possess two sets of qualities, and that neither avails without the other. He must have those qualities which make for efficiency; and he also must have those qualities which direct the efficiency into channels for the public good. He is useless if he is inefficient. There is nothing to be done with that type of citizen of whom all that can be said is that he is harmless. Virtue which is dependent upon a sluggish circulation is not impressive. There is little place in active life for the timid good man. The man who is saved by weakness from robust wickedness is likewise rendered immune from robuster virtues. The good citizen in a republic must first of all be able to hold his own. He is no good citizen unless he has the ability which will make him work hard and which at need will make him fight hard. The good citizen is not a good citizen unless he is an efficient citizen.

But if a man's efficiency is not guided and regulated by a

moral sense, then the more efficient he is the worse he is, the more dangerous to the body politic. Courage, intellect, all the masterful qualities, serve but to make a man more evil if they are merely used for that man's own advancement, with brutal indifference to the rights of others. It speaks ill for the community if the community worships these qualities and treats their possessors as heroes regardless of whether the qualities are used rightly or wrongly. It makes no difference as to the precise way in which this sinister efficiency is shown. It makes no difference whether such a man's force and ability betray themselves in a career of money-maker or politician, soldier or orator, journalist or popular leader. If the man works for evil, then the more successful he is the more he should be despised and condemned by all upright and far-seeing men. To judge a man merely by success is an abhorrent wrong; and if the people at large habitually so judge men, if they grow to condone wickedness because the wicked man triumphs, they show their inability to understand that in the last analysis free institutions rest upon the character of citizenship, and that by such admiration of evil they prove themselves unfit for liberty.

The homely virtues of the household, the ordinary workaday virtues which make the woman a good housewife and housemother, which make the man a hard worker, a good husband and father, a good soldier at need, stand at the bottom of character. But of course many others must be added thereto if a state is to be not only free but great. Good citizenship is not good citizenship if only exhibited in the home. There remain the duties of the individual in relation to the State, and these duties are none too easy under the conditions which exist where the effort is made to carry on the free government in a complex industrial civilization. Perhaps the most important thing the ordinary citizen, and, above all, the leader of ordinary citizens, has to remember in political life is that he must not be a sheer doctrinaire. The closet philosopher, the refined and cultured individual who from his library tells how men ought to be governed under ideal conditions, is of no use in actual governmental work; and the one-sided fanatic, and still more the mob-leader, and the insincere man who to achieve power promises what by no possibility can be performed, are not merely useless but noxious.

The citizen must have high ideals, and yet he must be able to achieve them in practical fashion. No permanent good comes from aspirations so lofty that they have grown fantastic and have become impossible and indeed undesirable to realize. The impractical visionary is far less often the guide and precursor than he is the embittered foe of the real reformer, of the man who, with stumblings and shortcomings, yet does in some shape, in practical fashion, give effect to the hopes and desires of those who strive for better things. Woe to the empty phrase-maker, to the empty idealist, who, instead of making ready the ground for the man of action, turns against him when he appears and hampers him when he does work! Moreover, the preacher of ideals must remember how sorry and contemptible is the figure which he will cut, how great the damage that he will do, if he does not himself, in his own life, strive measurably to realize the ideals that he preaches for others. Let him remember also that the worth of the ideal must be largely determined by the success with which it can in practice be realized. We should abhor the so-called "practical" men whose practicality assumes the shape of that peculiar baseness which finds its expression in disbelief in morality and decency, in disregard of high standards of living and conduct. Such a creature is the worst enemy of the body politic. But only less desirable as a citizen is his nominal opponent and real ally, the man of fantastic vision who makes the impossible better forever the enemy of the possible good.

We can just as little afford to follow the doctrinaires of an extreme individualism as the doctrinaires of an extreme social-

ism. Individual initiative, so far from being discouraged, should
be stimulated; and yet we should remember that, as society develops and grows more complex, we continually find that things
which once it was desirable to leave to individual initiative can,
under changed conditions, be performed with better results by
common effort. It is quite impossible, and equally undesirable,
to draw in theory a hard-and-fast line which shall always divide
the two sets of cases. This every one who is not cursed with the
pride of the closet philosopher will see, if he will only take the
trouble to think about some of our commonest phenomena. For
instance, when people live on isolated farms or in little hamlets,
each house can be left to attend to its own drainage and water-
supply; but the mere multiplication of families in a given area
produces new problems which, because they differ in size, are
found to differ not only in degree, but in kind from the old; and
the questions of drainage and water-supply have to be considered from the common standpoint. It is not a matter for abstract dogmatizing to decide when this point is reached; it is a
matter to be tested by practical experiment. Much of the discussion about socialism and individualism is entirely pointless, because of the failure to agree on terminology. It is not good to be
a slave of names. I am a strong individualist by personal habit,
inheritance, and conviction; but it is a mere matter of common
sense to recognize that the State, the community, the citizens
acting together, can do a number of things better than if they
were left to individual action. The individualism which finds its
expression in the abuse of physical force is checked very early in
the growth of civilization, and we of to-day should in our turn
strive to shackle or destroy that individualism which triumphs
by greed and cunning, which exploits the weak by craft instead
of ruling them by brutality. We ought to go with any man in the
effort to bring about justice and the equality of opportunity, to
turn the tool-user more and more into the tool-owner, to shift

burdens so that they can be more equitably borne. The deadening effect on any race of the adoption of a logical and extreme socialistic system could not be overstated; it would spell sheer destruction; it would produce grosser wrong and outrage, fouler immorality, than any existing system. But this does not mean that we may not with great advantage adopt certain of the principles professed by some given set of men who happen to call themselves Socialists; to be afraid to do so would be to make a mark of weakness on our part.

But we should not take part in acting a lie any more than in telling a lie. We should not say that men are equal where they are not equal, nor proceed upon the assumption that there is an equality where it does not exist; but we should strive to bring about a measurable equality, at least to the extent of preventing the inequality which is due to force or fraud. Abraham Lincoln, a man of the plain people, blood of their blood, and bone of their bone, who all his life toiled and wrought and suffered for them, at the end died for them, who always strove to represent them, who would never tell an untruth to or for them, spoke of the doctrine of equality with his usual mixture of idealism and sound common sense. He said (I omit what was of merely local significance):

> *I think the authors of the Declaration of Independence intended to include all men, but they did not mean to declare all men equal in all respects. They did not mean to say all men were equal in color, size, intellect, moral development or social capacity. They defined with tolerable distinctness in what they did consider all men created equal—equal in certain inalienable rights, among which are life, liberty and pursuit of happiness. This they said, and this they meant. They did not mean to assert the obvious untruth that all were actually enjoying that equality, or yet that they were about to confer it immediately upon them. They meant to set*

up a standard maxim for free society which should be familiar to all—constantly looked to, constantly labored for, and, even though never perfectly attained, constantly approximated, and thereby constantly spreading and deepening its influence, and augmenting the happiness and value of life to all people, everywhere.

We are bound in honor to refuse to listen to those men who would make us desist from the effort to do away with the inequality which means injustice; the inequality of right, of opportunity, of privilege. We are bound in honor to strive to bring ever nearer the day when, as far as is humanly possible, we shall be able to realize the ideal that each man shall have an equal opportunity to show the stuff that is in him by the way in which he renders service. There should, so far as possible, be equality of opportunity to render service; but just so long as there is inequality of service there should and must be inequality of reward. We may be sorry for the general, the painter, the artist, the worker in any profession or of any kind, whose misfortune rather than whose fault it is that he does his work ill. But the reward must go to the man who does his work well; for any other course is to create a new kind of privilege, the privilege of folly and weakness; and special privilege is injustice, whatever form it takes.

To say that the thriftless, the lazy, the vicious, the incapable, ought to have reward given to those who are far-sighted, capable, and upright, is to say what is not true and cannot be true. Let us try to level up, but let us beware of the evil of leveling down. If a man stumbles, it is a good thing to help him to his feet. Every one of us needs a helping hand now and then. But if a man lies down, it is a waste of time to try and carry him; and it is a very bad thing for every one if we make men feel that the same reward will come to those who shirk their work and those who do it.

Let us, then, take into account the actual facts of life, and not be misled into following any proposal for achieving the millennium, for recreating the golden age, until we have subjected it to hardheaded examination. On the other hand, it is foolish to reject a proposal merely because it is advanced by visionaries. If a given scheme is proposed, look at it on its merits, and, in considering it, disregard formulas. It does not matter in the least who proposes it, or why. If it seems good, try it. If it proves good, accept it; otherwise reject it. There are plenty of good men calling themselves Socialists with whom, up to a certain point, it is quite possible to work. If the next step is one which both we and they wish to take, why of course take it, without any regard to the fact that our views as to the tenth step may differ. But, on the other hand, keep clearly in mind that, though it has been worthwhile to take one step, this does not in the least mean that it may not be highly disadvantageous to take the next. It is just as foolish to refuse all progress because people demanding it desire at some points to go to absurd extremes, as it would be to go to these absurd extremes simply because some of the measures advocated by the extremists were wise.

The good citizen will demand liberty for himself, and as a matter of pride he will see to it that others receive liberty which he thus claims as his own. Probably the best test of true love of liberty in any country is the way in which minorities are treated in that country. Not only should there be complete liberty in matters of religion and opinion, but complete liberty for each man to lead his life as he desires, provided only that in so doing he does not wrong his neighbor. Persecution is bad because it is persecution, and without reference to which side happens at the most to be the persecutor and which the persecuted. Class hatred is bad in just the same way, and without regard to the individual who, at a given time, substitutes loyalty to a class for loyalty to a nation, or substitutes hatred of men because they happen to come in a certain social category, for judgment awarded them according to their conduct. Remember always that the same measure of condemnation should be extended to the arrogance which would look down upon or crush any man because he is poor and to envy and hatred which would destroy a man because he is wealthy. The overbearing brutality of the man of wealth or power, and the envious and hateful malice directed against wealth or power, are really at root merely different manifestations of the same quality, merely two sides of the same shield.

The man who, if born to wealth and power, exploits and ruins his less fortunate brethren is at heart the same as the greedy and violent demagogue who excites those who have not property to plunder those who have. The gravest wrong upon his country is inflicted by that man, whatever his station, who seeks to make his countrymen divide primarily in the line that separates class from class, occupation from occupation, men of more wealth from men of less wealth, instead of remembering that the only safe standard is that which judges each man on his worth as a man, whether he be rich or whether he be poor, without regard to his profession or to his station in life. Such is the only true democratic test, the only test that can with propriety be applied in a republic. There have been many republics in the past, both in what we call antiquity and in what we call the Middle Ages. They fell, and the prime factor in their fall was the fact that the parties tended to divide along the line that separates wealth from poverty. It made no difference which side was successful; it made no difference whether the republic fell under the rule of an oligarchy or the rule of a mob. In either case, when once loyalty to a class had been substituted for loyalty to the republic, the end of the republic was at hand. There is no greater need today than the need to keep ever in mind the fact that the cleavage between right and wrong, between good citizenship and bad citizenship, runs at right angles to, and not parallel with, the lines of cleavage between class and class, between occupation and occupation. Ruin looks us in the face if we judge a man by his position instead of judging him by his conduct in that position.

In a republic, to be successful we must learn to combine intensity of conviction with a broad tolerance of difference of conviction. Wide differences of opinion in matters of religious, political, and social belief must exist if conscience and intellect alike are not to be stunted, if there is to be room for healthy growth. Bitter internecine hatreds, based on such differences, are signs, not of earnestness of belief, but of that fanaticism which, whether religious or antireligious, democratic or antidemocratic, is itself but a manifestation of the gloomy bigotry which has been the chief factor in the downfall of so many, many nations.

Of one man in especial, beyond any one else, the citizens of a republic should beware, and that is of the man who appeals to them to support him on the ground that he is hostile to other citizens of the republic, that he will secure for those who elect him, in one shape or another, profit at the expense of other citizens of the republic. It makes no difference whether he appeals to class hatred or class interest, to religious or antireligious prejudice. The man who makes such an appeal should always be presumed to make it for the sake of furthering his own interest. The very last thing an intelligent and self-respecting member of a democratic community should do is to reward any public man because that public man says that he will get the private citizen something to which this private citizen is not entitled, or will gratify some emotion or animosity which this private citizen ought not to possess. Let me illustrate this by one anecdote from my own experience. A number of years ago I was engaged in cattle-ranching on the great plains of the western

United States. There were no fences. The cattle wandered free, the ownership of each one was determined by the brand; the calves were branded with the brand of the cows they followed. If on the round-up an animal was passed by, the following year it would appear as an unbranded yearling, and was then called a maverick. By the custom of the country these mavericks were branded with the brand of the man on whose range they were found. One day I was riding the range with a newly hired cowboy, and we came upon a maverick. We roped and threw it; then we built a fire, took out a cinch-ring, heated it in the fire; and then the cowboy started to put on the brand. I said to him, "It is So-and-so's brand," naming the man on whose range we happened to be. He answered: "That's all right, boss; I know my business." In another moment I said to him: "Hold on, you are putting on my brand!" To which he answered: "That's all right; I always put on the boss's brand." I answered: "Oh, very well. Now you go straight back to the ranch and get whatever is owing to you; I don't need you any longer." He jumped up and said: "Why, what's the matter? I was putting on your brand." And I answered: "Yes, my friend, and if you will steal for me then you will steal from me."

Now, the same principle which applies in private life applies also in public life. If a public man tries to get your vote by saying that he will do something wrong in your interest, you can be absolutely certain that if ever it becomes worth his while he will do something wrong against your interest.

So much for the citizenship of the individual in his relations to his family, to his neighbor, to the State. There remain duties of citizenship which the State, the aggregation of all the individuals, owes in connection with other States, with other nations. Let me say at once that I am no advocate of a foolish cosmopolitanism. I believe that a man must be a good patriot before he can be, and as the only possible way of being, a good citizen of the world. Experience teaches us that the average man who protests that his international feeling swamps his national feeling, that he does not care for his country because he cares so much for mankind, in actual practice proves himself the foe of mankind; that the man who says that he does not care to be a citizen of any one country, because he is the citizen of the world, is in fact usually an exceedingly undesirable citizen of whatever corner of the world he happens at the moment to be in. In the dim future all moral needs and moral standards may change; but at present, if a man can view his own country and all other countries from the same level with tepid indifference, it is wise to distrust him, just as it is wise to distrust the man who can take the same dispassionate view of his wife and mother. However broad and deep a man's sympathies, however intense his activities, he need have no fear that they will be cramped by love of his native land.

Now, this does not mean in the least that a man should not wish to do good outside of his native land. On the contrary, just as I think that the man who loves his family is more apt to be a good neighbor than the man who does not, so I think that the most useful member of the family of nations is normally a strongly patriotic nation. So far from patriotism being inconsistent with a proper regard for the rights of other nations, I hold that the true patriot, who is as jealous of the national honor as a gentleman of his own honor, will be careful to see that the nation neither inflicts nor suffers wrong, just as a gentleman scorns equally to wrong others or to suffer others to wrong him. I do not for one moment admit that a man should act deceitfully as a public servant in his dealings with other nations, any more than he should act deceitfully in his dealings as a private citizen with other private citizens. I do not for one moment admit that a nation should treat other nations in a different spirit from that in which an honorable man would treat other men.

In practically applying this principle to the two sets of cases there is, of course, a great practical difference to be taken into account. We speak of international law; but international law is something wholly different from private or municipal law, and the capital difference is that there is a sanction for the one and no sanction for the other; that there is an outside force which compels individuals to obey the one, while there is no such outside force to compel obedience as regards to the other. International law will, I believe, as the generations pass, grow stronger and stronger until in some way or other there develops the power to make it respected. But as yet it is only in the first formative period. As yet, as a rule, each nation is of necessity to judge for itself in matters of vital importance between it and its neighbors, and actions must be of necessity, where this is the case, be different from what they are where, as among private citizens, there is an outside force whose action is all-powerful and must be invoked in any crisis of importance.

It is the duty of wise statesmen, gifted with the power of looking ahead, to try to encourage and build up every movement which will substitute or tend to substitute some other agency for force in the settlement of international disputes. It is the duty of every honest statesman to try to guide the nation so that it shall not wrong any other nation. But as yet the great civilized peoples, if they are to be true to themselves and to the cause of humanity and civilization, must keep in mind that in the last resort they must possess both the will and the power to resent wrong-doing from others. The men who sanely believe in a lofty morality preach righteousness; but they do not preach weakness, whether among private citizens or among nations. We believe that our ideals should be so high, but not so high as to make it impossible measurably to realize them. We sincerely and earnestly believe in peace; but if peace and justice conflict, we scorn the man who would not stand for justice though the whole world came in arms against him.

And now, my hosts, a word in parting. You and I belong to the only two republics among the great powers of the world. The ancient friendship between France and the United States has been, on the whole, a sincere and disinterested friendship. A calamity to you would be a sorrow to us. But it would be more than that. In the seething turmoil of the history of humanity certain nations stand out as possessing a peculiar power or charm, some special gift of beauty or wisdom or strength, which puts them among the immortals, which makes them rank forever with the leaders of mankind. France is one of these nations. For her to sink would be a loss to all the world. There are certain lessons of brilliance and of generous gallantry that she can teach better than any of her sister nations. When the French peasantry sang of Malbrook, it was to tell how the soul of this warrior-foe took flight upward through the laurels he had won. Nearly seven centuries ago, Froissart, writing of the time of dire disaster, said that the realm of France was never so stricken that there were not left men who would valiantly fight for it. You have had a great past. I believe you will have a great future. Long may you carry yourselves proudly as citizens of a nation which bears a leading part in the teaching and uplifting of mankind.